ADVANCED FINANCIAL MANAGEMENT

PAWAN JHABAK
M.Com., P.G.D.Ed.M,
Vice-principal
Rustomjee Business School,
Dahisar (West), Mumbai - 68 and
Visiting Faculty at various Management Colleges,
India.

Himalaya Publishing House

MUMBAI • NEW DELHI • NAGPUR • BENGALURU • HYDERABAD • CHENNAI • PUNE • LUCKNOW • AHMEDABAD • ERNAKULAM • BHUBANESWAR • INDORE • KOLKATA • GUWAHATI

First Edition : 2012

Published by : Mrs. Meena Pandey for **Himalaya Publishing House Pvt. Ltd.**, "Ramdoot", Dr. Bhalerao Marg, Girgaon, **Mumbai - 400 004.** Phone: 022-23860170/23863863, Fax: 022-23877178 **E-mail: himpub@vsnl.com; Website: www.himpub.com**

Branch Offices :

New Delhi : "Pooja Apartments", 4-B, Murari Lal Street, Ansari Road, Darya Ganj, New Delhi - 110 002. Phone: 011-23270392, 23278631; Fax: 011-23256286

Nagpur : Kundanlal Chandak Industrial Estate, Ghat Road, Nagpur - 440 018. Phone: 0712-2738731, 3296733; Telefax: 0712-2721215

Bengaluru : No. 16/1 (Old 12/1), 1st Floor, Next to Hotel Highlands, Madhava Nagar, Race Course Road, Bengaluru - 560 001. Phone: 080-32919385; Telefax: 080-22286611

Hyderabad : No. 3-4-184, Lingampally, Besides Raghavendra Swamy Matham, Kachiguda, Hyderabad - 500 027. Phone: 040-27560041, 27550139; Mobile: 09390905282

Chennai : No. 8/2, Madley 2nd Street, Ground Floor, T. Nagar, Chennai - 600 017. Phone: 044-28144004/28144005; Mobile: 09345345051

Pune : First Floor, "Laksha" Apartment, No. 527, Mehunpura, Shaniwarpeth (Near Prabhat Theatre), Pune - 411 030. Phone: 020-24496323/24496333; Mobile: 09370579333

Lucknow : House No 731, Shekhupura Colony, Near B.D. Convent School, Aliganj, Lucknow - 226 022. Mobile: 09307501549

Ahmedabad : 114, "SHAIL", 1st Floor, Opp. Madhu Sudan House, C.G. Road, Navrang Pura, Ahmedabad - 380 009. Phone: 079-26560126; Mobile: 09377088847

Ernakulam : 39/176 (New No: 60/251) 1st Floor, Karikkamuri Road, Ernakulam, Kochi - 682011, Phone: 0484-2378012, 2378016; Mobile: 09344199799

Bhubaneswar : 5 Station Square, Bhubaneswar - 751 001 (Odisha). Phone: 0674-2532129, Mobile: 09338746007

Indore : Kesardeep Avenue Extension, 73, Narayan Bagh, Flat No. 302, IIIrd Floor, Near Humpty Dumpty School, Indore - 452 007 (M.P.). Mobile: 09301386468

Kolkata : 108/4, Beliaghata Main Road, Near ID Hospital, Opp. SBI Bank, Kolkata - 700 010, Phone: 033-32449649, Mobile: 09883055590, 07439040301

Guwahati : House No. 15, Behind Pragjyotish College, Near Sharma Printing Press, P.O. Bharalumukh, Guwahati - 781009, (Assam). Mobile: 09883055590, 09883055536

DTP by : HPH, Editorial Office, Bhandup **(Krunali)**.

Printed at : M/s. Aditya Offset Process (I) Pvt. Ltd., Hyderabad. On behalf of HPH.

PREFACE

"Genius is the ability to reduce the complicated to the simple"...

– Albert Einstien

I earnestly hope that the book will make complicated Subject A.F.M, simple to understand and score high marks in Exams.

I look forward for constructive suggestion from the reader.

I am thankful to one and all who have contributed directly or indirectly to make this book possible.

This book is user friendly and different. As one goes through the book one will feel the difference, and this will help to master finance in an enjoyable manner, with life time utility.

Recommended Books Authored by Pawan Jhabak

- 'Financial Management' for T.Y.BMS by Himalaya Publishing House, 2010
- 'Financial Management' for M.M.S. Sem II, by Himalaya Publishing House, 2010
- 'Portfolio Management' for T.Y.BMS/T.Y.BBI/T.Y.BFM by Himalaya Publishing House, 2011
- 'Advance Financial Management' for M.M.S. Sem. III by Himalaya Publishing House, 2011
- 'Financial Statement Analysis' for T.Y.BAF Sem. V by Himalaya Publishing House, 2011
- 'Financial Words All should know' General book by Himalaya Publishing House, 2011
- 'Financial and Management Accounting' MBA (edited) Jaro Publication'

Best Wishes
Million Thanks

Prof. Pawan Jhabak
Ex. Vice-principal
Rustomjee Business School
M: 9324343830
scorejhabak@gmail.com
scoreeducation.co.in

BIBLIOGRAPHY AND ACKNOWLEDGEMENT

I have benefited from scores of books and hundreds of articles. As it is impossible to list all of them, the overall reference book is mentioned.

- Prasanna Chandra, *Financial Management*, Tata McGraw-Hill, 2008.
- Khan & Jain, *Financial Management*, Tata McGraw-Hill, 2007.
- Dr. Jawaharlal, *Accounting for Management*, Himalaya Publishing House Pvt. Ltd., V Edition, 2010.

I would like to express my gratitude to:

- The Pioneers in the field of financial management who have shaped my understanding through their rich and varied contributions.
- Students for providing the stimulus for writing this book.
- My staff Sumedha, Sukhada, Anil Kumar and Staff of Himalaya Publishing House.
- My Grandmother Jhamkudevi, Wife Bharati and Daughter Param.

I eagerly look forward to suggestions for improvements in this book.

I wish you score the Best in Exams and reach at the highest level as Finance Professional.

BEST WISHES !!

Prof. Pawan Jhabak
Ex. Vice-principal
Rustomjee Business School
scorejhabak@gmail.com
M: 9324343830

About the Author

PAWAN JHABAK
M.Com., P.G.D.Ed.M
Vice-principal
Rustomjee Business School, Dahisar(West), Mumbai - 68
Cell No.: 9324343830

Visiting Faculty

- Vivekanand Education Society.
- LALA Lajpatrai College.
- Rajiv Gandhi Institute of Technology.
- Sydhnem Institute of Management.
- Amity Business School.
- Jaro Education

Ex. Visiting Faculty

- Narsee Monjee College.
- Usha Pravin Gandhi.
- Bhavan's College (Andheri).
- Rizvi College.
- S.K. Somaiya.
- Akbar Peerbhoy.
- Bhurani College.
- Poddar College.
- Mumbai Education Trust.
- Sydhnem College, etc.

"Suggestions for improvements from teachers, students and other readers will be greatly appreciated."

Send your suggestions to scorejhabak@gmail.com

We Can't Spell SUCCESS Without U !!!

CONTENTS

CHAPTER 1

INDIAN FINANCIAL SYSTEM

1.1 STRUCTURE OF FINANCIAL SYSTEM

The financial system implies a set of complex and closely connected institutions, agents, practices and markets. The following is a typical structure of financial system in any economy.

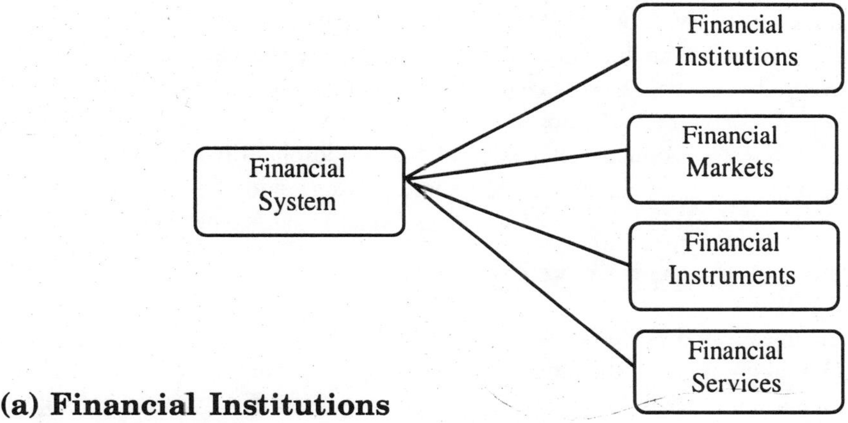

(a) Financial Institutions

Financial institutions are business organisations who act as mobilizers and depositories of savings, and suppliers of credit or finance. These institutions provide various financial services to the business organisations and common people. Financial institutions can be divided into banking and non-banking institutions (NBFC, MFI, etc).

(b) Financial Markets

Financial markets are the centres which provide facilities for buying and selling of financial claims and services. The participants in the financial market are financial institutions, brokers, dealers, borrowers and investors. They are interlinked by the laws, contracts and communication networks. Financial markets can be divided into two parts. The primary market which deals in new financial claims or instruments. It is also called as New Issue Market. The secondary market deals in securities which are already issued by the companies. Stock exchange is an example of secondary market. The primary markets mobilize savings and supply additional capital to the companies. Secondary markets do not supply direct capital but indirectly help the companies and investors in providing liquidity.

The capital market is co-extensive not only with the stockmarket but it is much wider than the stockmarket. The financial markets may be classified as organised or unorganised, formal or informal and domestic or foreign markets.

(c) Financial Instruments

Financial instruments are claims to the payment of sum of money in future or a periodic interval. For example, the important financial instruments are shares, debentures, bonds, fixed deposits, etc. Regular payment in the form of interest or dividend is paid by the company to the investors. These instruments are classified as primary or secondary instruments. The primary instruments are issued by the ultimate investors directly to the ultimate savers such as equity shares, debentures. Secondary instruments are issued by financial intermediaries to the ultimate savers as bank deposits, units and insurance policies. The financial instruments differ from each other in respect of their investment characteristics. The important characteristics are liquidity, transferability, volatility, maturity, risk and return. Market condition and risk appetite of investor play an important role in selection of financial instrument.

(d) Financial Services

A financial service is any kind of service of a financial nature offered by a financial service provider. All banking and insurance related services are included in this concept. These services are intangible and invisible. There should be proximity between the service provider and the consumer in order to complete a service transaction. These services cover a wide range of economic activities. Financial services have developed to meet the needs of investors. Banking and insurance are traditional financial services. The modern financial services include over-the-counter services, share transfer, pledging of shares, mutual funds, factoring, discounting, venture capital, credit cards, PMS, wealth management services, etc.

1.2 INTRODUCTION TO CAPITAL MARKETS

There are 22 stock exchanges in India, the first being the Bombay Stock Exchange (BSE), which began formal trading in 1875, making it one of the oldest in Asia. Over the last few years, there has been a rapid change in the Indian securities market, especially in the secondary market. Advanced technology and online-based transactions have modernized the stock exchanges. In terms of the number of companies listed and total market capitalization, the Indian equity market is considered large relative to the country's stage of economic development. The number of listed companies increased from 5,968 in March 1990 to about 10,000 by May 1998 and market capitalization has grown almost 11 times during the same period.

The debt market, however, is almost nonexistent in India even though there has been a large volume of Government bonds traded. Banks and financial institutions have been holding a substantial part of these bonds as statutory liquidity requirement. The portfolio restrictions on financial institutions'statutory liquidity requirement are still in place. A primary auction market for Government securities has been created and a primary dealer system was introduced in 1995. There are six authorized primary dealers. Currently, there are 31 mutual funds, out of which 21 are in the private sector. Mutual funds were opened to the private sector in 1992. Earlier in 1987, banks were allowed to enter this business, breaking the monopoly of the Unit Trust of India (UTI), which maintains a dominant position.

Before 1992, many factors obstructed the expansion of equity trading. Fresh capital issues were controlled through the Capital Issues Control Act. Trading practices were not transparent, and there was a large amount of insider trading. Recognizing the importance of increasing investor protection, several measures were enacted to improve the fairness of the capital market. The Securities and Exchange Board of India (SEBI) was established in 1988. Despite the rules it set, problems continued to exist, including those relating to disclosure criteria, lack of broker capital adequacy, and poor regulation of merchant bankers and underwriters.

There have been significant reforms in the regulation of the securities market since 1992 in conjunction with overall economic and financial reforms. In 1992, the SEBI Act was enacted giving SEBI statutory status as an apex regulatory body. And a series of reforms was introduced to improve investor protection, automation of stock trading, integration of national markets, and efficiency of market operations.

India has seen a tremendous change in the secondary market for equity. Its equity market will most likely be comparable with the world's most advanced secondary markets within a year or two. The key ingredients that underlie market quality in India's equity market are:

- exchanges based on open electronic limit order book;
- nationwide integrated market with a large number of informed traders and fluency of short or long position.

Among the processes that have already started are electronic settlement trade and exchange-traded derivatives. Before 1995, markets in India used open outcry, a trading process in which traders shouted and hand-signalled from within a pit. One major policy initiated by SEBI from 1993 involved the shift of all exchanges to screen-based trading, motivated primarily by the need for greater transparency. The first exchange to be based on an open electronic limit order book was the National Stock Exchange (NSE), which started trading debt instruments in June 1994 and equity in November 1994. In March 1995, BSE shifted from open outcry to a limit order book market.

Fragmented Market

Of the 22 stock exchanges in the country, 17 have introduced screen-based trading. With the expansion of trading networks of BSE and other stock exchanges beyond their original jurisdictions, an increasing number of investors in different parts of the country are within the reach of a national market system. This has raised informational efficiency and helped rapid market integration.

NSE, which provides a screen-based order driven system, has already extended its network to more than 100 centres in the country that are connected to its central computer via its satellite network. The Over-The-Counter Exchange of India (OTCEI) also provides a nationwide electronic system for trading relatively smaller stocks. BSE has introduced its own screen-based quote-driven trading system. However, the market is still fragmented and needs further integration.

Development of Secondary Market

While there has been increased activity in primary debt issues, the secondary market for debt is yet to become active. The entry of FIIs into the debt market and the launching of fixed income schemes and money market schemes by mutual funds are expected to activate the debt market. Several technical impediments that prevented more active secondary market trading in Government securities have been removed over the past few years. But still there are significant barriers to the active development of the secondary market for fixed income assets.

1.3 POLICY RECOMMENDATIONS

Over the last few years, there have been substantial reforms in the Indian capital market. But there are still many issues to be addressed to make it more efficient in mobilizing and allocating capital.

Investor confidence in stock investment is low. This must be regained in order to encourage capital mobilization through primary market issues. Further strengthening of investor protection, and improvements in transparency, corporate governance, and monitoring will be necessary. The capital market infrastructure, such as accounting standards and legal mechanisms, should also be improved to this end. On the supply side, to encourage corporate firms to rely more on stockmarkets for their source of financing, the issuing costs in terms of length of time required and administrative burden should be streamlined (Table 1).

Table 1: Matrix of Policy Recommendations

Issues	Policy Recommendation
A. Market infrastructure 1. Accounting principles 2. Legal mechanism **B.** Corporate governance **C.** Cost of capital issue **D.** Debt market 1. Diversification of investors 2. Stamp duty 3. Private placement **E.** Integration of stock exchanges and consolidation of intermediaries **F.** Risk management **G** Integration of the capital market with the banking sector	• Improve accounting principles, make them consistent with international practice. • Strictly enforce punitive measures for inaccurate accounting practice. • Establish prompt and effective settlement of disputes to protect small investors' interests. • Grant institutional investors voting power. • Allow hostile takeovers. • Require consolidated balance sheets for conglomerates-affiliated firms to better monitor cross-subsidization and internal transactions between affiliated firms. • Streamline the procedure for public subscription of securities to reduce transaction costs in terms of time lag and uncertainty. • Apply fully market-based interest rates for issuing Government securities. • Further reduce statutory liquidity requirements. • Further enhance the credibility of credit rating agencies. • Amend stamp duty regime by the Government of Maharashtra, where Mumbai is located, in the form of one time levy or consolidated fee payable by National Securities Depository, Ltd. (NSDL). • Indicate the framework within which the private placement has to function to protect investors from risk associated with subscriptions in the private placement market. • Provide favourable environment or some incentives for establishing central trading system through interconnectivity. • Encourage the corporatization and merger of brokers and merchant bankers through tax incentives. • Securities and Exchange Board of India to more closely monitor and inspect the intermediaries and stock exchanges and, if necessary, strengthen punitive measures. • Banking system to establish a good Electronic Funds Transfer (EFT) solution to enable direct payments of dividends to bank accounts, eliminate counterparty risk, and facilitate FIIs. • Encourage sound competition between the banking sector and the capital market through more banking liberalization.

1.4 REGULATORY FRAMEWORK OF CAPITAL MARKET

Securities and Exchange Board of India

Securities and Exchange Board of India (SEBI) was set up as an administrative arrangement in 1988. In 1992, the SEBI Act was enacted, which gave statutory status to SEBI. It mandates SEBI to perform a dual function: investor protection through regulation of the securities market, and fostering the development of this market. SEBI has been delegated most of the functions and powers under the Securities Contract Regulation (SCR) Act, which brought stock exchanges, their members, as well as contracts in securities which could be traded under the regulations of the Ministry of Finance. It has also been delegated certain powers under the Companies Act. In addition to registering and regulating intermediaries, service providers, mutual funds, collective investment schemes, venture capital funds, and takeovers, SEBI is also vested with power to issue directives to any person(s) related to the securities market or to companies in areas of issue of capital, transfer of securities, and disclosures. It also has powers to inspect books and records, suspend registered entities, and cancel registration.

On April 12, 1988, the Securities and Exchange Board of India (SEBI) was established with a dual objective of protecting the rights of small investors and regulating and developing the stockmarkets in India.

In 1992, the Bombay Stock Exchange (BSE), the leading stock exchange in India, witnessed the first major scam masterminded by Harshad Mehta. Analysts unanimously felt that if more powers had been given to SEBI, the scam would not have happened.

As a result, the Government of India brought in a separate legislation by the name of 'SEBI Act, 1992' and conferred statutory powers to it. Since then, SEBI had introduced several stockmarket reforms. These reforms significantly transformed the face of Indian stockmarkets.

SEBI introduced online trading and demat of shares which did away with the age-old paper-based trading, thus bringing more transparency into the trading system.

Objectives of SEBI

As an important entity in the market it works with following objectives:

1. It tries to develop the securities market.
2. Promotes investors interest.
3. Makes rules and regulations for the securities market.

Functions of SEBI

1. Regulates Capital Market.
2. Checks trading securities.
3. Checks the malpractices in securities market.
4. It enhances investor's knowledge on market by providing education.
5. It regulates the stockbrokers and sub-brokers.
6. To promote Research and Investigation.

SEBI from time-to-time have adopted many rules and regulations for enhancing the Indian capital market. The recent initiatives undertaken are as follows:

Sole Control on Brokers

- Under this rule in India every brokers and sub-brokers have to get registration with SEBI and Stock exchange.

For Underwriters

For working as an underwriter an asset limit of ₹ 10 crore has been fixed.

For Share Prices

According to this law all Indian companies are free to determine their respective share prices and premiums on the share prices.

For Mutual Funds

SEBI's introduction of SEBI (Mutual Funds) Regulation in 1993 is to have direct control on all mutual funds of both public and private sector.

Reserve Bank of India

Reserve Bank of India (RBI) has regulatory involvement in the capital market, but this has been limited to debt management through primary dealers, foreign exchange control, and liquidity support to market participants. It is RBI and not SEBI that regulates primary dealers in the Government securities market. RBI instituted the primary dealership of Government securities in March 1998. Securities transactions that involve a foreign exchange transaction need the permission of RBI.

Department of Company Affairs

In 1947, the Capital Issues (Control) Act was enacted, which formalized and continued initial controls on the issue of securities that were introduced during World War II. This Act was administered by the office of the Controller of Capital Issues (CCI), which was a part of the Ministry of Finance. In line with economic reforms, it was repealed in 1992 to liberalize capital issuance and pricing. While capital issurance used to be regulated by the office of the CCI, both private and public companies were governed by the Companies Act of 1956, which was and continues to be administered by the Department of Company Affairs (DCA) under the Ministry of Law, Justice and Company Affairs. Besides governing the incorporation, management, mergers, and winding up of companies, this Act also specifies certain aspects concerning capital issuance and securities trading, particularly the issue of prospectus for public offers, contents of the prospectus, completion of allotment, issue, and trading of securities, and transfer and registration of securities.

Stock Exchanges

SEBI issued directives that require that half the members of the governing boards of the stock exchanges be non-broker public representatives and include a SEBI nominee. To avoid conflicts of interest, stock brokers are a minority in the committees of stock exchanges set up to handle matters of discipline, default, and investor-broker disputes. The exchanges are required to appoint a professional, non-member executive director who is accountable to SEBI for the implementation of its directives on the regulation of stock exchanges. SEBI has introduced a mechanism to remedy investor grievances against brokers.

Disclosure

Similar to companies in capital markets in other countries, a company offering securities in the Indian capital market is required to make a public disclosure of all relevant information through its offer documents. These documents are as follows:

- Prospectus,
- Application form and the abridged prospectus (in case of an issue to the public), or
- Letter of offer (in case of a rights issue to existing shareholders or debenture-holders of a company with or without the right to renounce in favour of other persons).

After a security is issued to the public and subsequently listed on a stock exchange, the issuing company is required under the listing agreement to continue to disclose in a timely manner to the exchange, to the holders of the listed securities (the shareholders or the bondholders), and to the public (through the exchange or the media), any information necessary to enable the holders of the listed securities to appraise its position and to avoid the establishment of a false market in such listed securities. Such information include:

- the date of the meeting of the board of directors for corporate actions;
- the audited financial results on an annual basis and the unaudited ones on a semi-annual basis;
- any proposed change in the general character or nature of the company's business;
- any alterations of the company's capital; and any change of the company's directorate, including managing directors and auditors.

REVIEW QUESTIONS

1. Explain Structure of Financial System.
2. Explain function of SEBI in brief.

CHAPTER 2 LEVERAGE

2.1 LEVERAGE

Leverage refers to amplified benefit on comparatively lower level of owner investment or lower. Such enhancement of profit is usually seen because of fixed costs. These could be operating fixed cost or financial fixed cost. As sales volume increases fixed cost do not increase. Hence, it results in higher level of profit.

Fixed cost however also leads to higher level of break even-point. Higher break even point is a risk. Thus, highly leveraged firms feature high risk and high return. Leverages are also referred in the context of optimal utilization such as asset leverage and working capital leverage.

2.2 TYPES OF LEVERAGE

1. Operating Leverage

Operating leverage refers to enhancement of profits because of fixed operating expenses. As sales increase fixed cost do not increase which results in proportionately higher profits. Degree of Operating Leverage (DOL) calculated as

$$\text{DOL} = \frac{\text{Contribution}}{\text{PBIT}} = \frac{\text{\% Change in PBIT}}{\text{\% Change in Sales}}$$

Higher fixed expenses indicate higher operating break even point and hence higher business risk.

Fixed operating expenses are determined by nature of business and industry. For instance, heavy engineering units would have higher level of fixed overheads, whereas service industry would have lower overheads. Thus, DOL is dictated by these factors and managers have little liberty to adjust it at their will.

2. Financial Leverage

Financial leverage refers to higher level of profit because of higher fixed financial expenses. These include interest on loan and debentures as well as preference dividend. Degree of financial leverage is calculated as:

$$\frac{\text{PBIT}}{\text{PBT}} = \frac{\text{\% Change in PBT}}{\text{\% Change in PBIT}}$$

Higher financial leverage indicates higher financial break even point and higher financial risk. Capital structure to some extent is determined by nature of business and industry. However, finance managers have greater flexibility in choice of capital structure. They can decide quantum of borrowed capital and preference shares. Aggressive policies will lead to higher borrowings, higher DFL, which will result in high risk and high return profile.

Conservative policies would lead to lower level of borrowings, and therefore low risk low return profile.

It may be argued that capital intensive units are more likely to have higher debt to equity proportion and hence higher financial leverage. (e.g., Power Sector Units).

3. Combined Leverage

Combined leverage refers to higher profits because of fixed costs. These include fixed operating expenses as well as fixed financial expenses. Degree of Combined Leverage (DCL) is calculated as:

$$DCL = \frac{\text{Contribution}}{\text{PBT}} = \frac{\text{\% Change in PBIT}}{\text{\% Change in Sales}}$$

Alternate Formula

$$DCL = DOL \times DFL$$

DCL is a complete indicator of leverage benefits and leverage risks. DCL also indicates overall break even point. While operating fixed costs are determined by nature of business and industry. Financial fixed costs can be adjusted by appropriate choice of capital structure. Aggressive firms choose higher level of DCL, whereas conservative go for lower level of DCL.

Distinguish between Operating Leverage and Financial Leverage

The differences between the two leverages are as follows:

	Operating Leverage	Financial Leverage
1. Objective	The objective is to magnify the effect of changes in sales on operating profit.	The objective is to magnify the effect of changes in operating profits on earnings per share.
2. Relationship	It establishes relationship between operating profit and sales.	It establishes relationship between operating profit and return on equity.
3. Measurement	It measures a firm ability to use fixed cost assets to magnify the operating profits.	It measures a firm ability to use fixed cost funds to magnify the return to equity shareholders.
4. Relationship	It relates to the assets side of the balance sheet.	It relates to the liability side of the balance sheet.
5. Effect on income	It affects the profit before interest and tax.	It affects the profit after interest and tax.
6. Risk	It involves operating risk of being unable to cover fixed operating cost.	It involves financial risk of being unable to cover fixed financial cost.
7. Decision	It is concerned with investment decision.	It is concern with financial decision.
8. Stage	It is described as first stage leverage.	It is described as second stage leverage.
9. Formula	$DOL = \frac{\text{Contribution}}{\text{PBIT}}$	$DFL = \frac{\text{PBIT}}{\text{PBT}}$

Business Risk and Financial Risk

Business Risk

Higher operating fixed cost leads to higher operating break even point. Risk of not achieving operating break even point because of lower level of sales is called business risk. Higher business risk means higher DOL and possible higher profits after break even point. Business risk is measured in terms of operating leverage.

$$DOL = \frac{\text{Contribution}}{\text{PBT}} = \frac{\text{\% Change in PBIT}}{\text{\% Change in Sales}}$$

Business risk has effect on gross profit margin and return on capital employed. Business risk is determined by nature of business and industry.

Financial Risk

Higher financial expenses such as interest and preference dividend lead to higher financial break even point. Risk of not achieving financial break even is called financial risk. Higher financial risk means higher DFL and possible higher profits after break even point. Financial risk is measured in terms of financial leverage.

$$DFL = \frac{\text{PBIT}}{\text{PBT}} = \frac{\text{\% Change in PBT}}{\text{\% Change in PBIT}}$$

Financial risk has effect on net profit margin. Level of financial risk is a choice of finance manager and aggressive/conservative policies of the firm.

Break even analysis

It is a technique for studying the relationship among fixed costs, variable cost, sales volumes and profits. It occurs when the PBIT is equal to zero, as a result of which the earnings per share is also effectively zero. In other words, the break even point is the PBIT level where EPS is the same for two or more financial plans or alternatives. So it effectively analyses the effect of financing alternatives on earnings per share.

Thus, the operating break even point is defined as that level of sales at which PBIT is equal to zero. It is used to find the sales required to reach a target level of PBIT.

Income Statement Format

Particulars	Amt. (₹)
Sales	xxx
(-) Variable Cost	(xxx)
Contribution	xxx
(-) Fixed Cost	(xxx)
Earning Before Interest and Tax (EBIT)	xxx
(-) Interest	(xxx)
Earning Before Tax (EBT)	xxx
(-) Tax	(xxx)
Earning After Tax (EAT)	xxx

2.3 LEVERAGE: PROBLEMS + SOLUTION

Q. 1. Jigna Ltd., sells 1,00,000 units of product. Selling price is ₹ 10 per unit and variable cost is ₹ 3, if the fixed cost for the year amounts to ₹ 4,00,000, find out the effect on profit, if the company sells 1,10,000 units and 80,000 units.

Q.1: Solution

Particulars	Amt. (₹)	Amt. (₹)	Amt. (₹)
Units	1,00,000	1,10,000	8,0000
Sales	10,00,000	11,00,000	80,0000
(-) Variable cost	3,00,000	3,30,000	24,0000
Contribution	7,00,000	7,70,000	56,0000
(-) Fixed cost	4,00,000	4,00,000	40,0000
Profit	3,00,000	3,70,000	16,0000

Comment: The companies profit when the sales is 1,10,000 units is ₹ 3,70,000 and when the sales are 80,000 units, the profit is ₹ 1,60,000 i.e., 10% increase in sales. Increase in profit by 23.33% and 20% decrease in sales, reduces profit by 46.67%.

Q. 2. Ambika Ltd., sells 2,000 units per annum. The selling price per unit is ₹ 300 and the variable cost per unit is ₹ 70. The fixed operating cost is ₹ 60,000.

Calculate operating leverage.

Q.2: Solution

Particulars	Amt. (₹)
Sales (2,000 × 300)	6,00,000
(-) Variable cost (70 × 2,000)	1,40,000
Contribution	4,60,000
(-) Fixed Cost	60,000
PBIT	4,00,000

$$\text{Operating Leverage} = \frac{\text{Contribution}}{\text{PBT}}$$

$$= \frac{4,60,000}{4,00,000}$$

$$= 1.15$$

Q. 3. Y Ltd. sells its product at ₹ 20 per unit. Variable cost per unit is ₹ 15. Find out the "degree of operating leverage for sale of 3,000 units, and 3,500 units. What do you understand from the degree of operating leverage of these sales volumes? Fixed cost is ₹ 10,000."

Q.3: Solution

Particulars	Amt. (₹)	Amt. (₹)
Units	3,000	3,500
Sales	60,000	70,000
(-) Variable cost	45,000	52,500
Contribution	15,000	17,500
(-) Fixed cost	10,000	10,000
PBIT	5,000	7,500

$$\text{Operating Leverage (3,000 units)} = \frac{\text{Contribution}}{\text{PBIT}}$$

$$= \frac{15{,}000}{5{,}000}$$

$$= 3$$

$$\text{Operating Leverage (3,500 units)} = \frac{\text{Contribution}}{\text{PBIT}}$$

$$= \frac{17{,}500}{7{,}500}$$

$$= 2.3$$

Higher units/sales, results into lower operating/business risk and vice versa.

Q. 4.

Particulars	Amt. (₹)
Interest	10,000
Sales (1,000 units)	1,00,000
Variable Cost	50,000
Fixed Cost	30,000

Q.4: Solution

Particulars	Amt. (₹)
Sales	1,00,000
(-) Variable cost	50,000
Contribution	50,000
(-) Fixed cost	30,000
PBIT	20,000
(-) Interest	10,000
PBIT	10,000

$$\text{Financial Leverage} = \frac{\text{PBIT}}{\text{PBT}}$$

$$= \frac{20,000}{10,000}$$

$$= 2$$

Q. 5.

Shruti Ltd., has the following structure:

Particulars	**Amt. (₹)**
Equity share capital	5,00,000
10% preference share capital	5,00,000
8% debentures	5,50,000

The present EBIT is ₹ 2,50,000, tax rate is 50%. Calculate financial leverage.

Q.5: Solution

Particulars	**Amt. (₹)**
EBIT (Earning Before Interest Tax)	2,50,000
(-) Interest (550000 × 8%)	44,000
PBT	2,06,000

$$\text{Financial Leverage} = \frac{\text{PBIT}}{\text{PBT}}$$

$$= \frac{2,50,000}{2,06,000}$$

$$= 1.21$$

Q. 6. Y Ltd., has sales of ₹ 2,00,000. Variable cost is 50% of sales while the fixed operating cost amounts to ₹ 60,000. Interest on long-term loan amounted to ₹ 20,000.

You are requested to calculate the composite leverage and analyze the impact if sales increase by 10%.

Q.6: Solution

Particulars	**Amt. (₹)**	**Sales↑ 10%**
Sales	2,00,000	2,20,000
(-) Variable cost	1,00,000	1,10,000
Contribution	1,00,000	1,10,000
(-) Fixed cost	60,000	60,000
PBIT	40,000	50,000
(-) Interest	20,000	20,000
PBT	20,000	30,000

$$\text{Composite Leverage (at present)} = \frac{\text{Contribution}}{\text{PBT}}$$

$$= \frac{1,00,000}{20,000}$$

$$= 5$$

$$\text{Composite Leverage (at 10\% }\uparrow\text{)} = \frac{\text{Contribution}}{\text{PBT}}$$

$$= \frac{1,10,000}{30,000}$$

$$= 3.67$$

Analysis

Increase in sales reduces the combined risk and vice versa.

Q. 7. The following information is available in respect of two firms, P Ltd., and Q Ltd.

Particulars	P Ltd. (₹)	Q Ltd. (₹)
Sales	500	1,000
(-) variable cost	200	300
Contribution	300	700
(-) Fixed cost	150	400
EBIT	150	300
(-)Interest	50	100
Profit before tax	100	200

You are required to calculate different leverages for both the firms and also comment on their relative risk position.

Q. 7: Solution

Particulars	P Ltd. (₹)	Q Ltd. (₹)
(1) Operating Leverage ratio		
$= \frac{\text{Contribution}}{\text{PBIT}}$	$\frac{300}{150}$	$\frac{700}{300}$
	=2	=2.3
(2) Financial Leverage ratio $= \frac{\text{PBIT}}{\text{PBT}}$	$\frac{150}{100}$ = 1.5	$\frac{300}{200}$ = 1.5
(3) Combined Leverage ratio		
= OOL × DFL	2 × 1.5	2.3 × 1.5
	=3	=3.45

Comment:

1. **Operating Leverage:** Q Ltd., has comparatively higher operating risk.
2. **Financial Leverage:** The financial risk of both companies is same.
3. **Combined Leverage:** The combine risk is higher for Q Ltd.

Q. 8. A simplified Income Statement of Zenith Ltd., is given below. Calculate its degree of operating leverage, degree of financial leverage and degree of combined leverage.

Sales	?
Variable cost	2,00,000
Fixed cost	75,000
EBIT	2,08,000
Interest	1,10,000
Taxes (30%)	29,400
Net Income	68,600

Q.8: Solution

Revenue statement for year-----

Particulars	**(₹)**
Sales (bal. fig.) *	4,83,000
(-) Variable cost	2,00,000
Contribution	2,83,000
(-) Fixed cost	75,000
PBIT	2,08,000
(-) Interest	1,10,000
PBT	98,000
(-) Tax (30%)	29,400
PAT	68,600

$$\text{Operating Leverage Ratio} = \frac{\text{Contribution}}{\text{PBIT}}$$

$$= \frac{2,83,000}{2,08,000}$$

$$= 1.36$$

$$\text{Financial Leverage Ratio} = \frac{\text{PBIT}}{\text{PBT}}$$

$$= \frac{2,08,000}{98,000}$$

$$= 2.12$$

$$\text{Combined Leverage Ratio} = \frac{\text{Contribution}}{\text{PBT}}$$

$$= \frac{2,83,000}{98,000}$$

$$= 2.9$$

Q. 9.

1. Find out operating leverage from the following data:

Sales	₹ 50,000
Variable Costs	60%
Fixed Costs	₹ 12,000

2. Find out financial leverage from the following data:

Net Worth	₹ 25,00,000
Debt/Equity	3:1
Interest Rate	12%
Operating Profit	₹ 20,00,000

Q.9: Solution

(1)

Particulars	**(₹)**
Sales	50,000
(-) Variable cost (60%)	30,000
Contribution	20,000
(-) Fixed cost	12,000
PBIT	8,000

$$\text{Operating Leverage} = \frac{\text{Contribution}}{\text{PBIT}}$$

$$= \frac{20,000}{8,000}$$

$$= 2.5$$

(2)

Own Funds = Net worth = Equity = Shareholder fund = ₹ 25,00,000

$$\text{Debt Equity Ratio} = \frac{\text{Debt.}}{\text{Equity}}$$

$$\frac{3}{1} = \frac{\text{Debt.}}{25,000}$$

$$= 25,00,000$$

:. Debt = ₹ 75,00,000

:. Interest = ₹ 75,00,000 × 12%

= ₹ 9,00,000

Operating Profit	=	EBIT	20,00,000
		(-) Interest	9,00,000
		EBT	11,00,000

$$\text{Financial Leverage Ratio} = \frac{\text{EBIT}}{\text{EBT}}$$

$$= \frac{20,00,000}{11,00,000}$$

$$= 1.8$$

Q. 10. From the following information available for 4 firms, calculate the Earning before Interest and Tax (EBIT), Earnings per share (EPS), the operating leverage and the financial leverage.

	Firms			
	P	Q	R	S
Sales (in units)	20,000	25,000	30,000	40,000
Selling price per unit (₹)	15	20	25	30
Variable cost per unit (₹)	10	15	20	25
Fixed cost (₹)	30,000	40,000	50,000	60,000
Interest (₹)	15,000	25,000	35,000	40,000
Tax %	40	40	40	40
Number of Equity Shares	5,000	9,000	10,000	12,000

Q.10: Solution

Particulars	P	Q	R	S
Sales	3,00,000	5,00,000	7,50,000	12,00,000
(-) Variable cost	2,00,000	3,75,000	6,00,000	10,00,000
Contribution	1,00,000	1,25,000	1,50,000	2,00,000
(-) Fixed cost	30,000	40,000	50,000	60,000
PBIT	70,000	85,000	1,00,000	1,40,000
(-) Interest	15,000	25,000	35,000	40,000
PBT	55,000	60,000	65,000	1,00,000
(-) Tax (40%)	22,000	24,000	26,000	40,000
PAT	33,000	36,000	39,000	60,000
(-) Pref. dividend	-	-	-	-
Profit available to ESH a)...	33,000	36,000	39,000	60,000
No. of Equity Share b)...	5,000	9,000	10,000	12,000
EPS (a/b)	₹ 6.6	₹ 4	₹ 3.9	₹ 5

Operating Leverage				
$= \frac{\text{Contribution}}{\text{PBIT}}$	$\frac{1,00,000}{70,000}$	$\frac{1,25,000}{85,000}$	$\frac{1,50,000}{1,00,000}$	$\frac{2,00,000}{1,40,000}$
	= 1.42	= 1.47	= 1.5	= 1.42
Financial Leverage				
$= \frac{\text{PBIT}}{\text{PBT}}$	$\frac{70,000}{55,000}$	$\frac{85,000}{60,000}$	$\frac{1,00,000}{65,000}$	$\frac{1,40,000}{1,00,000}$
	= 1.27	= 1.41	= 1.54	= 1.4

Q. 11. A firm has sales of ₹ 75,00,000; Variable Cost ₹ 42,00,000 and Fixed Cost of ₹ 6,00,000. It has Debt of ₹ 45,00,000 at 9% and Equity of ₹ 55,00,000.

(a) What is firm's ROI?

(b) Does it have a favourable Financial Leverage?

(c) If the firm belongs to an industry, whose asset turnover is 3, does it have high or low asset leverage?

(d) What are the Operating, Financial and Combined Leverage of the firm?

(e) If the sales drop to ₹ 50,00,000; what will be the new EBIT?

Q. 11: Solution

Particulars	**(₹)**
Sales	75,00,000
(-) Variable cost (56%)	42,00,000
Contribution	33,00,000
(-) Fixed cost	6,00,000
PBIT	27,00,000
(-) Interest (9% × 45L)	4,05,000
PBT	22,95,000

(a) $$\text{ROI} = \frac{\text{EBIT}}{\text{Cap. Emp.}} \times 100$$

$$= \frac{27,00,000}{55,00,000 + 45,00,000} \times 100$$

$$= \frac{27,00,000}{1,00,000} \times 100$$

$$= 27\%$$

(b) Since ROI is greater than interest on borrowed fund, it can be said that the firm has favourable financial leverage.

(c) $$\text{Asset Turnover Ratio} = \frac{\text{Sales}}{\text{Net Assets}}$$

Or

$$= \frac{\text{Sales}}{\text{Capital Employed}}$$

$$= \frac{75,00,000}{1,00,00,000}$$

$= 0.75$

Comment: The firm has low asset leverage. It indicates inefficient utilization of asset/excess capacity

(d) Operating Leverage Ratio $= \frac{\text{Contribution}}{\text{PBIT}}$

$$= \frac{33,00,000}{27,00,000}$$

$= 1.22$

Financial Leverage Ratio $= \frac{\text{PBIT}}{\text{PBT}}$

$$= \frac{27,00,000}{22,95,000}$$

$= 1.17$

Combined Leverage Ratio $= \frac{\text{Contribution}}{\text{PBT}}$

$$= \frac{33,00,000}{22,95,000}$$

$= 1.43$

(e)		(₹)
	Sales	50,00,000
	(-) Variable cost (56%)	28,00,000
	Contribution	22,00,000
	(-) Fixed Cost	6,00,000
	EBIT	16,00,000

Hence, New EBIT will be ₹ 16,00,000.

Q. 12.

The selected financial data for A, B and C companies for the year ended 31st March, 2010 were as follows:

	A	B	C
Variable cost as a percentage of Sales	66 2/3	75	50
Interest Expenses (₹)	200	300	1,000
Degree of Operating Leverage	5	6	2
Degree of Financial Leverage	3	4	2
Income Tax Rate %	40	40	40

Prepare an income statement for each of the three companies. *(MU, BMS, Nov. 2002)*

Q.12: Solution

Particulars		A	B	C
Sales	100%	4,500	(100) 9,600	(100) 8,000
(-) Variable cost	66.66...%	3,000	(75) 7,200	(50) 4,000
Contribution	33.33...%	1,500	(25) 2,400	(50) 4,000
(-) Fixed cost		1,200	2,000	2,000
PBIT		300	400	2,000
(-) Interest		200	300	1,000
PBT		100	100	1,000
(-) Tax 40%		40	40	400
PAT		60	60	600

W.N. 1. A Ltd.,

$$\text{Degree of Financial Leverage} = \frac{\text{PBIT}}{\text{PBIT} - \text{I}}$$

$$3 = \frac{\text{PBIT}}{\text{PBIT} - \text{I}}$$

$$3 = \frac{\text{PBIT}}{\text{PBIT} - 200}$$

$$3\,(\text{PBIT} - 200) = \text{PBIT}$$

$$3\ \text{PBIT} - 600 = \text{PBIT}$$

$$3\ \text{PBIT} - \text{PBIT} = 600$$

$$2\ \text{PBIT} = 600$$

$$\text{PBIT} = 300$$

$$\text{Degree of Operating Leverage} = \frac{\text{Contribution}}{\text{PBIT}}$$

$$5 = \frac{\text{Contribution}}{300}$$

$$\text{Contribution} = 1{,}500$$

W.N. 2. B Ltd.,

$$\text{Degree of Financial Leverage} = \frac{\text{PBIT}}{\text{PBIT} - \text{I}}$$

$$4 = \frac{\text{PBIT}}{\text{PBIT} - \text{I}}$$

$$4 = \frac{\text{PBIT}}{\text{PBIT} - 300}$$

$$4\text{ PBIT} - 1{,}200 = \text{PBIT}$$
$$4\text{ PBIT} - \text{PBIT} = 12$$
$$3\text{ PBIT} = 1200$$
$$\text{PBIT} = 400$$

$$\text{Degree of Operating Leverage} = \frac{\text{Contribution}}{\text{PBIT}}$$

$$6 = \frac{\text{Contribution}}{400}$$

$$\text{Contribution} = 2{,}400$$

W.N. 3. C Ltd.,

$$\text{DFL} = \frac{\text{PBIT}}{\text{PBIT} - \text{I}}$$

$$2 = \frac{\text{PBIT}}{\text{PBIT} - \text{I}}$$

$$2 = \frac{\text{PBIT}}{\text{PBIT} - 1{,}000}$$

$$2\,(\text{PBIT} - 1{,}000) = \text{PBIT}$$
$$2\text{ PBIT} - 2{,}000 = \text{PBIT}$$
$$2\text{ PBIT} - \text{PBIT} = 2{,}000$$
$$\text{PBIT} = 2{,}000$$

$$\text{DOL} = \frac{\text{Contribution}}{\text{PBIT}}$$

$$2 = \frac{\text{Contribution}}{2{,}000}$$

$$\text{Contribution} = 4{,}000$$

Q. 13.

A firm has sales of ₹ 150 lakhs, variable cost of ₹ 84 lakh and fixed cost of ₹ 12 lakhs. It has a debt of ₹ 90 lakh at 9% and equity of ₹ 110 lakh.

(a) What is the firm's ROI?

(b) Does it have favourable financial leverage?

(c) If the firm belongs to an industry whose asset turnover is 2, does it have high or low asset leverage?

(d) What is the operating, financial and combined leverage of the firm?

(e) If the sales drop to ₹ 125 lakhs, what will be the new EBIT?

(f) At what level the EBT of the firm will be equal to zero?

Q.13: Solution

Particulars	(₹)
Sales	1,50,00,000
(-) Variable cost (56%)	84,00,000
Contribution	66,00,000
(-) Fixed cost	12,00,000
PBIT	54,00,000
(-) Interest	8,10,000
PBT	45,90,000

(a) $$\text{ROI} = \frac{\text{EBIT}}{\text{Cap. Emp.}} \times 100$$

$$= \frac{54,00,000}{90,00,000 + 1,10,00,000} \times 100$$

$$= \frac{54,00,000}{2,00,00,000} \times 100$$

$$= 27\%$$

(b) Since ROI is greater than interest on borrowed fund, it can be said that the firm has favourable financial leverages.

(c) $$\text{Asset turnover ratio} = \frac{\text{Sales}}{\text{Net Assets}}$$

Or

$$= \frac{\text{Sales}}{\text{Capital Employed}}$$

$$= \frac{1,50,00,000}{2,00,00,000}$$

$$= 0.75$$

Comment: The firm has low asset leverage which indicates inefficient utilization of assets/excess capital.

(d) Operating Leverage $= \frac{\text{Contribution}}{\text{EBIT}}$

$= \frac{66,00,000}{54,00,000}$

$= 1.22$

Financial Leverage $= \frac{\text{EBIT}}{\text{EBT}}$

$= \frac{54,00,000}{45,90,000}$

$= 1.18$

Combined Leverage $= \frac{\text{Contribution}}{\text{PBT}}$

$= \frac{66,00,000}{45,90,000}$

= ₹ 1.44

(e)	
Sales	125
(-) Variable cost (56%)	70
Contribution	55
(-) Fixed cost	12
EBIT	43

Hence, New EBIT is ₹ 43 lakhs

(f)		₹
Sales	100%	45,68,182
(-) Variable cost	56%	25,58,182
Contribution	44%	20,10,000
(-) Fixed cost		12,00,000
PBIT		8,10,000
(-) Interest		8,10,000
PBT		0

Ans: At sales level of ₹ 45,68,182

EBT of firm will be Zero.

Q. 14.

Calculate operating leverage and financial leverage under situations A, B and C and Financial Plans I, II and III respectively from the following information relating to the operation and capital structure of Rani Ltd. Also find out combination of operating and financial leverages, which gives the highest value and least value. How are these calculation useful to finance manager.

Installed Capacity (No. of Units)			1,200
Actual Production and Sales (No. of Units)			800
Selling Price per Unit (₹)			15
Variable Cost per Unit (₹)			10
Fixed Cost – Situation A (₹)			1,000
Fixed Cost – Situation B (₹)			2,000
Fixed Cost – Situation C (₹)			3,000
Financial Plan	I	II	III
Equity (₹)	5,000	7,500	2,500
12% debt (₹)	5,000	2,500	7,500

(MU, BMS, Nov. 2007)

Q.14: Solution

Revenue statement for the year______

Particulars	**(₹)**	**(₹)**	**(₹)**
Situation	**A**	**B**	**C**
Sales (800 × 15)	12,000	12,000	12,000
(-) Variable cost (800 × 10)	8,000	8,000	8,000
Contribution	4,000	4,000	4,000
(-) Fixed Cost	1,000	2,000	3,000
PBIT	3,000	2,000	1,000

Situation A Fixed cost ₹ 1,000

Financial Plan	**I**	**II**	**III**
PBIT	3,000	3,000	3,000
(-) Interest	600	300	900
PBT	2,400	2,700	2,100

$$\text{Operating Leverage} = \frac{\text{Contribution}}{\text{PBT}}$$

$$= \frac{4,000}{3,000}$$

$$= 1.33$$

$$\text{Financial Leverage} = \frac{\text{PBIT}}{\text{PBT}}$$

$$\text{Plan I} = \frac{3,000}{2,400} = 1.25$$

$$\text{Plan II} = \frac{3,000}{2,700} = 1.11$$

$$\text{Plan III} = \frac{3,000}{2,100} = 1.43$$

Situation B **Fixed Cost ₹ 2,000**

Financial Plan	I	II	III
PBIT	2,000	2,000	2,000
(-) Interest	600	300	900
PBT	1,400	1,700	1,100

$$\text{Operating Leverage} = \frac{\text{Contribution}}{\text{PBT}}$$

$$= \frac{4,000}{3,000}$$

$$\text{Financial Leverage} = \frac{\text{PBIT}}{\text{PBT}}$$

$$\text{Plan I} = \frac{2,000}{1,400} = 1.43$$

2,400

$$\text{Plan II} = \frac{2,000}{1,700} = 1.18$$

$$\text{Plan III} = \frac{2,000}{1,100} = 1.82$$

$= 2$

Situation C **Fixed Cost ₹ 3,000**

Financial Plan	I	II	III
PBIT	1,000	1,000	1,000
(-) Interest	600	300	900
PBT	400	700	100

$$\text{Operating Leverage} = \frac{\text{Contribution}}{\text{PBT}}$$

$$= \frac{4,000}{1,000}$$

$$= 4$$

$$\text{Financial Leverage} = \frac{\text{PBIT}}{\text{PBT}}$$

$$\text{Plan I} = \frac{1,000}{400} = 2.5$$

$$\text{Plan II} = \frac{1,000}{700} = 1.43$$

$$\text{Plan III} = \frac{1,000}{100} = 10$$

Situation A

Combined Leverage = Operating Leverage x Financial Leverage

Plan I = 1.33 × 1.25 = 1.66

Plan II = 1.33 × 1.11 = 1.48

Plan III = 1.33 × 1.43 = 1.90

Situation B

Combined Leverage = Operating Leverage x Financial Leverage

Plan I = 2 × 1.43 = 2.86

Plan II = 2 × 1.18 = 2.36

Plan III = 2 × 1.82 = 3.64

Situation C

Combined Leverage = Operating Leverage × Financial Leverage

Plan I = 4 × 2.5 = 10

Plan II = 4 × 1.43 = 5.72

Plan III = 4 × 10 = 40

Conclusion:

The highest combined leverage is under situation C, Plan III i.e., 40 and least is under situation A, Plan II, i.e., 1.48.

Utility of calculation of finance manager:

These calculation indicate how does variation in fixed cost and capital structure brings about change in risk and returns.

The finance manager should opt for the combination which will result into manageable risk and best possible returns.

Q.15.

Given below is the Balance Sheet of A Ltd.

Liabilities	(₹)	Assets	(₹)
ESC (₹ 10/Share)	10,00,000	Sundry Assets	31,00,000
10% Preference Shares	10,00,000		
8% Debentures	11,00,000		
	31,00,000		**31,00,000**

1. If ROI is 18% and Tax rate is 40%,

Calculate:

(a) DFL (b) EPS (c) DOL (d) DCL

Company's assets turnover ratio is 0.6 and the P/V ratio is 33.33% (1/3)

Q.15: Solution

W.N. 1. Capital Employed = ₹ 31 lakh

ROI = 18%

$$ROI = \frac{EBIT}{\text{Capital Employed}} \times 100$$

$$\therefore 18\% = \frac{EBIT \times 100}{31,00,000}$$

$$\therefore EBIT = 5,58,000$$

Income Statement	₹
Sales	18,60,000
(-) Variable cost	12,40,000
Contribution	6,20,000
(-) Fixed cost	62,000
EBIT	5,58,000
(-) Interest (debentures) (11,00,000 × 8%)	88,000
PBT	4,70,000
(-) Tax (40%)	1,88,000
PAT	2,82,000
(-) Preference dividend (1,00,000 × 10%)	1,00,000
Profit available to ESH (a)	1,82,000

No. of equity shares (b) 1,00,000 shares

(ESC/FV) (10,00,000 / 10)

(b) :. EPS (a ÷ b) = 1.82

(a) DFL (EBIT/PBT)

$$= \frac{5,58,00}{4,70,000} = 1.18$$

(c) DOL (C/EBIT)

$$= \frac{6,20,000}{5,58,000} = 1.111$$

(d) DCL (C/PBT)

$$= \frac{6,20,000}{4,70,000} = 1.319$$

W.N.1. Assets Turnover Ratio = $\frac{\text{Sales}}{\text{Net Assets}}$

= 0.6

∴ Sales = NA × ATR

= 31,00,000 × 0.6

= 18,60,000

W.N.2. C = 33.33% of Sales (PV ratio)

∴ C = 1/3 × 18,60,000

= 6,20,000

Q.16.

Chittaranjan Works is a rail coach manufacturing company and Infotech is a large size software development firm. Based on leverages you are required to advise an investor on the choice of investment in equity of these two firms:

Solution: Leverage is referred to higher profits because of fixed cost.

Operating Leverage:

Operating leverage refers to enhanced profits because of fixed operating expenses

Formula: $\text{DOL} = \frac{\text{Contribution}}{\text{PBT}} = \frac{\text{\% Change in PBIT}}{\text{\% Change in Sales}}$

Reason: Fixed operating expenses

Effects: Higher gross profit, higher operating break-even point, higher business risks.

Financial Leverage:

Financial leverage refers to possible higher profits because of fixed financial expenses such as interest and preference dividend.

Formula: $\text{DFL} = \frac{\text{PBIT}}{\text{PBT}} = \frac{\text{\% Change in PBT}}{\text{\% Change in PBIT}}$

Reason: Interest, Preference Dividend

Effects: Higher net profit, higher financial break-even point, higher financial risk.

Combined Leverage:

Combined Leverage refers to higher overall return because of operating fixed cost as well as financial fixed cost. (interest, preference dividend)

Formula: $DCL = \frac{\text{Contribution}}{\text{PBT}} = \frac{\text{\% Change in PBT}}{\text{\% Change in Sales}}$

Reason: Interest Preference dividend, Operating fixed costs.

Effects: Higher net profit, high overall break even point, higher overall risk.

Comparative Observations

Chittaranjan	Works	Infotech
(i) Industry	Rail coach manufacturing.	Software
(ii) Assets	Heavy assets such as huge land and building. Plant & Machinery.	Lower level of asset investment Just an office as premises.
(iii) Manpower	Unskilled and skilled and labour.	Professional expertiseLow.
(iv) Capital Requirement	High	Low

Determinants of Leverages

Chittaranjan Works

Chittaranjan	Works	Infotech
(i) Operating Leverage (DOL)	Higher factory overheads such as power, depreciation and maintenance	Low factory overheads. High (fixed) salary bill of professionals.
(ii) Financial Leverage (DFL)	Capital intensive, likely to borrow more	Less capital required, possibly lower borrowings

Comments:

(i) Chittaranjan Works

(a) Higher DOL because of overheads.

(b) Higher DFL (high borrowings).

(c) Higher DCL.

(d) High overall and financial break-even point.

(e) Indicates highly leveraged, high risk and high return profile with average higher break even point.

(ii) Infotech

(a) Higher DOL because of professional salaries.

(b) Lower DFL (low borrowings).

(c) Moderate DCL.

(d) Higher operating break even point but moderate overall break-even point.

(e) Indicates moderately leveraged, moderate risk and moderate return profile with break-even point.

Conclusion:

(a) Chittaranjan Works has high risk and high return profile. Business risk as well as financial risk is high. It is suitable for aggressive investor.

(b) Infotech has moderate risk and return profile. Business risk is high but financial risk is low. It is suitable for conservative investor.

(c) It may be noted that apart from leverages there are many other factors which influence investment decisions. In this case rail coach manufacturing is a defensive industry that survives better in recession. Software firms give better returns in bullish markets.

Practice Problems

Q.17.

Case Study: Observe the following data

Income Statement		
Sales	50 L	50 L
PBIT	5 L	5 L
- Interest	0.4 L	1.6 L
PBT	4.6 L	3.4 L
- Tax	2.3 L	1.7 L
PAT	2.3 L	1.7 L
Sources of Funds		
Equity	16 L	4 L
Debt	4 L	16 L

Company A has more profit than Company B. So, Company A is better. Do you agree? Discuss.

Q.18.

Interest ₹ 1200/- DFL 3, DOL 2, PV Ratio 1/3, Interest Rate @ 10%,

Debt: Equity is 2 : 1 Tax @ 50%

(A) Prepare Income Statement

(B) Calculate ROI

(C) Is financial leverage favourable?

(D) Calculate Asset Leverage

(E) If Industry Asset Leverage is 1.1, is this firm efficient?

REVIEW QUESTIONS

Q.1. Concept Testing.

(a) Types of Leverage Ratio.

(b) Operating Leverage vs. Financial Leverage

❑❑❑

CHAPTER 3

CAPITAL STRUCTURE

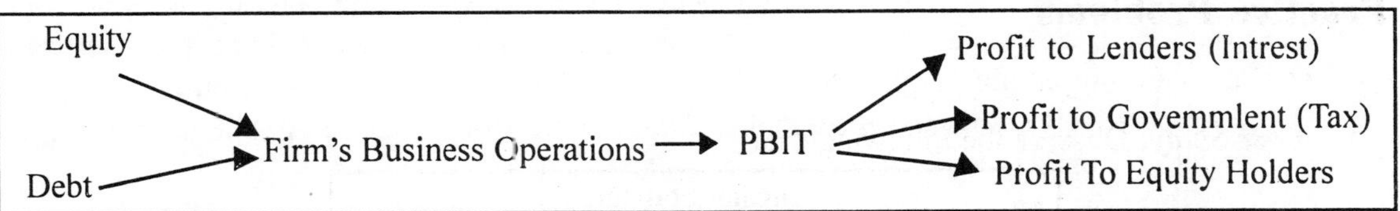

Capital Structure (The means of capital by which a firm is financed)

Capital Structure is a part of Financial Structure and is the mix of the various types of long-term sources of funds, i.e., debt/equity. Ex:

- Common Stock, i.e., Equity Share Capital
- Preferred Stock, i.e., Preference Share Capital
- Retained Earnings – (profit the company makes, but does not give to the shareholders in the form of dividends)
- Debt (e.g., Long Term Debt/Borrowed Funds)

The Target Capital Structure

Capital Structure: The combination of debt and equity used to finance a firm

Target Capital Structure: The ideal mix of debt, preferred stock, and common equity with which the firm plans to finance its investments.

3.1 FACTORS/DETERMINANTS FOR CAPITAL STRUCTURE PLANNING

Following are the important factors to be considered while planning a capital structure:

1. **Financial Leverage:** The financial manager should take the advantage of debt capital as much as possible because use of debt capital increases the earnings on equity since interest payments give a tax shield. However, an important fact to be kept in view is that beyond a particular point of leverage, weighted average cost of capital may go up. Also, higher financial leverage results into higher financial risk.
2. **Operating Leverage:** This leverage depends on the operating fixed cost of the firm. If a higher percentage of a firm's total costs are fixed operating costs, the firm is said to have a high degree of operating leverage. Operating leverage measures the operating risk of a firm. Operating risk is the variability of operating profit or EBIT to sales. A financial manager should attempt at an appropriate combination of the two leverages.

3. **EBIT/EPS Analysis:** This analysis is an important tool of measuring a company's performance. Normally a financial plan, which will give maximum value of EPS will be selected as the most desirable mix. The greater the level of EBIT, the more beneficial it is to employ debt capital in capital structure. However, EPS analysis ignores risk.
4. **Cost of Capital:** The financial manager aims to select a combination of debt and equity, that maximizes the value of the firm and minimises the overall cost of capital. It should always be borne in mind that overall cost of capital is an important variable in the decision-making relating to selection of debt-equity mix.
5. **Growth and Stability of Sales:** The growth and stability of sales is an important factor in selection of desired mix of debt and equity. The firms with stable sales are likely to employ high degree of leverage. For e.g., the sale of consumer goods show wide fluctuation. Therefore, they do not employ large amount of debt. On the other hand, sales of public utilities are comparatively stable and predictable. Therefore, it is observed that public utilities services relatively employ higher debt in their capital structure.
6. **Cash Flow Analysis:** The capital structure of a firm should be so planned that it should be able to service its fixed charges of interest and principal under any reasonable predictable adverse circumstances. The companies expecting larger and stable cash inflows in future can employ a large amount of debt in their capital structure. If companies having unstable cash inflows in future employ sources of finance with fixed charges, it will be risky. In planning the capital structure, financial manager must consider coverage ratios. The greater the coverage, the greater will be the amount of debt capital that a firm may use.
7. **Flexibility:** It means the ability of the company to adapt its capital structure in response to changing conditions. The main point is that company should be able to raise funds without undue delay and cost whenever needed to finance the profitable investment. Debt capital is more flexible than equity capital, because it can be redeemed when circumstances are favourable. Equity does not enjoy flexibility as equity shares cannot be redeemed except on liquidation or buyback which is an expensive exercise. Preference shares can be redeemed under certain circumstances.
8. **Control:** Ordinary or equity shareholders have the legal right to vote. In fact, they are the real owners and they can exercise the control over the overall affairs. In the event of issuing fresh equity shares, there remains a risk of loss of control for promoters. When a choice is made between debt and equity to raise additional funds, normally debt is preferred to equity in order to avoid loss of controlling stake. However, now banks and FIs introduced a lot of restrictions (restrictive covenants) in the loan agreement to protect their interest. At times, the loan agreement includes the right to nominate a director to oversee the activities of the firm.
9. **Size and Nature of the Company:** It is also an important consideration in selection of sources of finance. A small firm finds it extremely difficult to raise long-term loans and normally small companies depend on share capital and retained earnings for long-term capital. A large company relatively enjoys greater degree of flexibility in designing its capital structure. A firm should make best use of its size in planning its capital structure. Nature of industry is also an important consideration in designing the capital structure. For e.g., Real Estate Industry or IT Industry or Power Sector Industry or Telecom Industry, etc., have different capital structure requirement.
10. **Marketability/Capital Market Conditions:** The conditions in capital market are continuously changing. At one time the capital market favours the debenture issue and at other time it readily accept share issues. Based on the changing market sentiments, decision should be taken regarding raising the funds through debt or equity.

11. **Floatation Costs (cost of raising finance):** Floatation costs are incurred only when the funds are raised. Normally, cost of floating a debt is less than the cost of floating an equity issue. It is not a very significant factor, but it should be considered in designing a capital structure. QIP floating cost is less than public issue floating cost.
12. **Legal Constraints:** In a regulated economy, a firm has to comply with legal requirements in this respect. E.g., Dual listing not allowed in India, Capital a/c convertibility not allowed in India, FDI investment cap. in certain sectors (e.g., Retail, Banking, Telecom, Aviation, etc.,)

Features of Optimum Capital Structure

- **Profitability:** It is that capital structure which minimizes cost of financing and maximizes earning per equity share.
- **Solvency:** A firm should plan the capital structure in such a way that it does not run the risk of becoming insolvent. Excess use of debt threatens the solvency of the company.
- **Flexibility:** It should be such that it can provide funds whenever the company needs it, to finance for profitable activities.
- **Conservatism:** Debt content is capital structure should be in limits so that the company can service the debt comfortably.
- **Control:** It should be such that it involves minimum risk of loss of control of the company, for the promoters.

3.2 THEORY OF CAPITAL STRUCTURE

1. Net Income (N) Approach	2. Net Operating Income (NOI) Approath
As per NI Approach, we calculate WACC and use it as a benchmark to compare with ROI of proposed investment. If ROI>WACC, we accept the proposal.	As per NOI Approach, we estimate ROI of proposed investment. We deduct the cost of debt (and cost of pref if any) from ROI to get Kerence, (ROE). If Kerence, [ROE]> Expectation of shareholders, we accept the proposal.
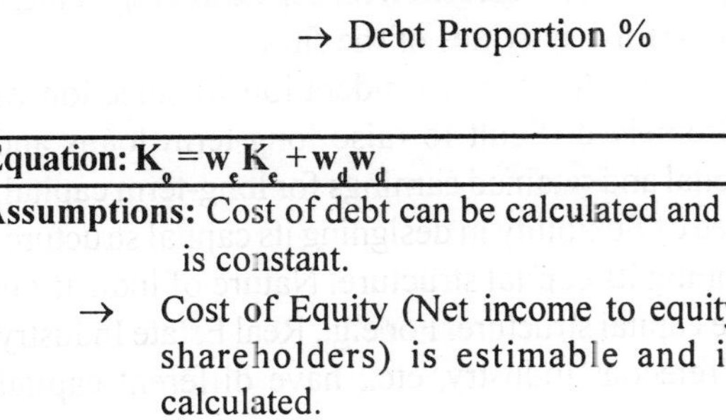 Cost% ; K_e ; ← K_o ; K_d ; → Debt Proportion %	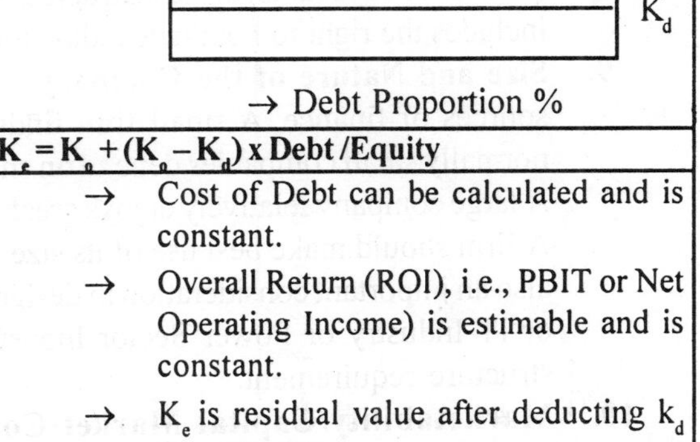 Cost% ; K_e ; K_o ; K_d ; → Debt Proportion %
Equation: $K_o = w_e K_e + w_d w_d$	$K_e = K_o + (K_o - K_d)$ x Debt/Equity
Assumptions: Cost of debt can be calculated and is constant. → Cost of Equity (Net income to equity shareholders) is estimable and is calculated. → Overall cost (WACC) is weighted average of K_e and K_d. → K_e and K_d are independent variables and k_o is dependent.	→ Cost of Debt can be calculated and is constant. → Overall Return (ROI), i.e., PBIT or Net Operating Income) is estimable and is constant. → K_e is residual value after deducting k_d from WACC. → K_o & K_d are independent variables and k_e is dependent.

3. **Traditional Approach:** According to the traditional financial structure theory the cost of capital is not independent of the capital structure of the firm and that there is an optimal capital structure. There are two types of risks:

   (a) **Business Risk:** Business risks includes factors such as market fluctuations, availability of material, etc., and it will always be there more or less in the same measure.

   (b) **Financial Risk:** Financial risks keeps on increasing after a certain stage as more and more debt capital commitments are undertaken.

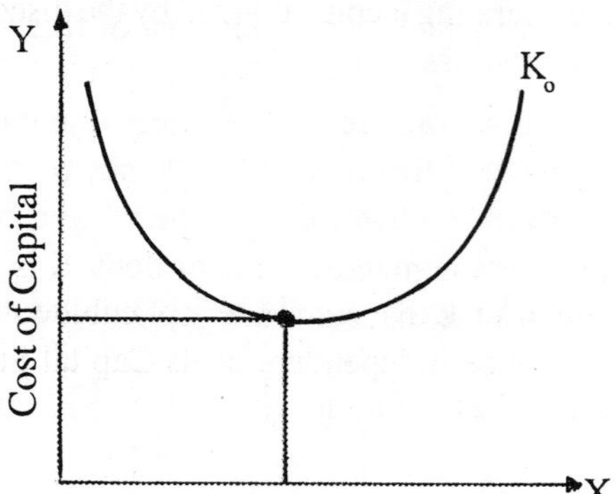

Fig. 3.1: Traditional Approach indicating inter-relationship between Cost of Capital and Capital Structure

This theory states that there exists a correlation between the weighted average Cost of Capital and the Debt-Equity Ratio. The relation between the two when presented graphically takes the form of an U-shaped curve. Cost of Capital will be very high if the Debt-Equity ratio is zero. When debt is injected into the capital structure step-by-step the weighted average cost of capital will progressively come down only up to the lowest (optimum) point and then the cost of capital will go up with the further introduction of debt; since the debentureholders have to be offered a higher rate of interest, to compensate higher risk.

4. **Modigliani-Miller Approach:** The Franco Modigliani and Merton H. Miller (M.M.) Approach on cost of capital states that there is no correlation between cost of capital and debt-equity ratio. This approach states that the average cost of capital of any firm is independent of its capital structure and equal to the capitalisation rate of pure equity stream of its class. The value of the firm and cost of capital is the same for all the firms irrespective of the proportion of debt included in a firms capital structure.

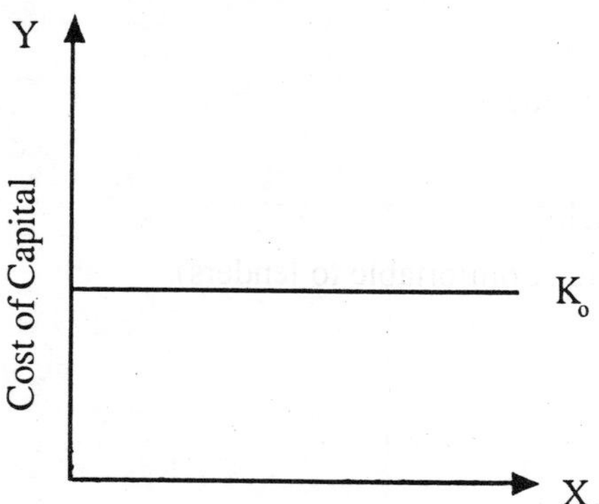

Fig. 3.2: Modigliani-Miller Approach to Cost of Capital and Capital Structure

Assumptions:

(i) Perfect Capital Market.

(ii) Rational Investors and Managers.

(iii) Homogeneous Expectations.

(iv) Equivalent Risk Classes.

(v) Absence of Taxes.

"The value of a firm is equal to its expected operating income divided by the discount rate appropriate to its risk class. It is independent of its capital structure."

In symbols

$$V = D + E = O/r$$

Where V is the market value of the firm, D is the market value of debt, E is the market value of equity, O is the expected operating income, and r is the discount rate applicable to the risk class which the firm belongs. Hence, the value of the firm will be Independent of its Capital Structure, as per MM theory.

3.3 PROBLEMS + SOLUTION

Q.1. Your friend approaches you with a proposal to set-up a manufacturing unit having gestation period of 50 to 55 months and fund requirement of around ₹15 crores. Explain to him the various sources to raise the fund for the project.

Q.1: Solution

Observations:

(a) Individual Promoter.

(b) Manufacturing unit, good asset base.

(c) Funds requirement ₹ 150 million (₹ 15 crore)

(d) Gestation period 50-55 months (4-5 years)

Possible Sources of Capital – Equity, Debt.

Equity: It is owners capital with claim on profits after paying external liabilities.

Merits (to issuing firm):

- No legal obligation to pay dividend.
- No charge on assets.
- Improves borrowing capacity.
- Improves Debt: Equity ratio (Comfortable to lenders)

Demerits:

- Voting Rights.
- Dilution of control
- Tax not saved on dividend paid.

Ways to Raise Equity

(a) **Promoters:** Promoters should invest to the extent possible, as it does not dilute control. Limited fund availability with the promoters, however, should not hamper growth.

(b) **Private Placements:** Equity can be placed with business associates, friends and other such network. Advantage is control is diluted, but to known people. Also they not bring only money, but also bring business contacts/community. This improves business. Disadvantage is they really use voting rights and dilution of control is real. Nominee on board is common.

(c) **Public Issue:** IPO offer can fetch virtually unlimited money. Advantage is that, public is not interested in control. They do not vote. Practically no dilution of control. Disadvantage is people are passive, they bring only funds and no other value addition. Also public issue is time-consuming and costly.

(d) **Venture Capital:** It is a risk capital invested at very early stage of business. It is suitable for technology/new upcoming areas of ventures.

(e) **Retained Earnings:** Re-investment of profits is always good. It is low cost and less time-consuming. It does not dilute control of the existing shareholders/promoters.

→ Debt: It is borrowed capital.

Merits: → Fixed Interest.

→ Saves Tax.

→ Offers Leverage Benefits.

→ No Loss of controlling stake/voting power.

Demerits: → Charge on assets.

→ Interest to be paid irrespective of profits/loss.

Ways to raise Debt:

i. Term Loan : From Banks (negotiated.)

ii. Debentures : By public issue.

Factors Determining Capital Structure in a Given Case:

(a) **Business Track Record:** Appears to be a new business, so external funds will have limitation.

(b) **Nature of Business:** Manufacturing Unit doesn't seem to be a high technology unit. Not suitable for venture capital. Offers good asset - backup and good for borrowing.

(c) **Quantum of Investment:** ₹ 15 crore - Small size. Not suitable for public issue.

Suggested Capital Structure.
Manufacturing Unit.
₹ 15 crore

Equity (7.5 crore) — Debt

- Promoters (To extent possible)
- Private Placements (Balance, friends and relatives)

- Term Loan from bank with factory assets as security

Q.2. X Ltd., a widely held company is considering a major expansion of its production facilities and the following alternatives are available:

(₹ in crore)

Particulars	Alternatives		
	A	B	C
Share capitals ('10)	50	20	10
14% debentures	-	20	15
Loan from financial institution @ 18 p.a. Rate of Interest	-	10	25

Expected rate of return before tax is 25%. The company at present has low debt. Corporate taxation 50%.

Which of alternatives you would choose?

Q.2: Solution

Evaluation of financing Alternative

Particulars		A	B	C
EBIT		12.5	12.5	12.5
(-) Interest (20 x 14%) + (10 x 18) = 4.6		-	4.6	6.6
(15 x 14%) + (25 x 18) = 6.6		12.5	7.9	5.9
EBT(-) Tax @ 50%		6.25	3.95	2.95
EAT		6.25	3.95	2.95
(-) Preference dividend		-	-	-
Earnings for ESH	(a)	6.25	3.95	2.95
No of Equity Shares	(b)	5	2	1
∴ EPS (a ÷ b)	(₹)	1.25	1.98	2.95

Recommendation: On the basis of EPS it is advised to select Alternative C.

Q.3. One-up Ltd., has equity share capital of ₹ 5,00,000 divided into shares of ₹ 100 each. It wishes to raise further ₹ 3,00,000 for expansion-cum-modernization scheme. The company plans the following financing alternatives:

- By issuing equity shares only.
- ₹ 1,00,000 by issuing equity shares and ₹ 2,00,000 through debentures or term loan @ 10% per annum.
- By raising term loan only at 10% per annum.
- ₹ 1,00,000 by issuing equity shares and ₹ 2,00,000 by issuing 8% preference shares.
- You are required to suggest the best alternative giving your comment assuming that the estimated earning before interest and taxes (EBIT) after expansion is ₹ 1,50,000 and corporate of tax is 35%.

Q.3: Solution

Evaluation of Financing Alternatives

Particulars		Alternatives			
		1	2	3	4
EBIT		1,50,000	1,50,000	1,50,000	1,50,000
(-) Interest		-	20,000 (10% × 2L)	30,000 (10% × 3L)	-
EBT/PBT		1,50,000	1,30,000	1,20,000	1,50,000
(-) Tax @ 35%		52,500	45,500	42,000	52,500
EAT/PAT/NPAT		97,500	84,500	78,000	97,500
(-) Preference dividend		-	-	-	16,000
Earnings for ESH	a)...	97,500	84,500	78,000	81,500
No of equity shares	→ Existing	5,000	5,000	5,000	5,000
	→ New	3,000	1,000	-	1,000
	b)....	8,000	6,000	5,000	6,000
EPS (a/b)		₹ 12.19	₹ 14.08	₹ 15.60	₹ 13.58

Recommendation: The company is advised to select alternative 3, i.e., 10% term loan since it results into highest EPS, i.e., ₹ 15.60

Q.4. The existing capital structure of ABC Ltd., is as follows:

	₹
Equity shares of ₹ 100 each	40,00,000
Retained Earnings	10,00,000
9% Preference Shares	25,00,000
7% Debentures	25,00,000

Company earns a return of 12% and the tax on income is 50%.

Company wants to raise ₹ 25,00,000 for its expansion project for which it is considering following alternatives:

- Issue of 20,000 equity shares at a premium of ₹ 25 per share.
- Issue of 10% preference shares.
- Issue of 9% debentures.
- Projected that the Price Earning ratios in the case of Equity, Preference and Debenture financing ₹ 20, 17 and 16, respectively.

Which alternative would you consider to be the best? Give reason for your choice.

(MU, BMS, May 2008)

Q.4: Solution

Evaluation of Financing Alternatives

Particulars			Alternatives		
			1	2	3
EBIT			15,00,000	15,00,000	15,00,000
(-) Interest	- Existing		(1,75,000)	(1,75,000)	(1,75,000)
	- New		–	–	(2,25,000)
EBT/PBT			13,25,000	13,25,000	11,00,000
(-) Tax @ 50%			6,62,500	6,62,500	5,50,000
EAT/PAT/NPAT			6,62,500	6,62,500	5,50,000
(-) Preference dividend	→ Existing		(2,25,000)	(2,25,000)	(2,25,000)
	→ New		–	(2,50,000)	–
Equity Earnings	a). . . .		4,37,500	1,87,500	3,25,000
No of Equity Shares Existing		40,000	40,000	40,000	40,000
New	b). . . .		60,000	40,000	40,000
EPS (a/b)			7.29	4.69	8.13
MPS = PE x EPS			₹ 145.8	₹ 79.73	₹ 130.08
			(29 × 7.29)	(17 × 4.69)	(16 × 8.13)

Capital Employed = Existing + New

= 100,00,000 + 25,00,000

= 125,00,000

ROI $= \frac{\text{PBIT}}{\text{Capital Employed}} \times 100$

$\therefore$ PBIT $= \text{Cap. Emp.} \times \frac{\text{ROI}}{100}$

$= 1,25,00,000 \times \frac{12}{100}$

= ₹ 15,00,000

Recommendation: Select Alternative 1, i.e., Issue of 20,000 Equity Shares, since it results into highest MPS, i.e., ₹ 145.8

Q.5. The Modern Chemicals Ltd., requires ₹ 25,00,000 for a new plant. This plant is expected to yield earnings before interest and taxes of ₹ 5,00,000. While deciding about the financial plan, the company considers the objectives of maximizing earnings per share. It has three alternatives to finance the project by raising debt of ₹ 2,50,000 or ₹ 10,00,000 or ₹ 15,00,000 and the balance in each case, by issuing equity shares. The company's shares are currently selling at ₹ 150, but it expected to decline to ₹ 125 in case the funds are borrowed in excess of ₹ 10,00,000. The funds can be borrowed as under up to ₹ 2,50,000 10% p.a., between ₹ 2,50,001 to ₹ 10,00,000 15% p.a., between 1000001 and above 20% p.a. The tax rate applicable to the company is 50%. Which form of financing should the company choose?

Q.5: Solution

Particulars	Alternatives		
	1	2	3
Debt	2,50,000	10,00,000	15,00,000
Equity Share Capital	*22,50,000	15,00,000	10,00,000
Total Capital	25,00,000	25,00,000	25,00,000
Issue price	150	150	125
∴ No. of Equity shares	15,000	10,000	8,000
EBIT	5,00,000	5,00,000	5,00,000
(-) Interest			
250000 x 10%	25,000	25,000	25,000
Bal. 750000 x 15%	–	1,12,500	1,12,500
Bal. 500000 x 20%	–	–	1,00,000
EBT	4,75,000	3,62,500	2,62,500
(-) Tax @ 50%	2,37,500	1,81,250	1,31,250
EAT	2,37,500	1,81,250	1,31,250
(-) Preference dividend	–	–	–
Earnings for ESH (a)	2,37,500	1,81,250	1,31,250
No. of Equity shares (b)	15,000	10,000	8,000
∴ EPS (a÷b)	₹ 15.83	₹ 18.13	₹ 16.41

Recommendation: Select Alternative 2, i.e., debt ₹ 10,00,000 since it results into the highest EPS ₹ 18.13

Q.6. Excel Ltd., is considering three financing plans. The key information is as follows:

(a) Total investment to be raised ₹ 2,00,000.

(b) Plan of financing proportion:

Plan	Equity	Debt	Preference Shares
A	100%	–	–
B	50%	50%	–
C	50%	–	50%

(c) Cost of Debt 8%. Cost of Preference Shares 8%.

(d) Tax rate 50%.

(e) Equity Shares of the face value of ₹ 10 each will be issued at a premium of ₹ 10 per share.

(f) Expected PBIT is ₹ 80,000.

Determine for each plan:

(i) Earnings per share (EPS), and

(ii) The financial break even point.

Q.6: Solution

(i) Computation of EPS

Particulars	Plan A (₹)	Plan B (₹)	Plan C (₹)
EBIT	80,000	80,000	80,000
Less: Interest	–	8,000	–
EBT	80,000	72,000	80,000
Less: Tax @ 50%	40,000	36,000	40,000
EAT	40,000	36,000	40,000
Less: Preference Dividend	–	–	8,000
Amount Available to Equity Shareholders	40,000	36,000	32,000
EPS = $\frac{\text{Amount Available to Equity Shareholders}}{\text{Number of Equity Shares}}$	$\frac{40,000}{10,000}$	$\frac{36,000}{5,000}$	$\frac{32,000}{5,000}$
EPS =	₹ 4.0	₹ 7.2	₹ 6.4

Recommendation: Plan B, i.e., to raise ₹ 1lakh by equity capital and ₹ 1 lakh by 8% debt is recommended since it gives the highest EPS.

Working Notes:

(1) Capital Structure

Source	Plan A		Plan B		Plan C	
	%	₹	%	₹	%	₹
(i) Equity Share Capital	100	2,00,000	50	1,00,000	50	1,00,000
(ii) 8% Debt	–	–	50	1,00,000	–	–
(iii) 8% Preference Share Capital	–	–	–	–	50	1,00,000
Total Capital	**100**	**2,00,000**	**100**	**2,00,000**	**100**	**2,00,000**

(2) Number of Equity Shares

(i) Number of Equity Shares = $\frac{\text{Equity Capital Amount}}{\text{Issued Price per Share}}$

Plan A	Plan B	Plan C
= $\frac{₹\ 2,00,000}{20}$	= $\frac{₹\ 1,00,000}{20}$	= $\frac{₹\ 1,00,000}{20}$
= 10,000 Shares	= 5,000 Shares	= 5,000 Shares

Issue Price Share = Face Value Per Share + Premium Per Share

= ₹10 + ₹ 10

= ₹ 20 per share.

(ii) Calculation of Financial Break-even Point

At financial break-even level of EBIT; EPS = Zero i.e. amount available to ESH is Nil.

Particulars	Plan A ₹	Plan B ₹	Plan C ₹
Financial Break-even Level of EBIT	Zero	8,000	16,000
Less: Interest	–	8,000	–
EBT	–	–	16,000
Less: Tax @ 50%	–	–	8,000
EAT	–	–	8,000
Less: Preference Dividend	–	–	8,000
Amount Available to Equity Shareholders	Zero	Zero	Zero

Financial break even level of EBIT;

for Plan A = Zero

for Plan B = ₹ 8,000

for Plan C = ₹ 16,000

Q.7. Expected PBIT ₹ 20 lakh

Options of capital structure

	A	B	C
Equity	20	20	40
10% Debt	80	60	40
15% Preference	–	20	20

Tax @ 40%, Equity divided into shares of face value ₹ 10. Which option is preferred?

Q.7: Solution

Particulars	A	B	C
PBIT	20	20	20
(-) Interest	8	6	4
PBT	12	14	16
(-) Tax	4.8	5.6	6.4
PAT	7.2	8.4	9.6
(-) Pref. dividend	–	3	3

	A	B	C
$\frac{\text{Equity Earning}}{\text{No. of Shares}}$	$\frac{7.2}{2}$	$\frac{5.4}{2}$	$\frac{6.6}{2}$
EPS	3.6	2.7	1.65

Option A is Preferred

Practice Problems

Q.8. The following financial information pertains to VX Ltd., as at 31st March, 2010.

Balance Sheet	**(₹ in lakhs)**
Fixed Assets (at cost less depreciation)	200
Net Current Assets	60
Total Assets	260
Less: Long-term debt	215
Net Assets	45
Represented by:	
Equity capital	40
Retained earnings	5
	45

Profit and Loss Account	**(₹ in lakhs)**
Net Profit before interest and tax	52
Interest paid	20
Tax paid	12
Dividends declared	18

The company has identified a profitable investment opportunity and requires funds to the tune of ₹ 20 lakh for fixed assets purchase and ₹ 5 lakh for working capital.

You are required to state the sources of funds that are available to company and also discuss the problem chooses debt to fund the new project.

REVIEW QUESTIONS

Q.1. Concept Testing.

(a) Target Capital Structure.

(b) Net Income Approach.

(c) MM Theory of Capital Structure.

Q.2. Explain factors/determinants of Capital Structure Planning.

CHAPTER 4

DIVIDEND POLICY

That part of the profits of a company that is distributed to shareholders. Dividend disbursements are based on a percentage of the par value of the stock or are a certain sum per share of no-par-value stock. They become payable only when approved by the board of directors and are usually declared at regular intervals. Obviously, dividends should not be paid unless the company has accumulated a profit or surplus. Dividends may be both interim (and normally paid during the financial year) or final (and recommended by the directors for approval for the shareholders at the annual general meeting). Dividends are shown in the appropriation section of the profit and loss account (Income statement). A proposal final dividend is shown in the balance though it is not a legal obligation at the date of the balance sheet. Preference share dividends may be either cumulative or non cumulative. If they are non-cumulative, shareholders are not entitled to receive later a dividend which has been passed through lack of profits. Arrears of cumulative dividends, on the other hand, must be disclosed in the notes to the accounts and paid before dividends on the ordinary shares are resumed.

4.1 MODELS OF DIVIDEND POLICY

To distribute dividend or not is a debatable issue. A person investing in shares for fixed income will always want dividend while a person investing in the shares for capital gains will deem it indifferent. There have been many theories/arguments as to whether distribution of dividend is really important or not. Some of them are as follows:

Walter's Model

Argument: A firm's dividend policy will be determined by the relationship between the return on investment (ROI) and the expected rate of return.

Quantitatively $P = (D+(E-D)\ r/k)/k$

Where P, D, E have the same connotations as above and r is the internal rate of return on the investments and k is the cost of capital.

Assumptions:

1. All financing through the retained earnings; no external source.
2. With additional business undertaken, firm's business risk won't change. Thus, ROI (r) and required rate of return on capital (k) are constant.
3. There's no change in key variables, which are E and D.
4. Perpetual life of the firm.

Justification:

The firm would have an optimum relation of r and k, i.e., if r > k, then the firm will retain earnings. But if r < k then the firm would distribute dividend so that shareholders can earn some ROI from elsewhere. If r = k, it becomes matter of indifference.

Gordon's Model

Argument: Being risk averse, an investor will always prefer present income to future income.

Quantitatively $P = Y(1-b)/(k-br)$

Where p is the price per share   Y is the earnings per share

b is the retention ratio   1– b is the payout ratio

br is the growth rate   r is the return on investment

k is the rate of return required by shareholders

on comparing r and k, the relationship between market price and the payout ratio is exactly the same as compared to the Walter model.

Assumptions:

1. Firm is an all equity firm.
2. ROI (r) and expected rate of return on capital (k) are constant.
3. Firm has perpetual life.
4. The retention ratio is constant.
5. Growth rate is constant and is less than expected rate of return on capital (k).
6. Investors are risk averse.
7. They put premium on certain investments and discount on uncertain.

Justification:

'Bird in the hand is worth two in the bush.' ---- is the bottom line of this argument.

If investors are risk averse, the rational investors in general would prefer dividend – they'll avoid risk. The payment of current dividend removes any chance of risk. If firm retains earnings, dividends obviously will be received in future. Future dividend is uncertain. Thus, the rational investors will prefer current dividends, and discount future dividends.

The argument that deems dividends to be irrelevant is the famous MM Model.

MM Model (Modigliani and Miller Model)

Argument: Dividend policy has no effects on share price of a firm and is therefore of no consequence. What matters is the investment policy through which the firm can increase its earnings and therefore the value of the firm.

Assumptions:

1. Perfect capital markets, i.e., all investors are rational, information is available to all, free of cost, there are no transactional costs, securities are infinitely divisible, no floatation costs, etc.

2. No taxes or no difference in tax rates applicable to dividends and capital gains.
3. Firm has a given investment policy which does not change, i.e., risk extent will be constant.

Justification:

If a company retains earnings instead of giving it out as dividends, the shareholder enjoys capital appreciation, which is equal to the amount of earnings retained. If it distributes dividends, the shareholder will enjoy dividend in amount by which capital would have appreciated had the company retained its earnings. Thus, it's quite irrelevant whether dividend is given or not.

4.2 LEGAL AND PROCEDURAL ASPECTS OF DIVIDEND

Dividend can be defined as:

A **cash payment** using **profits** that's announced by a company's Board of Directors to be **distributed among the stockholders.**

Conceptually, dividends may be in the form of **cash, stock or property. The Board of Directors must declare all dividends.**

Through the stocks, an investor can make income either through the capital gains or through the periodic dividends. A company announces dividend either quarterly, semi-annually or yearly. Thus, it is a **steady periodic** source of income. It is in the proportion to the share of capital, which the investor actually holds in the company. Though dividend is usually offered, it is necessary to note that a **company is under no obligation to pay the dividends.** It may or may not pay the dividends. Even if it pays; **there is no set level as to the payment of dividend.** That is there is no minimum or maximum limit on the amount of dividend that can be paid.

Most often, the dividend comes in the form of cash: a company will pay a small percentage of its profits to the owner of each share of stock. However, it is not unheard of for companies to pay dividends in the form of stock. Dividends can be determined by a fixed rate known as **preferred dividends**, or a variable rate based on the company's latest profits known as **common dividends**.

Usually, amount of profit made is announced in the AGMs or quarterly/semi-annual result. The company declares amount of dividend on each share (Usually as percentage of face value). At this point of time, the BoD announces that 'The dividend of the set amount will be paid to shareholders of record as of the record date and will be paid or distributed on distribution date'.

Record date is a concept to enable proper distribution of dividend.

A company issues shares, and once it starts operating, the shares begin to be traded in the stock market. Thus ownership of a single share might pass even 1000 hands within a year. Thus, at the time of distributing dividends it would have been very difficult to determine the exact owner of a share, if concept of 'Record Date' wouldn't have existed. A company usually maintains record of its shareholders. It declares a date called 'Record Date', prior to which all the transferred names have to be entered into the company's records. The company will give dividends only to those investors whose names are found in company's records on the record date. Thus, even if share is sold on the day after record date, the concerned seller-investor will receive the dividend.

This is done because a dividend payout automatically reduces the value of the company (It comes from the company's cash reserves), and the investor would have to absorb that reduction in value.

Dividend is quite unpredictable; but a trend might be understood by studying past pattern, future expectations, industry trends, etc.

On the distribution date, which as the name suggests is the date when dividends are distributed, the shareholders on record as on record date will be mailed cheques.

The legal aspects of dividend distribution in the Indian Context (As per company law) are as follows:

1. Companies can pay only cash dividends (with the exception of bonus shares).
2. Dividends can be paid only out of the profits earned during the financial year after providing for depreciation and after transferring to reserves such percentage of profits as prescribed by the law. The companies (Transfer to reserves) Rules, 1975, provide that before dividend declaration a percentage of profit as specified below should be transferred to the reserves of the company.
   - Where the dividend proposed exceeds 10% but not 12.5% of the paid-up capital, the amount to be transferred to the reserves shall not be less than 2.5% of the current profits.
   - Where the dividend proposed exceeds 12.5% but not 15%, the amount to be transferred to the reserves shall not be less than 5% of the current profits.
   - Where the dividend proposed exceeds 15% but not 20%, the amount to be transferred to the reserves shall not be less than 7.5% of the current profits.
   - Where the dividend proposed exceeds 20%, the amount to be transferred to reserves shall not be less than 10%.
3. Due to inadequacy or absence of profits in any year, dividend may be paidout of the accumulated profits of previous years. In this context, the following conditions as stipulated by the companies (Declaration of Dividends out of reserves) Rules, 1975, have to be satisfied:
   - The rate of the dividend declared shall not exceed the average of the rates of which dividend was declared by it in 5 years immediately preceding that year or 10% of its paid-up capital, whichever is less.
   - The total amount to be drawn from the accumulated profits earned in the previous years and transferred to the reserves shall not exceed an amount equal to one-tenth of the sum of its paid-up capital and free reserves and the amount so drawn shall first be utilized to set off the losses incurred in the financial year before any dividend in respect of preference or equity shares is declared.
   - The balance of reserves after such drawal shall not fall below 15% of its paid-up capital.
4. Dividends cannot be declared for past years for which the accounts have been closed.

4.4 RETAINED EARNINGS AS A PRUDENT INVESTMENT POLICY

DRIP's: These days, because of lack of investment initiatives, industries are encouraging the investors to reinvest their dividends. The concept is called **DRIP or the Dividend Re-investment Plan**. As per this plan, the shareholder will be given choice of accepting dividend or reinvesting it. If he/she opts for the latter, his dividend is credited to his/her individual DRIP A/c and the equivalent shares will be allotted to him.

To Pay or Not to Pay: Since the company is under no obligation as to payment of dividend, '**Should a company pay dividend**' is an important issue of discussion. In general it can be said that the younger companies in growth markets are far more likely to pay a small or no dividend so that they can find further expansion. In contrast, more mature companies in slower growing markets are likely to pay higher dividends because they do not have opportunity to invest in the expansion.

Thus, regular dividends are paidout to make holding the stock more appealing to investors, a move the company hopes will increase demand for the stock and therefore increase the stock's price.

4.5 FACTORS AFFECTING DIVIDEND POLICY

Following reasons result into payment of dividends.

- **Investor Preference for Dividends:** If taxes and transaction costs are ignored, dividends and capital receipts could be perfect substitutes. Yet principles of self-control and aversion for regret lead to investor preference for dividends.
- **Self control and Dividends:** Individuals often lack self-control. So they rely on rules and programmes, which check their temptations. In the realm of personal financial management, individuals like to protect their principal from their spending tendencies. A simple way to do this is to limit their spending to the dividend income so that the capital amount is maintained intact.
- **Aversion to Regret and Dividends:** Although the dividend and the capital receipts are perfectly substitutable, when taxes and transaction costs are abstracted away, empirical evidence suggests that most people feel more regret when they sell the stock because they can readily imagine the consequences of that action.
- **Information Signaling:** Management often has significant information about the prospects of the firm that it cannot (or prefers not to) disclose to the investors. The information gap between management and shareholders generally causes stock prices to be less than what they would be under conditions of information symmetry. According to signalling theory, these firms need to take actions that cannot be easily imitated by firms that do not have such promising projects. One such action is to pay more dividends. Increasing dividends suggest to the market that the firm is confident of its earning prospects that will enable it to maintain higher dividends in future as well. By the same token, a decrease in dividends is perceived as a negative signal, because firms are reluctant to cut dividends. This leads to consequent drop in stock prices.
- **Funds Requirement:** The dividend pay-out ratio of firms depends on the firm's future requirements for funds. Long-term financial forecasting of funds can assess this requirement. Usually firms, which have plans for substantial financial investment, need funds to exploit the available opportunities. Thus, they keep their dividend payout ratio low. On the other hand, firms, which have very few investment avenues have larger dividend payout ratio.
- **Liquidity:** It is another factor which influences the dividend payout ratio as dividends involved cash payment. Firms, which desire to pay dividends, may not do so, because of insufficient liquidity. This usually happens in the case of profitable and expanding firms, which have very low liquidity because of substantial investments.
- **Availability of External Sources of Financing:** Firms which have easy access to external sources of funds enjoy a great deal of flexibility in deciding the dividend payout ratio. For such firms, dividend payout decision is somewhat independent of its investment decision as well as its liquidity position. Such firms are usually more generous in their dividend policies.

While on the other hand, firms, which do not have easy access to external sources of funds, have to rely on the internal sources of funds or investment purposes. Such firms are usually very conservative in their dividend policy decisions.

- **Difference in the Cost of External Equity and Retained Earnings:** The cost of equity in all cases except for those raised by way of rights issue is higher than the cost of retained earnings. Depending on the extent of this difference in cost, firms decide the relative proportion of external equity and retained earnings to be used. This affects the dividend policy decision of the company.
- **Control:** Raising money from external resources may lead to dilution of control, in case money is raised by issuing public equity. Internal financing on the other hand does not lead to any dilution of control. Hence, if management and shareholders are averse to dilution of control, then firms prefer to rely more on retained earnings. Thus, such companies may adopt, the conservative dividend policy.
- **Taxes:** In India, dividend income for the individuals is free; however, capital gains are taxable. Thus, in that case shareholders who are in high tax bracket may prefer dividend income rather than capital gains. However, if tax on dividends is viewed from point of view of corporates, they have to pay dividend tax. Thus, this may influence the companies' dividend policy.
- **Clientele Effect:** Investors have diverse preferences. Some want more dividend income; others want more capital gains; still others want a balanced mix of both. Over a period of time, investors naturally migrate to the firms, which have a dividend policy that matches their preferences. The concentration of investors in companies with dividend policies that are matched to their preferences is called clientele effect. The existence of clientele effect implies that: A) Firms get the investors they deserve, and B) It will be difficult for firm to change an established dividend policy.

4.6 DISCUSS RETAINED EARNINGS AS A PRUDENT INVESTMENT POLICY

Depreciation charges and retained earnings represent the internal sources of finance available to the company. If depreciation charges are used for replacing wornout equipment, retained earnings represent the only internal source for financing expansion and growth. Companies normally retain 30% to 80% of profit after tax for financing growth. Hence, these are an important source of long-term financing.

Retained earnings can be reviewed for their advantages and disadvantages from

1. Firm's Point of View

Advantages:

(a) They are readily available internally. They do not require talking to outsiders.

(b) They effectively represent infusion of additional equity in the firm. Use of retained earnings, in lieu of external equity, eliminates issue costs and losses on account of underpricing.

(c) There is no dilution of control when a firm relies on retained earnings.

Disadvantages:

(a) The amount that can be raised by way of retained earnings may be limited. Further, the quantum of retained earnings tends to be highly variable.

(b) The opportunity cost of retained earnings is quite high, since it is nothing but the dividends foregone by the equity shareholders.

2. Shareholder's Point of View:

Advantages:

(a) Compared to dividend income, the capital appreciation that arises as a sequel to retained earnings is subject to a lower rate of tax.

(b) Reinvestment of profits may be convenient for many shareholders as it relieves them to some extent of the problem of investing on their own.

Disadvantages:

(a) Shareholders who want a current income higher than the dividend income may be highly averse to converting a portion of capital appreciation into current income, as it calls for selling some shares.

(b) Many firms do not fully appreciate the opportunity cost of retained earnings.

4.7 PAYMENT OF DIVIDENDS vs. ISSUE OF BONUS SHARES

Why do investors have strong preference for dividend rather than bonus share?

In a closely held co. Is it preferred to issue bonus shares or dividends?

A dividend is a portion of a company's earnings that is returned to shareholders. Dividends provide an added incentive (in the form of a return on the investment) to own stock in stable companies even if they are not experiencing much growth. Many companies – mature and young, large and small – pay a regular dividend to their stockholders. Companies use dividends to pass on their profits directly to their shareholders. Dividend can be defined as follows:

A cash payment using profits that's announced by a company's Board of Directors to be distributed among the stockholders.

In other words, dividends refer to a **part of the firm's net earnings**, which is paid to the shareholders. Net earnings mean the profit remaining after the payment of interest and taxes (PAT), some part of this may be transferred to the reserves and surpluses, while the remaining part is usually distributed as dividend. The shareholders are the actual owners of the company and should therefore get a return on the investment made by them.

Through the stocks, an investor can make income either through the capital gains or through the periodic dividends. A company announces dividend either quarterly, semi-annually or yearly. Thus, it is a **steady periodic** source of income. It is in the proportion to the share of capital, which the investor actually holds in the company. Though dividend is usually offered, it is necessary to note that a **company is under no obligation to pay the dividends**. It may or may not pay the dividends. Even if it pays; **there is no set level as to the payment of dividend.** That is there is no minimum or maximum limit on the amount of dividend that can be paid.

As mentioned earlier, the dividend can be paidout either quarterly, semi-annually or even annually. Sometimes, the companies may also declare an extra or special dividend, usually to share profits made due to some temporary changes in the market, or on special occasion in the company – genesis (E.g., HDFC completing 25 years).

Most often, the dividend comes in the form of cash: a company will pay a small percentage of its profits to the owner of each share of stock. However, it is not unheard of for companies to pay dividends in the form of stock. Dividends can be determined by a fixed rate known as **preferred dividends**, or a variable rate based on the company's latest profits known as **common dividends**.

Bonus shares are the shares issued top existing shareholders as a result of capitalization of reserves. In the wake of a bonus issue:

- The shareholders' proportional ownership remains unchanged.
- The book value per share, the earnings per share, the market price per share decrease, but the number of shares increase.

Following are the reasons for issue of bonus shares.

- The bonus issue tends to bring the market price per share within a more popular range.
- It increases the number of outstanding shares. This promoters more active trading.
- The nominal rate of dividend tends to decline. This may dispel the impression of profiteering.
- The share capital base increases and the company may achieve a more respectable size in the eyes of investing community.
- Shareholders regard a bonus issue as a firm indication that the prospects of the company have brightened and they can reasonably look for increase in total dividends.
- It improves the prospects of raising additional funds. In recent years many firms have issued bonus shares prior to issue of convertible debentures or other financing instruments.

Thus, the motives differ as regards to the issue of bonus shares and payment of dividends.

Since compared to receipt of dividends, receipt of additional stock is a risk. Hence, investors do not prefer it.

Similarly, in case of a closely held company, since no active trading occurs, there is no point in increasing the investor liquidity. Thus, practice of issuing bonus shares is **rarely followed** in a closely held company.

Bonus Shares	Dividend
1. No liquidity in hand.	Liquidity in hand in form of cash.
2. More number of shares with the same amount of investment as it is free.	No such addition to the shares held by the individual.
3. Company is perceived to have huge profits, huge reserves.	Company is perceived to be financially stable.
4. No tax is paid when bonus shares are received.	Company pays dividend distribution tax.
5. The fall in share price after the bonus becomes effective is much steeper.	The decrease in the market price of the share is comparatively lower.

Types of Dividend Policies

- **Generous Dividend and Bonus Policy:** Such firms reward shareholders generously by stepping up total dividend payment overtime. Typically, these firms maintain the dividend rate at a certain level (15-25%) and issue bonus shares when reserves position and earnings potential permit. Such firms naturally have a strong shareholder orientation.

- **More or Less Fixed Dividend Policy:** Some firms have a target dividend rate which is usually in the range 10% to 20% which they consider as a reasonable compensation to equity shareholders. Such firms normally do not issue bonus shares. Infrequently, may be once in a few years, the dividend rate may be slightly raised to provide somewhat higher compensation to equity shareholders to match the higher returns from other forms of investment.
- **Erratic Dividend Policy:** Firms which follow this dividend policy seem to be indifferent to the welfare of equity shareholders. Dividends are paid erratically whenever management believes that it will not strain its resources.

State Reasons for Using Internal Funds as a Source of Finance

Many companies use retained profit as a source of finance. Instead of paying dividends to shareholders and borrowing funds from outside, Profit After Tax can be used as capital or a source of finance OR a part of Profit After Tax can be used for payment of dividends and remaining can be used as internal funding. Terms like, retained profits, retained earnings and internal funding indicate same thing. Following are the reasons for using internal funds as a source of finance:

- **Non-expensive:** Retained earnings are self-evidently the cheapest form of finance. No interest is charged on retained earnings and at the same time, no shares are issued. As a result, there are no professional fees to be paid.
- **No change of Ownership:** Normally, existing owners of the business are reluctant to transfer the ownership in the new hands. Due to internal funding, ownership remains with existing management.
- **Time:** Reputed companies can get loans quite easily. But it takes several months to attract a suitable equity partner. A detailed study of capabilities of equity partner is required. It should also be kept in mind that chosen equity partner has to show interest in the company.
- **Exit Strategies:** Normally, private equity investors require an exit within three to five years. This means after every three to five years, company is bound to choose a new equity partner.
- **History:** History shows that companies which are looking to build a substantial size over a 10 to 15 years period and want to retain control and ownership of the original shareholders and management team, retained earnings is the best source of finance.

Hence, Berkshire Hathway, has not declared any dividend till date on shares.

4.8 EVALUATE INTERNAL FUNDS AS A SOURCE OF FINANCE

Instead of paying dividends to shareholders and borrowing funds from outside, Profit After Tax can be used as capital or a source of finance OR a part of Profit After Tax can be used for payment of dividends and remaining can be used as internal funding. Terms like, retained profits, retained earnings and internal funding indicate same thing. According to history, internal funding is used for a steady growth over a period over 10 to 15 years. On internal funding, no professional fees have to be paid. Company need not go for the search of the private equity partner and at the same time, control and ownership are retained by existing partners and shareholders.

On opposite side, as outsiders are not allowed to interfere in the business of the company due to fear of losing control, company does get talented and experienced people on the board. Companies, which are growth-oriented, have to depend on private equity partner for working capital requirements.

One more aspect to be considered while evaluating internal funds as a source of finance is that the banks, while giving loans or overdraft facilities, follow 'one-to-one' gearing rule which means that bank may be reluctant to lend more than the sum of the share capital plus retained profits. If the share capital is to remain unchanged, the only way a company can increase the amount a bank will be prepared to lend is through increasing retained profit.

Now, it must be clear that it is up to individual company to decide whether to go for internal funding or private equity. As long as the management team understands the urgency of maximizing retained profits, company can be made fully self-sufficient in funding, with help from the bank. It can also be said that internal equity is not just about providing the comfort of full control to owner managers who might otherwise have to seek external equity investors, it is also about necessity of survival and success.

4.9 PROBLEMS AND SOLUTIONS

Q.1. The earnings per share of B Ltd., is '4 and the rate of capitalisation applicable is 10%. The company has before it an option of acopting (i) 50% (ii) 75%, and (iii) 100% Dividend payout ratio, compute the market price of company's shares as per Walter's model if it can earn a return of 10% on its retained earnings.

Q.1: Solution

Computation of market price of company's share:

D/P Ratio 50% 75% 100%

$$P = \frac{D + \frac{r}{K_e}(E - D)}{K_e}$$

Where P = Market Price per Share.

E = Earnings per Share.

D = Dividend per Share.

(E - D) = Retained Earnings per Share.

r = Rate of return on investment.

Ke = Capitalisation Rate.

D = 50% of 4	D = 75% of 4	D = 100% of 4
= 2	= 3	= 4
E = 4	E = 4	E = 4
r = 10%	r = 10%	r = 10%
Ke = 10%	Ke = 10%	Ke = 10 %
$\therefore P = \frac{2 + \frac{0.10}{0.10}(4 - 2)}{0.10}$	$\therefore P = \frac{3 + \frac{0.10}{0.10}(4.3)}{0.10}$	$\therefore P = \frac{4 + \frac{0.10}{0.10}(4.4)}{0.10}$
$= \frac{4}{0.10}$	$= \frac{4}{0.10}$	$= \frac{4}{0.10}$
= ₹ 40	= ₹ 40	= ₹ 40

Q. 2. Following are the details regarding three companies X Ltd., Y Ltd., and Z Ltd.,

X Ltd.,	Y Ltd.,	Z Ltd.,
r = 15%	r = 15%	r = 10%
Ke = 10%	Ke = 10%	Ke = 10%
E = ₹ 8	E = ₹ 8	E = ₹ 8

Calculate the value of equity share of each of the company applying Walter's model; when dividend payout ratio is (a) 50% (b) 75% and (c) 25%. You are required to offer your comments on the result.

Q.2: Solution

Value of equity shares as per Walter's Model

D/P Ratio	X Ltd.	Y Ltd.	Z Ltd.
(1) 50%	$\frac{4 + \frac{0.15}{0.10}(8. - 4)}{0.10}$ = ₹ 100	$\frac{4 + \frac{0.05}{0.10}(8. - 4)}{0.10}$ = ₹ 60	$\frac{4 + \frac{0.10}{0.10}(8. - 4)}{0.10}$ = ₹ 80
(2) 75%	$\frac{6 + \frac{0.15}{0.10}(8. - 6)}{0.10}$ = ₹ 90	$\frac{6 + \frac{0.05}{0.10}(8. - 6)}{0.10}$ = ₹ 70	$\frac{6 + \frac{0.10}{0.10}(8. - 6)}{0.10}$ = ₹ 80
(3) 25%	$\frac{2 + \frac{0.15}{0.10}(8. - 2)}{0.10}$ = ₹ 110	$\frac{2 + \frac{0.05}{0.10}(8. - 2)}{0.10}$ = ₹ 50	$\frac{2 + \frac{0.05}{0.10}(8. - 2)}{0.10}$ = ₹ 80

Comments: The value of 'X' Ltd.'s share is the highest at ₹ 110 when Dividend Payout Ratio is lowest, i.e., 25%. The value of 'Y' Ltd., goes on declining with every increase in the earnings retained by it. In case of Z Ltd., the value of share continues to be ₹ 80 in all three situations.

Gordon Growth Valuation Model

The Gordon Growth Model is a theoretical model used to value the shares of a company. The model considers the retentions of earnings and growth of dividends. Therefore, it is called 'Dividend Growth Model'. The main proposition of model is that the value of a share reflects the value of the future dividends accruing to that share. Therefore, the dividend payments and growth are relevant in valuation of shares. The model holds that share price is equal to the sum of share's discounted future dividend payments. The value of a share, as per Gordon Growth Model, is determined as follows:

$$Po = \frac{D_o(1+g)}{K_e - g} = \frac{D_1}{K_e - g}$$

Where,

Po = Current ex-dividend market price of a share.

D_o = Current Year's dividend.

D_1 = Expected dividend.

K_1 = Cost of equity capital.

g = Expected future growth rate of dividends.

The shareholder's required rate of return (K_e) can also be calculated by using the Capital Asset pricing model. The model requires the estimation of future growth of dividends. The Gordon Growth Model using dividend capitalisation can also be used as follows:

$$Po = \frac{E1\ (1 - b)}{Ke - br}$$

Where,

Po = Current ex-dividend market price of equity share.

E1 = Expected earnings per share

b = Retention Ratio

(1 – b) = Dividend payout Ratio

Ke = Cost of Capital or Capitalisation rate

br = g = Growth rate of earnings and dividends

The implications of the Gordon Growth Model is that when the rate of return is greater than the discount rate the price per share increases as the dividend ratio increases. The price per share remains unchanged when the rate of return and discount rate are equal.

The Gordon Growth Valuation Model is based on the following assumptions:

(i) The firm is an all-equity firm and has no debt in its capital structure.

(ii) Retained earning is the only source of financing.

(iii) The internal rate of return is the firm's cost of capital 'K'. It remains constant and is taken as the appropriate discount rate.

(iv) Future growth rate of dividend is expected to be constant.

(v) Growth rate of the firm is the product of retention ratio and its rate of return.

(vi) Cost of capital is always greater than the growth rate.

(vii) Corporate taxes do not exist.

(viii) The growth rate g = br, is constant for ever.

Q. 3. X Ltd., has an investment of ₹ 5,00,000 in assets and 50,000 shares outstanding at ₹ 10 each. It earns a rate of 15% on its investment and has a policy of retaining 50% of the earnings. If the appropriate discount rate is 10%, determine the price of company's share using Gordon's Growth Model. What will be the share price if the company has a payout of 80% or 40%?

Q.3: Solution

Gordon's Share Valuation Model.

$$P_o = \frac{D_1}{Ke - g} \text{ or } \frac{E_1 (1 - b)}{ke - br}$$

Where, Po = Current ex-dividend Market Price.

D_1 = Expected Dividend

Ke = Rate of return required by shareholders

g = Growth rate of earnings and dividends

E_1 = Earnings per share.

b = Fraction of earnings the firms ploughs back

r = Rate of return earned on investments.

(1) If dividend payout is 50%,

$$Po = \frac{(10 \times 0.15)(1 - 0.2)}{0.10 - (0.15 \times 0.5)}$$

$$= \frac{0.75}{0.025}$$

= ₹ 30

(2) If dividend payout is 80%,

$$Po = \frac{(10 \times 0.15)(1 - 0.2)}{0.10 - (0.15 \times 0.5)}$$

$$= \frac{1.20}{0.07}$$

= ₹ 17.14

(3) If dividend payout is 40%,

$$Po = \frac{(10 \times 0.15)(1 - 0.6)}{0.10 - (0.15 \times 0.60)}$$

$$= \frac{0.6}{0.01}$$

= ₹ 60

Q.4. Ruchi Soya Ltd., is an established company having its shares quoted in the stockmarket. The company has distributed dividend at 20% p.a. The paid-up capital of the company was 50 lakh shares of ₹ 10 each. Annual growth rate in dividend expected is 3%. The expected rate of return on its equity capital is 15%. Calculate the value of shares of Ruchi Soya Ltd., based on Gordon's dividend growth model.

Q. 4: Solution

$$Po = \frac{Do\,(1 + g)}{Ke - g}$$

$$= \frac{2\,(1 + 0.03)}{(0.15 - 0.03)}$$

$$= \frac{2.06}{0.12}$$

= ₹ 17.17

According to MM Hypothesis, the market value of a share in the beginning of the period is equal to the present value of dividends paid at the end of the period plus the market price of the share at the end of the period. The value can be determined with the help of the following formula:

$$P_o = \frac{D_1 + P_1}{(1 + K_e)}$$

Where, P_o = Current Market Price of a Share.

K_e = Cost of equity Capital.

D_1 = Dividend to be received at the end of period.

P_1 = Market Price of a Share at the end of period.

The above equation can be modified as under:

$$P1 = Po\,(1 + K_e) - D_1$$

The MM Hypothesis is based on the following assumptions:

(i) Capital markets are perfect.

(ii) Information is freely available to the investors and there are no transaction costs.

(iii) The firm has a fixed investment policy.

(iv) There are no taxes or there are uniform taxes.

(v) Risk or uncertainty does not exist.

Q. 5. D Ltd., belongs to a risk-class for which the appropriate capitalisation rate is 10%. It has 25,000 shares outstanding. The current market price of the share is ₹ 100. The company is contemplating the declaration of dividend of ₹ 5 per share at the end of the current year. The company expects to have a net income of ₹ 2,50,000 and has a proposal for making new investments of ₹ 5,00,000. You are required to calculate:

(a) Market price per share when dividend is declared.

(b) Market price per share when dividend is not declared.
(c) Number of new shares to be issued.
(d) Show that the payment of dividend does not affect the value of the firm.

Q. 5: Solution

(1) Calculation of market price when dividend is declared:

$P1 = P_o (1 + K_e) - D_1$

$= 100 (1 + 0.1) - 5$

$= 100 \times 1.1 - 5$

$= 110 - 5$

$=$ ₹ 105.

(2) Calculation of market price per share when dividend is not declared.

$P1 = Po (1 + K_e) - D_1$

$= 100 (1 + 0.1) - 0$

$=$ ₹100 (1.1)

$=$ ₹110

(3) Calculation of number of new share to be issued:

Particulars	Dividend Declared	Dividend not Declared
Net income (₹)	2,50,000	2,50,000
Less: Dividend paid	1,25,000	-
Retained earnings	1,25,000	2,50,000
New Investments	5,00,000	5,00,000
Amount to be raised by issue of new shares	3,75,000	2,50,000
Market price per share	₹ 105	₹ 110
∴ Number of new shares to be issued	$\frac{3,75,000}{105}$	$\frac{2,50,000}{110}$
	=3,571	=2,273

(4) Verification of MM Dividend Irrelevancy Theory:

Particulars	Dividend Declared	Dividend not Declared
Existing shares	25,000	25,000
New shares to be issued	3,571	2273
Total Shares	28,571	27,273
Market price per share	₹ 105	₹ 110
Total market value of shares at the end of the year	30,00,000	30,00,000

Thus, whether dividends are paid or not, the value of the firm remains the same.

Q.6. Bajaj Ltd., has 1,20,000 shares outstanding and selling at ₹ 20 each in the market. The company hopes to make a net income of ₹ 3,50,000 during the year ended 31st March, 2009. The company is considering to pay a dividend of ₹ 2 per share at the end of the current year. The capitalisation rate for class of this company has been estimated to be 15% using MM Dividend Valuation Model.

(a) What will be the price of a share at the end of the year: (i) if dividend is paid, and (ii) if dividend is not paid?

(b) How many new shares must the company issue if the dividend is paid and the company needs ₹ 7,40,000 for an approved investment expenditure during the year?

Q.6: Solution

(a) Calculation of market price per share under MM Dividend Valuation Model:

$P1 = Po\ (1 + K_e) - D_1$

(i) If dividend is declared:

$P1 = Po\ (1 + K_e) - D_1$

$= 20\ (1 + 0.15) - 2$

$= 20\ (1 + 1.15) - 2$

$= 23$

(ii) If dividend is not declared:

$P1 = Po\ (1 + Ke) - D1$

$= 20\ (1 + 0.15) - 0$

$= 20\ (1.15)$

$= 23$

= ₹ 23

(iii) Calculation of the number of new shares to be issued:

Particulars	Dividend Declared	Dividend not Declared
Net income (₹)	3,50,000	3,50,000
Less: Dividend paid	2,40,000	-
Retained earnings	1,10,000	3,50,000
New Investments	7,40,000	7,40,000
Amount to be raised by issue of new shares	6,30,000	3,90,000
Market price per share	21	23
∴ Number of new shares to be issued	30,000	16,957

Q. 7. The following information is available in respect of a company:

Capitalisation rate (Ke) = 0.12

EPS = ₹ 15

Rate of return on investments (r): (i) 0.15 (ii) 0.10

The company wants to know the effect on the market price of its shares under the two possibilities of r (i.e., 0.15 and 0.10) under two options: (i) if it does not declare any dividend, and (ii) if it declares ₹ 15 as dividend. Using Walter's Model explains the results obtained by you.

(MU, MMS, Dec. 2008)

Q.7: Solution

Calculation of Market Price of Company's Share

D/P Ratio	100%	0%
$P = \dfrac{D + \dfrac{r}{K_e}(E - D)}{K_e}$	$\dfrac{15 + \dfrac{0.15}{0.12}(15 - 15)}{0.12}$	$\dfrac{0 + \dfrac{0.15}{0.12}(15 - 0)}{0.12}$
(i) If r = 15%	$= \dfrac{15}{0.12}$	$= \dfrac{18.75}{0.12}$
	₹ 125	₹ 156.25

D/P Ratio	100%	0%
$P = \dfrac{D + \dfrac{r}{K_e}(E - D)}{K_e}$		
(i) If r = 10%	$\dfrac{15 + \dfrac{0.10}{0.12}(15 - 15)}{0.12}$	$\dfrac{0 + \dfrac{0.10}{0.12}(15 - 0)}{0.12}$
	$= \dfrac{15 + 0}{0.12}$	$= 0 + \dfrac{12.50}{0.12}$
	₹ 125	₹ 104

Using Walter's Model, the market price of a share remains the same in case the value of 'r' is changed and dividend is declared by the company. However, the value of share is reduced if the value of 'r' is reduced and if the company does not declare dividend.

Q. 8. A company expects to generate the following net income and incur the following capital expenditure in the next five years as per the following details:

(₹ in lakh)

Year	1	2	3	4	5
Net Profit	75	60	45	40	25
Capital Expenditure	40	45	55	47	50

The total number of outstanding shares are 18,00,000 and Current Dividend is ₹ 6.5 per share; you are required to:

(a) Determine the Dividend Per Share, if the company follows a residual dividend policy.

(b) Determine the amount of external financing if the current dividend is maintained.

(c) Determine the amounts of external financing if the company maintains a 50% Dividend Payout Ratio.

(d) Identify under which of the above three policies the aggregate dividends are maximized and under which policy the amount of external financing is minimized.

Q.8: Solution

Particulars	Year 1	Year 2	Year 3	Year 4	Year 5
Net Profit	75	60	45	40	25
(-) Capital Exp.	40	45	55	47	50
Residual Profit	35	15	NIL	NIL	NIL
A. Dividend per share Residual profit/No. of shares	1.94	0.83	NIL	NIL	NIL
External Finance Required	NIL	NIL	10	7	25
B. Funds reqd. for dividend (current div. 6.5 × 18)	117	117	117	117	117
(+) Funds reqd. for C.E.	40	45	55	47	50
Int. Funds	157	162	172	164	167
(-) Net Profit	75	60	45	40	25
External Finance Required	82	102	127	124	142

Q. 9. Pradeep Enterprises is a fast growing firm in a manufacturing sector. Following is the balance sheet of the company for the year ending 2010-2011:

Particulars		₹ in ('000)
Equity Shares of ' 10 each	300	
Accumulated Profits	170	
Profits for the year	100	
6% Debenture	80	
Total:		650
Fixed Asset	400	
Working Capital	250	
Total:		650

The management of the company has been following a dividend payout of 40% constantly in the past.

However, it is not sure as to whether it should continue the practice as it has enough investment opportunities in store. It has therefore approached you for advice and needs you to answer the following questions with reason if any:

(a) If it continues the earlier dividend policy what is the rate of dividend it will be declaring and how much is the cash outflow.

(b) Can it give out bonus shares in lieu of dividend to avoid the cash outflow in the form of dividend payment?

(c) If it wants to give out dividends @ 40%, how much is the cash outflow then?

(d) If the current market price of the share is ₹ 50. What would be the P/E ratio?

(e) If in the future years it incurs a loss due to incorrect investments then can it still payout dividends?

Q.9: Solution

$$\text{Dividend Payout Ratio} = \frac{\text{DPS}}{\text{EPS}} \times 100$$

$$= \frac{\text{DPS}}{3.33} \times 100$$

$$\therefore \text{DPS} = ₹\ 1.33$$

$$\text{EPS} = \frac{\text{NPAT} - \text{Pref. Div.}}{\text{No. of Equity Shares}}$$

$$= \frac{1,00,000}{30,000}$$

$$= ₹\ 3.33$$

$$\text{Rate of Dividend} = \frac{\text{DPS}}{\text{FV / Paid - up Value}} \times 100$$

$$= \frac{1.33}{10} \times 100$$

$$= 13.33$$

[A] Cash outflow = No. of Shares x DPS

= 30,000 × 1.33

= ₹ 40,000

or

= PAT × 40%

= 1,00,000 × 40% = 40,000

[B] No, the company cannot give out Bonus Shares in lieu of Dividend to avoid cash outflow, as it is forbidden by SEBI Regulations

[C] Dividend per Share = Rate of Div. × FV

$$= \frac{40}{100} \times 10$$

$$= ₹\ 4$$

∴ Cash outflow = No. of Shares × DPS

= 30,000 × 4 = ₹ 1,20,000

1) $$\text{P/E Ratio} = \frac{\text{MPS}}{\text{EPS}} = \frac{50}{3.33} = 15 \text{ times}$$

[D] Yes, the company can declare dividend in future year if it incurs a loss, after satisfying below condition of Company's Act 1956:-

1. First set off current year loss against Accumulated Profits of the previous year.
2. The Rate of Dividend Declared cannot exceed average rate of Dividend of last five years.
3. The balance left in reserves should not follow below 15% of the paid-up capital

Q. 10. BPR Ltd., – is a listed company set up by new entrepreneurs for the manufacture of refractories. Refractory is a consumable which, if not made available to the still industry, would render operations impossible because it is the refractory which confines the heat inside the furnace. But unfortunately for the Greenfield promoters, the steel industry worldwide has hit a trough. The domestic industry, in particular, is being buffered by falling demand growth and large-scale imports at the same time. BPR which has been in existence for less than a year has not yet achieved the projected first year capacity of 60%.

For the above company, state whether you would expect it to distribute high or low proportion of earnings as dividend and whether you would expect them to have a relatively high or low price earning ratio.

Q. 10: Solution

Comments:

1. As the company has not achieved projected 1st year capacity and the steel industry has just now entered in recession phase, the company is advised to distribute lower proportion of earnings as dividend.

   This will help to generate profits to meet future contingencies.
2. As the future growth prospects and earning prospects are not too good, the shares of the company will be traded at relatively low P/E Ratio.

Q. 11. IFL Ltd., – is an acknowledged leader in the pump industry with over 60% of the market share. The product range consists of a wide range of power-driven pumps including submersible pumps, special pumps for application in fertiliser, chemical and petrochemical industries. The company paying steady dividends had a turnover growth at an annual Compound Annual Growth Rate (CAGR) of 28% over the last five years and the company had been maintaining its market share in spite of the intense competition. But unexpectedly for the current financial year, the company reported a net loss of over ₹ 10 crore. This has mainly been attributed to the loss of a major order as well as IFL extending credit period to customers.

For the above company, state whether you would expect it to distribute high or low proportion of earnings as dividend and whether you would expect them to have a relatively high or low price earning ratio.

Q. 11: Solution

IFL Ltd.,

Facts of the case study:

1. IFL Ltd., is an acknowledge leader with over 60% market share.
2. The company has diversified product portfolio/range of pumps.
3. The company is paying steady dividend in past years.
4. Turnover growth is at a CAGR of 28%.
5. Unexpectedly for the current financial year, the corporate Net Loss of ₹ 10 crore.
6. The reason for lower profitability/loss is:-
   (i) Loss of a major order and extending credit period to customers.
   (ii) Loss of a major order

Observations:

1. IFL Ltd., is a reputed company.
2. The company follows steady dividend per share policy in spite of increase in profits. FV to rate of dividend 50%

   $$\frac{5}{10}\times 100 \quad \frac{5}{15}, \quad \frac{5}{20}, \quad \frac{5}{25}, \quad \frac{5}{30}, \quad \frac{5}{35}$$

   = 50% EPS keeps on changing

   =14% DPS remain the same
3. Healthy growth in turnover/profits and low dividend policy (Low Dividend Payout Ratio) will result into huge retained earnings.
4. The reasons for loss are temporary and it is viewed that future outlook of the company is good.

Recommendations/Conclusions:

1. The company is advised to follow the same rate of dividend or marginally higher rate of dividend.

   This will result into distributing high proportion of earnings as dividends.

   This is because company has huge retained earnings, future outlook is good, etc.

   One needs to compare the company's P/E with other company's in the same field and not with the company's previous P/E.
2. It is the market leader and it is expected that the company will bounce back in future, the shares of the company will be traded at relatively high P/E ratio.
3. The company is advised to improve the receivable management and take efforts to secure large orders.

Q. 12. The director of the following Indian company has approached you with their concern for the current business scenario and future prospects.

Cadbury Products Limited is an established company in the field of dairy products, chocolates and ice-creams. It has a decent track record of dividend, which average @ 40% p.a., the company has also a good record of bonus issue. The last bonus issue was made in September 2000.

The Company feels that due to the conspiracy hatched by its competition with the help of widespread network of distributors, the company's product were shown to have been contaminated and it was also widely shown on the media that under the wrappers of many of their chocolates and ice-cream, there was a layer of fungus and decayed dry fruits. The snaps and live interview of the consumers complaining about the inferior quality and "totally unsafe for human consumption" shouts, drastically brought down the sale in the last quarter of the financial year 2003-2004.

The directors immediately undertook damage controlling steps and through wide scale advertisement campaign tried to restore the public confidence. However, the current year's performance is very much lower than the earlier years and any prudent financial consultant would not recommend dividend more than 20% this year.

The directors are of the opinion that the sale would again pick-up of from the 2nd quarter of the next year and than will be normal thereafter.

Give your guidance in above case, with special reference to the issues related to dividend/bonus policy and future share price behaviour on the stock exchange.

Q. 12: Solution

Cadbury Products Limited

Facts

1. Cadbury's Product Limited is an established, in the field of dairy products, chocolates and ice-creams.
2. The company has a decent track record of dividend which average 40% p.a.
3. The company also has a good record of bonus issue.

   The last bonus issue was made in September 2000.
4. The company's products were known to have been contaminated.
5. This brought down the sale in the last quarter of financial year 03-04.
6. The directors immediately undertook damage-controlling steps to restore public confidence.
7. Current year performance is very much low than earlier year and prudent financial consultant would not recommend more than 20% this year.
8. The directors are of opinion that the sale would again pick-up from 2nd quarter of next year and then will be normal thereafter.

Observations:

1. It is a reputed FMCG leader.
2. The company believes in sharing wealth with shareholders in the form of cash dividend.
3. The company tries to maximise wealth by stock dividend at regular intervals.

   The last bonus issue was made 3½ years back.
4. Due to conspiracy hatched by competitor the company's product were shown on the media to be of inferior quality and to tally unsafe for human consumption.

5. The reduction in sales is a temporary phenomena and wide scale advertisement campaign and other measures would result into sales picking up from 2nd quarter of next year.

Recommendations:

1. The company is advised to declare marginally higher rate of dividend than last year. This will enhance confidence of shareholders, regarding financial liquidity of the company.
2. The company is advised to introduce double packaging and improve storage facilities.
3. Because of sufficient retained profits and expectations of shareholders, the company is advised to declare bonus issue.
4. The company is also advised to train its sales staff and come up with incentive schemes for the distributors/retailers.

Conclusion:

1. Marginally higher rate of dividend, bonus issue and other measures will have a good impact on a future share price/shareholders wealth of the company.

Q. 13. The director of the following Indian company has approached you with their concern for the current business scenario and future prospects.

Infosys Software Ltd., is a well-established company in the field of software development, e-service provider and man power consultancy service. Its clientele is mainly in the banking, airways and transport sector. Almost 60% of the revenue comes from overseas clients. It has shown a steady growth and progress for last five years and has paid dividend of 15%, 15%, 17%, 20% and 25%, and still a large amount of profits where ploughed back every year. Till December 2003 everything going was smoothly, but all of a sudden the overseas countries having maximum business associates, saw the rise of anti-outsourcing agitations. The problem got further aggravated by rupee becoming stronger day-by-day against the US dollar. The company some how managed to complete the ongoing contract but is not so sure of the future prospectus. The company is also in the process of finalizing new business ventures with "non-affected countries" and also taking steps to expand its operations more in India. The company is hopeful of getting the better results for all its efforts.

Give your guidance in above case, with special reference to the issues related to dividend/bonus policy and future share price behaviour on the Stock Exchange.

Q. 13: Solution

Infosys Software Ltd.

Facts

1. Infosys Software Ltd., is a well-established software company.
2. Its clientele is mainly in banking, airways and transport sector.
3. Almost 60% of the revenue comes from overseas clients.
4. The company has shown steady progress and has paid dividend of 15%, 15%, 17%, 20% and 25%.
5. Till December 2003 everything was normal but all of a sudden the company squartise of anti-outsourcing agitation.
6. The problem got further aggravated by rupee becoming stronger under US dollar.

7. The company completed the ongoing contract but it is not so sure of future prospects.
8. The company is in process of finalising new business venture and also taking steps to expand its operation in India.

Observations:

1. Infosys Software Ltd., is a reputed software company.
2. It is a diversified company having its operation in different like banking, airways and transport sector.
3. The company believes in sharing wealth with the shareholders, i.e., the company believes in shareholders wealth maximisation because it has paid steady increase of dividend.
4. Till December 2003 everything was normal, but after that company had to face the problem of anti-outsourcing agitation and after that situation got worse by rupee becoming stronger day-by-day against the US dollar.
5. In spite of all these problems the company somehow manage to complete its existing contract.
6. The company is also in the project of finalising new business ventures with "non-affected countries" and is also taking steps to expand its operations more in India.

Recommendations:

1. The company though follows a steady dividend policy is advised to increase marginally so as to be retained the existing shareholders and also try attracting more.
2. The company is advised to concentrate on its new business ventures with non-affected countries as well as try to expanding operations more in India.
3. The company is also advised to make a bonus issue out of its retained profits, this will have positive outlook to the shareholders towards the company.

Conclusion:

1. Marginally higher rate of dividend at regular intervals bonus issue and company's concentration on its future projects will have the company to maintain its position in the market and these steps may give the company new dimensions to expand domestically as well as internationally.

Q. 14. Emami Ltd., is a Stock Exchange listed company making good profits every year. However, the Board of Directors are very conservative and has declared dividend at fixed rate of ₹ 4 per share, when EPS is always above ₹ 50 for the last five years. The last bonus issue was made six years ago. The salary packages are also not attractive. As a result there is a high turnover of employees and low volume of company's share on bourses. The young members of the director's family wish to make the company more dynamic, employee friendly and darling of shareholders so as to make it the most valued one. What steps you would suggest to achieve these objectives?

Q. 14: Solution

Emami Ltd.

Facts

1. Emami Ltd., is a stock listed company making good profits every year.
2. The Board of Directors are paying dividend @ 8% p.a., for the last five years.

3. The last bonus issue was six years ago.
4. The salary packages are not attractive.
5. Due to unattractive salary packages there is high turnover of employees.
6. There is low volume of company's share on bourses.
7. The young members of the directors family wish to make the company more dynamic, employee-friendly and darling of shareholders.

Observations:

1. Emami Ltd., is a well-established company making profits steadily every year.
2. The Board of Directors is paying a very low rate of dividend, i.e., 8% and ploughing back 92% of the revenue since last five years.
3. The company is just ploughing back its profits and is least concerned in declaring bonus.

   The company has not declared any bonus for the last six years.
4. The company's salary packages are unattractive thus dissatisfying its employees, which is in turn is leading to high turnover of its employees.

Recommendations:

1. The company is advised to declare a higher rate of dividend as compared to the present rate (₹15-20).

   This will lead to more shareholder wealth maximisation, thus retaining the existing ones and also attracting prospective ones.
2. The company is also advised to declare bonus, which it has not declared for the past six years.

   This will help attracting prospective investors.
3. The company is advised to improve the salary packages of its employees, by giving ESOP performance based incentives, etc.

Practice Problems

Q. 15. Following is the EPS record PP Ltd., company over the past ten years.

Year ending March	EPS (₹)	Year ending March	EPS (₹)
2009	20	2004	12
2008	19	2003	6
2007	16	2002	9
2006	15	2001	3
2005	16	2000	2

Determined the annual dividend paid each year in the following cases.

(i) If the company's dividend policy is based on a constant dividend payout policy of 50% for all the years.

(ii) If the policy is to pay ₹ 8 per share dividend and increase it to ₹ 10 when earning exceed ₹ 14 per share for 2 consecutive years.

(iii) If the policy is to pay ₹ 7 per share dividend each year except when EPS exceeds ₹ 14 per share, when an extra dividend equal to 80% of earnings beyond ₹ 14 would be paid?

Q. 16. What is Capitalization of Reserves? What are the guidelines issued by SEBI within this regard? How does it affect the Balance Sheet of a company?

Q. 17. The directors of M/s. Rich-e-Rich Ltd., are planning to declare interim dividend, as a financial consultant of the company, the directors want you to send them a brief write-up on the factors to be considered before declaring interim dividend. Kindly prepare a brief write-up.

Q. 18. Royal Industries has for many years enjoyed a moderate stable growth in sales and earnings. In recent years it is facing stiff competition in a plastic product-line and consequently its sales have been declining. Apprehending further decline in its sales, its management is planning to move eventually out of plastic business altogether and develop a new diversified product-line in growth-oriented industries. To execute the proposed investment plan of this year a capital outlay of ₹ 12 crore as in necessary to purchase new facility to start manufacturing a new product. The estimated rate of return on fresh investment is 20 per cent per annum.

The company has been paying a dividend of ₹ 1.50 per share on 4 crore outstanding shares. The dividend policy has been to maintain a stable dividend of rupee one raising it only when it appears that earnings have reached a new permanently higher level. The directors may change such a policy if there are compelling reasons to do so. Total earnings of the current year are ₹ 10 crore. The current price of the equity share is ₹ 15 and firm's Debt/Assets ratio is 40%. Current costs of various forms of financing are:

- Debentures 13%, New equity shares sold at ₹ 15, Required rate of return is 10 per cent.
- What would be an appropriate policy for the company?
- What assumptions, if any, do you make in your investors preference for dividends vs. capital gains?

Q. 19. PCR Ltd., was a financially sound company in the not so distant past. On equity of ₹ 5.40 crore, it has a net worth of approximately ₹ 120 crore, and a gross block ₹ 202.04 crore which has steadily grown at 10% Compound Annual Growth Rate. This company which has technical collaboration with Yogyo Corporation Ltd., Japan, is considered by analyst to be firmly established and an asset player. Recently declared result for financial year 1997 mirrors the tight money situation prevailing due to economic factors and lacklustre markets rather than operational inefficiency of the company though the lacklustre performance was only to be expected by the company and economy watchers.

For the above company, state whether you would expect it to distribute high or low proportion of earnings as dividend and whether you would expect them to have a relatively high or low price earning ratio.

Q. 20. GMFF Ltd., manufactures resin bounded silicon carbide crucible which are used by non-ferrous foundries for melting and maintaining of aluminium alloys. Buoyed by the rapid growth in auto-ancillaries and steady growth in domestic appliances and capital goods, GMFF currently holds approximately 40% of the market share. Coupled with the user industry growing at approximately 20% per annum and competitors yielding ground, GMFF should see its already dominant position enhanced to a market share of approximately 60% in the next couple of years.

For the above company, state whether you would expect it to distribute high or low proportion of earnings as dividend and whether you would expect them to have a relatively high or low price earning ratio.

Q. 21. Annual Report - 2000-2001

The Tata Iron and Steel Company Limited (TISCO)

Directors' Report

To The Members

The directors hereby present their Ninety-fourth Annual Report on the business and operations of the company and the financial accounts for the year ended 31st March, 2001.

Financial Result

Total revenue increased by 13% from ₹ 6,943.33 crore to ₹ 7,814.58 crore on account of marginally higher sales volumes, improved product-mix and better price realization in the first half of the year.

After a good first quarter, a combination of factors, such as excess global production, the slow down of US economy and higher import from Russia and CIS countries at low prices, pushed steel prices down for most of the rest of the year. However, in the face of such adverse circumstances, the company ended the year on a satisfactory note, through aggressive cost-cutting, better product-mix and a marginal improvement in realization over the previous year. All the major profit centres reported better performance. Gross profit was higher at ₹ 1,757.14 crore as against ₹ 1,285.60 crore in the previous year, an increase of 3%. Provision for depreciation was higher at ₹ 492.25 crore (1999-2000: ₹ 426.54 crore), mainly due to commissioning of the major part of the Cold Rolling Mill Complex during the year. Net interest and expenses towards employee separation compensation- amounted to ₹ 376.61 crore and ₹ 201.52 crore respectively, (1999-2000: ₹ 359.96 crore and ₹ 157.99 crore), yielding a profit before taxes of ₹ 602.44 crore (after providing for extraordinary items), an increase of 26% and the highest ever achieved by your company. After providing ₹ 49 crore towards taxes, profit after taxes increased by 31% to ₹ 553.44 crore. The performance of the major divisions is discussed separately.

Q. 22. Prepare Dividend Policy Analysis:

Case of ACC Ltd.,

Year	EPS (₹)	DPS (₹)	Average Share Price (₹)	Book Value	Dividend Payout Per Share (₹)	Dividend Yield Ratio	Earning Yield	ROE
1991	5.90	1.70	153.00	53.49	28.8%	1.1%	3.9%	11.0%
1992	5.31	2.00	95.50	55.77	37.7%	2.1%	5.6%	9.5%
1993	4.01	3.00	109.75	57.91	74.8%	2.7%	3.7%	6.9%
1994	5.73	2.50	88.25	57.55	43.6%	2.8%	6.5%	10.0%
1995	11.60	3.00	121.25	66.81	25.9%	2.5%	9.6%	17.4%
1996	7.58	3.50	245.00	66.38	46.2%	1.4%	3.1%	11.4%
1997	5.48	3.50	287.00	67.31	63.9%	1.2%	1.9%	8.1%
1998	9.07	4.00	240.00	72.10	44.1%	1.7%	3.8%.	12.6%
1999	11.96	5.00	268.75	91.99	41.8%	1.9%	4.5%	13.0%
2000	16.90	6.00	262.00	125.00	35.5%	2.3%	6.5%	13.5%
Average	**8.35**	**3.42**	**187.05**	**71.43**	**44.2%**	**2.0%**	**4.9%**	**11.3%**

❑❑❑

CHAPTER 5

VALUATION OF DEBENTURES

From this exhibit you can feel the power of compound interest. As Albert Einstein once remarked: "I don't know what the seven wonders of the world are, but I know the eighth – compound interest". You may be wondering why your ancestors did not display foresight. Hopefully, you will show concern for your posterity.

Exhibit 5.1 Value of ₹ 1,000 Invested at 10 per cent Simple and Compound Interest

Year	Simple Interest					Compound Interest				
	Starting Balance	+	Interest	=	Ending Balance	Starting Balance	+	Interest	=	Ending Balance
1	1000	+	100	=	1100	1000	+	100	=	1100
5	1400	+	100	=	1500	1464	+	146	=	1610
10	1900	+	100	=	2000	2358	+	236	=	2594
20	2900	+	100	=	3000	6116	+	612	=	6728
50	5900	+	100	=	6000	106,718	+	10672	=	117,390
100	10900	+	100	=	11000	12,527,829	+	1,252,783	=	13,780,612

5.1 ANALYSIS AND VALUATION OF DEBT

Debt instruments are fixed income securities like bonds and debentures. Bonds and debentures are issued by public and private sectors undertakings. A bond or debentures is a debt security issued by a borrower issued by the firms with a promise to make payment of interest and principal under clearly defined terms and conditions.

Characteristics of debt securities

1. Tradeable.
2. Obligation to pay principal/par value.
3. Tenor/term to maturity.
4. Obligation to pay interest.
5. Periodicity of payment of interest.

Types of debentures/bonds

1. **Bearer and Registered:** Bearer debentures are transferable by means of delivery and they instruments. Registered debentures are issued specifically on the name of particular persons, who is registered by the company as debenture holders. The payment of interest and repayment of capital is made to those whose names are registered with the company and duly entered in the register of debenture holders.

2. **Secured and Unsecured:** Secured debentures are the debentures which are secured by a charge on the assets or properties of the company. Unsecured debentures are the debentures, which do not carry any security in respect of repayment of interest or the principal.
3. **Redeemable and Irredeemable:** Redeemable debentures provide for the payment of principal amount on the expiry of a certain period. Redeemable debentures can be reissued even after they have been redeemed until they have been cancelled. Irredeemable debentures are retained as a part of the capital structure of the company. They are also known as perpetual debentures. They are not refundable during the lifetime of the company.
4. **Convertible and Non-convertible:** Convertible debentures give options to the debenturesholders to convert them into equity or preference shares at a stated rate of exchange, after a certain period. Non-convertible debentures are not convertible into equity or preference shares afterwards. Convertible debentures are very popular at present.

Risks of Bonds

The risks involved in bonds to the investor are as follows:

1. Purchasing power risk.
2. Default risk.
3. Interest rate risk.

Interest Rate Risk

The earning of companies and the performance of their shares are sensitive to interest rate changes. Therefore, potential variability of investment returns due to interest rate fluctuations is known as interest rate risk. The prices of debt securities and all other types of securities with fixed payment are dependent upon the level of market interest rates. When the interest rates rise, bond value will generally fall. The return on other types of securities also depends upon interest rates. The degree of sensitivity to interest rate changes will naturally differ from company-to-company.

Recently, companies have started issuing 'floating rate bonds'. The rates of interest on these bonds are linked to some floating rates such as prime lending rate or the banks minimum lending rate. When market interest rate rise, the bond rate rises and when it falls, the bonds rate also falls. This is a good way to circumvent the interest rate risk. Interest rate is a major risk to the holder of high quality bonds. Interest risk arises due to the inverse relationship between interest rates and prices of the debt instrument. The changes in the interest rates have the greatest impact on the market price of short-term bonds. Also the interest income on short-term bonds portfolio may fluctuate from period-to-period, as interest rates change.

Rating of Debt Securities

Compulsory Rating of Debt Issue: Rating is necessary for debt instrument and world over debt instruments are rated. In India in case of issue of a fully, partly or non-convertible debentures with maturity or conversion period of 18 months or more, credit rating from a recognized rating agency is compulsory. A fresh credit rating is required in case of rollover debentures. Whereas, there is no mandatory rating for public issue of shares.

Determinants of Interest Rates

Interest rates are determined by the supply and demand for loanable funds. The demand for and supply of these funds will determine the interest rate. There are two types of interest rates, nominal and real interest rates. The nominal rates is the published or quoted interest. It is the return to the lender or investor rate on a security or loans; on the other hand, the real rate of interest is the return to the lender or investor measured in terms of its actual purchasing power. Nominal interest rate = Real interest rate + inflation.

For example, the real rate is 7% and the expected rate of inflation is 5%, then the nominal rate will be 7+5 = 12%.

The factors which influence interest rates on various financial investments are as follows:

1. **Maturity Period:** Difference in maturity periods of time. Thus, the longer the period, the higher is the interest rate.
2. **Default risk/creditworthiness:** The degree of default risks or uncertainty of return would also determine the interest rates.
3. **Tax incentives on Products:** The tax provision on the financial instrument, incentives or disincentives for the taxes on the interest income would also influence the demand for different types of financial assets which in turn determine the interest rates [for e.g., Notified Infrastructure Bonds.]
4. **Marketability:** Marketability of financial assets with facilities for discounting or rediscounting also imparts liquidity to the instruments. The financial instrument which have a good marketability have lower rate of interest.

Summary

Debenture or bond is the loan which is taken from the public. The debentures carry a fixed rate of interest. The debentures are redeemable. The debentures are secured. The difference between bond and debenture is that the debentures are generally issued by Pvt. Company and bonds are issued by Public Company or Govt. Company.

Required rate of return = Cost of Capital = Discounting factor = PV

5.2 ILLUSTRATION

Illustration 1: A debenture of 100 face value carries an interest rate of 15 per cent is redeemable after 7 years at a premium of 5 per cent. If the required rate return is 16 per cent, what is the present value of the debentures. The current market price of the bond is 150 advise the investor.

Solution:

Year	Interest/Cash Inflow	PV @ 16%	PV of Cash Inflow
1	15	0.862	12.93
2	15	0.743	11.15
3	15	0.641	9.62
4	15	0.552	8.28
5	15	0.476	7.14
6	15	0.410	6.154
7	15	0.354	2.48
	(15 + 105)	PV of Bond	97.75

Present Value of Bond = 97.75

MPS = 150

Comment:

The present value of the bond means the real worth of a bond. Since the present value of the bond is less than the market price it is advisable to sell the bond.

Illustration 2: What is the value of a bond of ₹ 10,000 with a 7% coupon rate, 5 years before maturity. The required rate of return is 8%. What is the present value of the debentures. The current market price of the bond of the bond is ₹ 11,000

Solution:

Year	Interest/Cash Inflow	PV @ 16%	PV of Cash Inflow
1	700	0.926	648.2
2	700	0.857	599.9
3	700	0.794	555.8
4	700	0.735	514.5
5	10,700	0.681	7286.7
	(700 + 10,000)	PV of Bond	9605.1

Comment:

Since the market price of the bond is 11,000 which is less than the present value of the bond, it is advisable to sell the bond.

OR

= 700 × 3.993 + 10,000 × 0.681

= 2,795.10 + 6810

= 9,605.10

Illustration 3: A Bond of ₹ 1,000 face value with a coupon of 7 per cent is redeemable after 5 years at a premium of 5 per cent. The required rate of return is 8%. The current market price of the bond is ₹ 940. Whether investment at current market price of the bond advisable. The present values of rupee one at 8% discounting rate are 0.926, 0.857, 0.794, 0.735 and 0.681.

Solution:

Year	Interest/Cash Inflow	PV @ 16%	PV of Cash Inflow
1	70	0.926	64.82
2	70	0.857	59.99
3	70	0.794	55.58
4	70	0.735	51.45
5	120	0.681	762.72
	(70 + 1,050)	PV of Bond	994.56

Present Value of Bond = ₹ 994.56

It is advisable to buy the bond since the market price of the bond 940 is less than the present value of bond of ₹ 994.56

Illustration 4: A bond of ₹ 1,000 face value carrying interest rate of 14% is redeemable after 6 years at a premium of 5%. If the required rate of return is 15%. What is the present value of the bond.

Solution:

Year	Interest/Cash Inflow	PV @ 16%	PV of Cash Inflow
1	140	0.870	121.8
2	140	0.756	105.84
3	140	0.658	92.12
4	140	0.572	80.08
5	140	0.497	69.58
6	1190	0.432	514.08
	(140 + 1,050)	PV of Bond	983.5

Present Value of Bond = ₹ 983.5

Illustration 5: A GOI bond of ₹ 1,000 each has a coupon rate of 8 per cent annum and maturity period is 20 years. If the current market prices is ₹ 1,050, find YTM?

Solution:

$$YTM = \frac{I + \left(\dfrac{R_V - M_P}{n}\right)}{\dfrac{R_V + M_P}{2}} \times 100$$

Where,

YTM = Yield to maturity

I = Interest

RX = Redemption Value

MP = Market Price

n = Number of years

$$YTM = \frac{I + \left(\dfrac{R_V - M_P}{n}\right)}{\dfrac{R_V + M_P}{2}} \times 100$$

$$= \frac{80 + \left(\dfrac{1{,}000 - 1{,}050}{20}\right)}{\dfrac{1{,}000 + 1{,}050}{2}} \times 100$$

$$= \frac{80 + (-2.5)}{1,025} \times 100$$

$$= \frac{77.5}{1,025} \times 100$$

$$= 7.56\%$$

Illustration 6: You are considering an investment in one of the following Bonds:

	Coupon Rate	Maturity	Price/₹100
Par Value			
Bond A	12%	10 Year	70
Bond B	10%	06 Year	60

(i) What is YTM of each bond?

(ii) Which bond would you recommend for investment?

Solution:

(i) Bond A:

$$YTM = \frac{I + \left(\frac{R_V - M_P}{n}\right)}{\frac{R_V + M_P}{2}} \times 100$$

$$= \frac{12 + \left(\frac{100 - 70}{10}\right)}{\frac{100 + 70}{2}} \times 100$$

$$= \frac{12 + 3}{85} \times 100$$

$$= \frac{15}{85} \times 100$$

$$= 17.65\%$$

(ii) Bond B:

$$YTM = \frac{I + \left(\frac{R_V - M_P}{n}\right)}{\frac{R_V + M_P}{2}} \times 100$$

$$= \frac{10 + \left(\frac{100 - 60}{6}\right)}{\frac{100 + 60}{2}} \times 100$$

$$= \frac{10 + 6.67}{80} \times 100$$

$$= \frac{16.67}{80} \times 100$$

$$= 20.84\%$$

Comment:

I will recommend Bond B for Investment since it has higher YTM.

Illustration 7: A bond of ₹ 1000 has a coupon rate of 6% p.a. and maturity period is 3 years. The bond is currently selling at ₹ 900. What is the yield to maturity in investment of this bond.

Solution:

$$YTM = \frac{I + \left(\frac{R_V - M_P}{n}\right)}{\frac{R_V + M_P}{2}} \times 100$$

$$= \frac{60 + \left(\frac{1,000 - 900}{3}\right)}{\frac{1,000 + 900}{2}} \times 100$$

$$= \frac{60 + 33.33}{950} \times 100$$

$$= 9.82\%$$

Illustration 8: A bond pays an interest annually and sells for ₹ 835. It six years left to maturity and a par value of ₹ 1,000. What is the coupon rate if YTM is 12 %.

Solution:

$$YTM = \frac{I + \left(\frac{R_V - M_P}{n}\right)}{\frac{R_V + M_P}{2}} \times 100$$

$$= \frac{I + \left(\dfrac{1{,}000 - 835}{6}\right)}{\dfrac{1{,}000 + 835}{2}} \times 100$$

$$12 = \frac{I + 27.5}{917.5} \times 100$$

$$\frac{12 \times 917.5}{100} = I + 27.5$$

$$110.1 = I + 27.5$$

$\therefore$ I = 82.6

1,000 = 82.6

100 = (?)

$\therefore$ Coupon Rate = 8.26%

Illustration 9: Calculate the present value of Debenture of Mahesh Ltd.,

Year	Coupon rate
1-2	8%
3-4	10%
5-7	12%

The face value of the debenture is 100. Debentures are redeemed at 5% premium. The required rate of return 16%.

Solution:

Year	Interest/Cash Inflow	PV @ 16%	PV of Cash Inflow
1	8	0.862	6.896
2	8	0.743	5.944
3	10	0.641	6.41
4	10	0.552	5.52
5	12	0.476	5.712
6	12	0.410	4.92
7	117	0.354	41.418
	(12 + 105)	PV of Bond	76.82

Present Value of Bond = 76.82

Illustration 10: A ₹ 100 par value bond bears a coupon rate of 14 per cent and matures after five years. Interest is payable semi-annually. Compute the value of the bond if the required rate of return is 16 per cent.

Solution:

In this case the number of half-yearly periods is 10, the half-yearly interest payment is ₹ 7, and the discount rate applicable to a half-yearly period is 8 per cent. Hence, the value of the bond is:

$$V = \sum_{t=1}^{10} \frac{7}{(1.08)^t} + \frac{100}{(1.08)^{10}}$$

$$= 7\ (PVIFA_{8\%,\ 10yrs}) + 100\ (PVIF_{8\%,\ 10yrs})$$

$$= 7\ (6.710) + 100\ (0.463)$$

$$= 46.97 + 46.30$$

$$= ₹\ 93.27$$

Illustration 11: Consider the following data for Government securities:

Face Value	Interest Rate (%)	Maturity (Years)	Current Price
1,00,000	0	1	91,000
1,00,000	10.5	2	99,000
1,00,000	11.0	3	99,500
1,00,000	11.5	4	99,900

Calculate the forward rates.

Solution:

To get forward interest rates, begin with the one-year Treasury bill

$$91{,}000 = 1{,}00{,}000/(1 + r_1) \rightarrow r_1 = 0.099$$

Next consider the two-year Government security

$$99{,}000 = \frac{10{,}500}{(1.099)} + \frac{1{,}10{,}500}{(1.099)(1+r_2)}$$

$$r_2 = 0.124$$

Then consider the three-year Government security

$$99{,}500 = \frac{11{,}000}{(1.099)} + \frac{11{,}000}{(1.099)(1.124)} + \frac{1{,}11{,}000}{(1.099)(1.124)(1+r_3)}$$

$$r_3 = 0.115$$

Finally, consider the four-year Government security

$$99{,}500 = \frac{11{,}500}{(1.099)} + \frac{11{,}500}{(1.099)(1.124)} + \frac{11{,}500}{(1.099)(1.124)(1.115)} + \frac{1{,}11{,}500}{(1.099)(1.124)(1.115)(1+r_4)}$$

$$r_4 = 0.128$$

Extra Practice Problem

Illustration 12: A bond of ₹ 1,000 face value carrying a interest of 14%. Is redeemable after 6 years at a premium of 5%. If required return is 15%, what is present value of bond?

REVIEW QUESTIONS

Q.1. Concept Testing

(a) Characteristics of Debt Securities

(b) Determinants of Interest Rates

(c) YTM

❑❑❑

CHAPTER 6 VALUATION OF EQUITY

6.1 CONCEPT

Equity shares can be described more easily than fixed income securities. However, they are more difficult to analyse. Fixed income securities typically have a limited life and a well-defined cash flow stream. Equity shares have neither. While the basic principles of valuation are the same for fixed income securities as well as equity shares, the factors of growth and risk create greater complexity in the case of equity shares.

Equity analysts employ two kinds of analysis, viz., fundamental analysis and technical analysis. Fundamental analysts assess the fair market value of equity shares by examining the assets, earnings prospects, cash flow projections, and dividend potential. Fundamental analysts differ from technical analysts who essentially rely on price and volume trends and other market indicators to identify trading opportunities.

Equity Valuation Methods

6.2 BALANCE SHEET VALUATION

(1) Net Assets Value Method (NAV method)

or Intrinsic value method

or Asset backing method

or Liquidation method

or Break-up value method

Note: For calculating NAV per share, it should be ASSUMED that company is liquidated on the date of valuation of shares.

Particulars	**(₹)**	**(₹)**
Market value's of all Real Assets		xxx
(-) Agreed values of all outsiders liabilities		-xx
Net Assets for all shareholders		xxx
(-) payment to Pref. shareholders		
(a) % Pref. share capital	xx	
(b) Premium on Redemption, if any	xx	
(c) Arrears of Pref. dividend, if anyNet assets for Equity shareholders	xx	-xx
		xxxxx

$$\text{NAV per share} = \frac{\text{Net Assets for Equity Shareholders}}{\text{No. of Equity Shares}}$$

(2) Yield value method or Market value method

$$\text{Yield value per share} = \frac{\text{ARR}}{\text{NRR}} \times \text{Paid – up value per share}$$

(A) Actual Rate of Return (ARR)

= Expected Rate of Equity dividend in future.

$$= \frac{\text{FMP for equity dividend}}{\text{Equity share capital}} \times 100$$

(B) NRR → as given in the problem

(C) $\text{Yield value per share} = \frac{\text{ARR}}{\text{NRR}} \times \text{Paidup value per share}$

(3) Fair value method:

$$\text{Fair value per share} = \frac{\text{NAV per share + Yield value per share}}{2}$$

6.3 BALANCE SHEET VALUATION ILLUSTRATIONS

Illustration 1: The Balance Sheet of Ganesh Ltd., as on 31-3-2009 was as under:

Liabilities	(₹)	Assets	(₹)
2,000 Equity shares of ₹ 100 each	2,00,000	Land and Building	1,25,000
General Reserve	50,000	Machinery	75,000
Profit and Loss A/c	25,000	Investment at Cost (Market Value 37,500)	45,000
Creditors	45,000	Debtors	50,000
Provision for Taxation	20,000	Stock	37,500
Provident Fund	17,500	Cash and Bank	25,000
Total	**3,57,500**	**Total**	**3,57,500**

Additional Information:

(i) Land & Building and Machinery are valued at ₹ 1,37,500 and ₹ 55,000 respectively.

(ii) Of the total debts ₹ 2,500 are bad.

(iii) Goodwill is to be valued at ₹ 25,500.

(iv) The normal dividend declared and paid by such type of companies is 15% on the paid-up capital.

(v) The average rate of dividend, declared and paid-up by the company is 18% on its paid-up capital.

Calculate the fair value of an equity share of the company.

Solution:

Calculation of NAV/Shares

Particulars	(₹)	(₹)
Market Value of all Real Assets		
Land and Building	1,37,500	
Machinery	55,000	
Investment	37,500	
Debtors	47,500	
Stock	37,500	
Cash and Bank	25,000	
Goodwill	25,500	3,65,500
(-) Agreed Value of Outsiders Liabilities		
Creditors	45,000	
Prov. for Tax	20,000	
Provident fund	17,500	82,500
Net assets available to all SH.= } Net assets available to all ESH →		2,83,000

$$\therefore \text{NAV/Share} = \frac{\text{Net assets for ESH}}{\text{No. of Eq. Shares}}$$

$$= \frac{2,83,000}{2,000}$$

$$= ₹\ 141.5$$

$$\text{Yield Value/Share} = \frac{\text{ARR}}{\text{NRR}} \times \text{Paidup value/share}$$

$$= \frac{18}{15} \times 100$$

$$= ₹\ 120$$

$$\text{Fair Value/Share} = \frac{\text{NAV + Yield}}{2}$$

$$= \frac{141.5 + 120}{2}$$

$$= ₹\ 130.75$$

Extra Practise Problem

Illustration 2: Following is the Balance Sheet of Satyam Ltd., for the year 31.12.2008:

(₹ in crore)

Liabilities	(₹)	Assets	(₹)
Share Capital (@ ₹10/- par)	136	Fixed Assets	883
Reserves	7,222	Investments	494
Secured Loans	24	Current Assets	7,446
Current Liabilities	1,441		
Total	**8,823**	**Total**	**8,823**

Mr. Raju, the chairman of Satyam Ltd., declared a scam in the company on 1.1.2009. The following were the details:

(1) There was cash which was non-existent cash of ₹ 5,040 crore.

(2) Interest not receivable recorded ₹ 376 crore.

(3) Total liability is understated by ₹ 1,230 crore.

(4) Actual debtor position of ₹ 490 cr. as against ₹ 651 crore. reported in the books.

L&T which has a Net asset value of ₹ 405.10 per share wants to buy a stake in the company and has asked you to calculate:

(i) Intrinsic value on 1.1.2009

(ii) Exchange Ratio

6.4 EQUITY SHARE VALUATION MODELS

1. Dividend Discount Model

The dividend discount model defines the intrinsic value of a share as the present value of future dividend. This is the most widely used model of equity share valuation.

(a) Zero Growth Model

$$V = \frac{D_1}{K_e}$$

Where, D_1 = Expected dividend

= Dividend at the end of year one.

= D0 (1 + g)

Ke = Cost of Equity/Capitalisation rate

= Required rate/Discount rate

$$= \frac{D_1}{MPS} \times 100 + g$$

(b) Constant Growth Model (Gordon Model)

$$V = \frac{D_1}{K_e - g}$$

Where, g = growth rate

(c) Multiple Growth Model

$$V = V_A + V_B$$

$$= \text{PV of dividend} + \frac{D_n(1+g_2)}{K_e - g_2} \times \text{PV of } n^{th} \text{ year}$$

Where,

D_n = Dividend at end of g1 period

PV of nth year = Discount rate at end of g1 period.

2. Price – Earning Ratio Model

$$\text{P/E Ratio} = \frac{MPS}{EPS}$$

Under P/E ratio model, Earnings per share is estimated for a stock for a future period, then EPS is multiplied with

(i) Industry P/E ratio, or

(ii) Current P/E ratio of company, or

(iii) Competitor P/E ratio, or

iv) Forecast P/E ratio, in order to estimate value of a share.

6.5 ILLUSTRATION

Illustration 1: Akshay Ltd., is a zero growth company paying dividend of ₹ 8 per share and selling for ₹ 60 per share. The required rate of return is 10%. Find the value of the company's shares.

Solution:

$$D_1 = D_0 (1 + g)$$

$$= 8 (1 + 0)$$

$$= 8$$

$$V = \frac{D_1}{Ke - g}$$

$$= \frac{8}{0.10}$$

= ₹ 80 per share

Comment:

Since the market price per share ₹ 60 less than the intrinsic value it is advisable to buy the shares.

Illustration 2: Tata Ltd., paid dividend @ ₹ 1.80 per share. The forecast is the dividend will grow by 5% per year into the infinite future. If the capitalization rate is 11% and the current market price of the company's shares is ₹ 40, find out its intrinsic value.

Solution:

$$D_1 = D_0 (1 + g)$$

$$= 1.80 (1 + 0.05)$$

$$= 1.89$$

$$V = \frac{D_1}{Ke - g}$$

$$= \frac{1.89}{0.11 - 0.05}$$

$$= \frac{1.89}{0.06}$$

= ₹ 31.5 per share

Comment:

Since the market price per share is ₹ 40 it is more than the intrinsic value, it is advisable to sell the shares.

Illustration 3: Mamta Ltd., has expected dividend of ₹ 10. Earning and dividend are expected to grow at a rate of 20 per cent. The capitalization rate and current market price are 25% and ₹ 280 respectively. Is the share fairly priced?

Solution:

$$V = \frac{D_1}{Ke - g}$$

$$= \frac{10}{0.25 - 0.20}$$

$$= \frac{10}{0.05}$$

= ₹ 200 per share

Comment:

Since the market price per share is ₹ 280 which is more than the intrinsic value, i.e., ₹ 200 per share, it is advisable to sell the shares.

Illustration 4: BSES paid ₹ 2.50 as dividend per share on its equity shares for the last year. Dividends are expected to grow at 10 per cent per year for an indefinite future. (a) What is its expected rate of return if its current market price is ₹ 20? (b) If the required rate of return is 12% what would be the value of stock? (c) Is it worth investing in the share?

Solution:

$$D_1 = D_o (1 + g)$$

$$= 2.50 (1 + 0.10)$$

$$= 2.75$$

(a) $$Ke = \frac{D_1}{MPS} + g$$

$$= \frac{2.75}{20} + 0.10$$

$$= 0.2375$$

$$= 23.75\%$$

(b) $$V = \frac{D_1}{Ke - g}$$

$$= \frac{2.75}{0.12 - 0.10}$$

$$= \frac{2.75}{0.02}$$

$$= ₹\ 137.5 \text{ per share}$$

(c) Yes. Since value is higher than market price.

Illustration 5: Prof. Navin wishes to invest in the shares of 'A' Ltd., whose expected dividend in the first year is ₹ 4. In the past, company's dividend per share has grown at an average rate of about 5 per cent per annum. Prof. Navin expects that the dividend will grow at the same in future. The required rate of return on the shares is 20% per annum. The market of the share is ₹ 16. Advise Prof. Navin whether he should buy the share?

Solution:

$$V = \frac{D_1}{Ke - g}$$

$$= \frac{4}{0.20 - 0.05}$$

$$= \frac{4}{0.15}$$

$$= ₹\ 26.67 \text{ per share}$$

Comment:

Since the market price per share is ₹ 16 which is lesser than the intrinsic value of ₹ 26.67 per share, it is advisable to buy the shares.

Illustration 6: Sonam Ltd., paid dividend of 10%. Face value per share is ₹ 10 per share; Earnings and dividends are expected to grow at a rate of 20 per cent. The required rate of return and the current market price are 25% and ₹ 240, respectively. Is it fairly priced?

Solution:

$$D_1 = 1\ (1 + g)$$
$$= 1\ (1 + 0.20)$$
$$= 1.2$$

$$V = \frac{D_1}{Ke - g}$$

$$= \frac{1.2}{0.05}$$

= ₹ 24 per share

Comment:

Since the market price per share is ₹ 240 which is higher than the intrinsic value of ₹ 24 per share, it is advisable to sell the shares. It is overpriced.

Illustration 7: Sunrise Ltd., is currently paying dividend of ₹ 1.50 on its face value of ₹ 10. Earnings and dividends are expected to grow at 5% annual rate indefinitely. Investors require 9% rate of return on their investments. The company is considering several business strategies and wishes to determine the effect to these strategies on the market price of its share.

(a) Continuing the present strategy will result in the expected growth rate and required rate of return as above.

(b) Expanding sales will increase the expected dividend growth rate at 7% but will increase the risk of the company. As a result, the investor's required rate of return will increase to 12%.

(c) Integrating into retail stores will increase the dividend growth rate at 6 per cent and increase the required rate of return to 10 per cent.

You are required to find out the best strategy from the point of view of the market price.

Solution:

$$D_1 = Do\ (1 + g)$$
$$= 1.50\ (1 + 0.05)$$
$$= 1.575$$

(a) $$V = \frac{D_1}{ke - g}$$

$$= \frac{1.575}{0.09 - 0.05}$$

= ₹ 39.375 per share

(b) $D_1 = D_0 (1 + g)$

$= 1.50 (1 + 0.06)$

$= 1.605$

$$V = \frac{D_1}{ke - g}$$

$$= \frac{1.605}{0.12 - 0.07}$$

= ₹ 32.1 per share

(C) D_1 = Do (1 + g)

= 1.50 (1 + 0.06)

= 1.59

$$V = \frac{1.59}{0.10 - 0.06}$$

= ₹ 39.75 per share

Comment:

Strategy C is the best since it results into the highest market price.

Illustration 8: Samrudhi Ltd., paid ₹ 2.50 as dividend per share on its equity shares for year ended 31st March, 2010. Dividends are expected to grow at 10 per cent annum for an indefinite future. The current market price of the share is ₹ 2,080.

1. What is the expected rate of return?
2. If the required rate of return is 12%, what would be the value of stock?
3. Is it worth investing in the share?

Solution:

(1) D_1 = Do (1 + g)

= 2.50 (1 + 0.10)

= 2.75

$$Ke = \frac{D_1}{MPS} + g$$

$$= \frac{2.75}{20} + 0.10$$

= ₹ 0.2375 per share

$= 23.75\%$

$$V = \frac{D_1}{ke - g}$$

$$= \frac{2.75}{0.12 - 0.10}$$

$$= \frac{2.75}{0.02}$$

= ₹ 137.5 per share

(2) **Comment:**

Since the market price per share is ₹ 2,080 which is higher than the intrinsic value of ₹ 137.5 per share, it is advisable to sell/not buy the shares.

Illustration 9: MNO Ltd., shares are quoted at ₹ 80 on BSE currently. The company pays rupee one per share as dividend and the investors expect a growth rate of 5% per year. Compute:

(i) Expected rate of return

(ii) If the anticipated growth rate is 10% p.a., calculate the indicative market price

(iii) Advise on the basis of the indicative market price computed above whether it is profitable to invest in the shares of MNO Ltd., at its current price on BSE.

Solution:

$D_1 = Do\ (1 + g)$

$= 1\ (1 + 0.05) \qquad = 2\ (1 + 0.10)$

$= 1.05 \qquad = 2.2$

$$Ke = \frac{D_1}{MPS} + g$$

$$= \frac{1.05}{20} + 0.05$$

= ₹ 0.1025 per share

= 10.25%

$$V = \frac{2.20}{0.1275 - 0.10}$$

$$= \frac{2.20}{0.275}$$

= 80

Comment:

Since the market price per share is ₹ 80 which is equal to value it is advised to hold the share.

Note: Whenever expected dividend, dividend for next year, dividend at the end of year given, do not calculate, D1 = Do (1 + g)

Illustration 10: Meghna Ltd., dividend for next year of ₹ 1.80 per share. The forecast is that dividend will grow by 8 per cent per annum into the infinite future. If the required rate of return is 10% and the current market price of the company's stock is ₹ 60, find out the intrinsic value of the company's share. Is it worth investing in the company?

Solution:

$$V = \frac{D_1}{ke - g}$$

$$= \frac{1.80}{0.10 - 0.08}$$

$$= \frac{1.80}{0.02}$$

= ₹ 90 per share

Comment:

Since the market price per share is ₹ 60 which is less than the intrinsic value of share, i.e., ₹ 90 per share, it is advisable to buy the shares.

Illustration 11: A Ltd., paid a dividend of ₹ 3 per share in the last year. The dividend is expected to grow at a constant rate of 5% in the future. If the required rate of return is 10%, what would be intrinsic value of the share?

Solution:

$$D_1 = Do\ (1 + g)$$

$$= 3\ (1 + 0.05)$$

$$= 3.15$$

$$V = \frac{D_1}{ke - g}$$

$$= \frac{3.15}{0.10 - 0.05}$$

$$= \frac{3.15}{0.05}$$

= ₹ 63 per share

Illustration 12: As per the financial accounts for the last year, the company has paid dividend @ 20% . The paid-up equity capital is₹ 6,00,000 and 10% preference share capital ₹ 1,00,000. Operating profit is ₹ 4,00,000. The tax rate is 32%. The company expects a growth rate of 5%. Compute Value per Equity Share.

(a) Dividend Growth Approach.

(b) Dividend Approach.

(c) Earnings Growth Approach.

(d) Earning Approach.

Solution:

$$D_1 = D0\ (1 + g)$$

$$= 2\ (1 + 0.05)$$

$$= 2.1$$

(a) Dividend Growth Approach:

$$V = \frac{D_1}{ke - g} A$$

$$= \frac{2.1}{0.10 - 0.05}$$

$$= ₹\ 42 \text{ per share}$$

(b) Dividend Approach

$$V = \frac{D_1}{Ke}$$

$$= \frac{2}{0.10}$$

$$= ₹\ 20 \text{ per share}$$

(c) Earning Growth Approach

	₹
Operating Profit	4,00,000
(-) Interest	-
NPBT	4,00,000
(-) Tax @ 32%	1,28,000
NPAT	2,72,000

$$EPS = \frac{\text{NPAT} - \text{Preferenced Dividend}}{\text{No. of Equity Shares}}$$

$$= \frac{2,72,000 - 10,000}{60,000}$$

$$= ₹\ 4.37 \text{ per share}$$

$E_1 = E_0 (1 + g)$

$= 4.37 (1 + 0.05)$

$= 4.59$

$$V = \frac{E_1}{ke - g}$$

$$= \frac{4.59}{0.10 - 0.05}$$

$$= \frac{4.59}{0.5}$$

= ₹ 91.8 per share

(d) Earning Approach

$$V = \frac{E_1}{Ke}$$

$$= \frac{4.37}{0.10}$$

= ₹ 43.7 per share

Note: In absence of FV, It is taken as 10.

In absence of Ke, it is assumed 10 or any value above than growth rate.

Illustration 13: Anand Ltd., dividend for next year of ₹ 1.80 per share. The forecast is that dividend will grow by 5 per cent per annum into the infinite future. If the required rate of return is 10% and the current market price of the company's stock is ₹ 40, what is the expected rate of return of the stock? Should you make investment in the stock?

Solution:

$D_1 = Do (1 + g)$

$= 1.80 (1 + 0.05)$

$= 1.89$

$$V = \frac{D_1}{ke - g}$$

$$= \frac{1.89}{0.11 - 0.05}$$

$$= \frac{1.89}{0.06}$$

= ₹ 31.5 per share

Comment:

Since market price is higher than value, it is advised to sell/not buy shares of Anand Ltd.

Illustration 14: A mining company's iron reserves are being depleted, as a result of which the company's earnings and dividend is declining at rate of 8%. If the previous year dividend was ₹ 10 and the required rate of return is 15%, what would be the current price of equity share of the company?

Solution:

$$D_1 = Do\ (1 + g)$$

$$= 10\ (1 - 0.08)$$

$$= 9.2$$

$$V = \frac{D_1}{ke - g}$$

$$= \frac{9.2}{0.15 - (-0.05)}$$

$$= \frac{9.2}{0.15 + 0.05}$$

$$= \frac{9.2}{0.2}$$

$$= 46 \text{ per share}$$

Illustration 15: The Chemical and Fertilizers Ltd., has been growing at the rate of 18% in the recent years. This abnormal growth rate is expected to continue for another 4 years and then likely to grow at normal rate of 6%. Dividend paid last year was ₹ 3 per share. Find out the intrinsic value of share if the required rate of return is 12%.

Solution:

$$D_1 = D0\ (1 + g)$$

$$= 3\ (1 + 0.18)$$

$$= 3.54$$

$$V = \frac{D_1}{ke - g}$$

Year	Dividend	PVIF 12%	PV of Dividend
1	3.54	0.893	3.16
2	4.18	0.797	3.33
3	4.93	0.712	3.51
4	5.82	0.636	3.70
		(A)	13.70

$$P_4 = \frac{D_4\ (1+g)}{Ke-g}$$

$$= \frac{5.82\ (1+0.06)}{0.12-0.06}$$

$$= \frac{5.82\ (1.06)}{0.06}$$

$$= 102.82 \times PV\ @\ 12\%\ (4\ years)$$

$$= 102.82 \times 0.636$$

$$(B) = ₹\ 65.39$$

Now,

$$(A + B) = 13.70 + 65.39$$

$$= ₹\ 79.09$$

Note: When two growth rates are given calculate as above.

Illustration 16: An investor has invested in a company which is growing at a rate of 15% for 5 years. Thereafter dividend is expected to grow at 7%. The capitalization rate is 10% and current dividend is rupee one per share. Determine the value per share.

Solution:

$$D_1 = 1\ (1 + 0.15)$$

$$= 1.15$$

$$V = \frac{D_1}{ke - g}$$

Year	Dividend	PVIF 12%	PV of Dividend
1	1.15	0.909	1.05
2	1.32	0.826	1.09
3	1.52	0.751	1.14
4	1.75	0.683	1.20
5	2.01	0.621	1.25
		(A)	5.73

$$P_5 = \frac{D_5\ (1+g)}{Ke-g}$$

$$= \frac{2.01\ (1+0.07)}{0.10-0.07}$$

$$= \frac{2.15}{0.03}$$

$$= 71.67 \times 0.621$$

(B) $= 44.51$

Now,

(A + B) $= 5.73 + 44.51$

$= 50.24$

Extra Practice Problems

Illustration 17: OM Ltd., paid a dividend of ₹ 0.75 per share. Over the next year it is expected to pay dividends of ₹ 2 per share. In the third year it is expected to pay dividend at ₹ 3 per share. The dividend will grow by 10 per cent per year indefinitely. If the required rate of return is 15% and current market price is ₹ 55, find the intrinsic value of the company's share.

Illustration 18: The after tax profits of SCORE Ltd., are expected to be ₹ 18 crore. The company does not have any preference shares outstanding, whereas the equity capital is ₹ 90 crore dividend into shares of ₹ 10 each. The company is operating in an industry whose P/E multiple is 10. Using P/E ratio model determine the price at which the stock should be purchased.

Illustration 19: Sukhada Ltd., paid ₹ 2.50 as dividend per share on its equity shares for the last year. Dividends are expected to grow at 10 per cent per year for an indefinite future. (a) What is its expected rate of return if its current market price is ₹ 20? (b) If the required rate of return is 12%, what would be the value of stock? (c) Is it worth investing in the share?

Illustration 20: What will be the intrinsic value of equity shares of 'SE' Ltd., based on the following data.

Last dividend	3 per share
Growth rate for 1-3 years	20% p.a.
Growth rate for 4-6 years	10% p.a.
Growth rate beyond 6 years	5% p.a.

The investor's required rate of return is 14%.

6.6 CAPITAL ASSET PRICING MODEL (CAPM)

The major implication of CAPM is that the expected return of an asset will be related to a measure of risk for that asset known as beta. CAPM specifies the manner in which expected return and beta are related.

According to CAPM, the relationship between Risk and Return is $K_e = R_F + \beta\ (K_M - R_F)$

Where K_e = Required or expected rate of return on security

R_F = Risk free rate of return

β = Beta coefficient of a security

K_M = Expected rate of return on market portfolio

CAPM is the name given to a set of **principles describing how people behave in the market.** This theory attempts to describe how investor's behaviour should affect security prices rather than explaining what investors actually observe in the market. This theory is useful because it is relatively simple and its implications have been widely explored with actual data and found to be substantially consistent with most of the theory's predictions.

Basic Assumptions

The Capital Asset Pricing Model is based on the following assumptions:

1. The investor's objective is to maximise the utility of terminal wealth.
2. Investors make choices solely on the basis of risk and return.
3. Investors have homogeneous expectations.
4. Investors have identical one-period time horizons.
5. Information is freely available.
6. There is a risk-free asset and investors can borrow and lend any amount of money at the risk-free rate.
7. There are no taxes, transaction costs, or other market imperfections.
8. Total assets quantity is fixed and all assets are marketable and divisible.
9. Capital markets are in equilibrium.

Capital Market Line (CML)

The next step in deriving the asset pricing model is to define a set of criteria for identifying preferred investments. Probably the most straightforward method is the mean-variance criteria. It utilizes only the mean and variance of expected returns to identify the investments that dominate.

Introduction of risk-free asset with borrowing and lending at the risk-free rate leads to the Capital Market Line. **The CML is a linear relationship between expected return and total risk.**

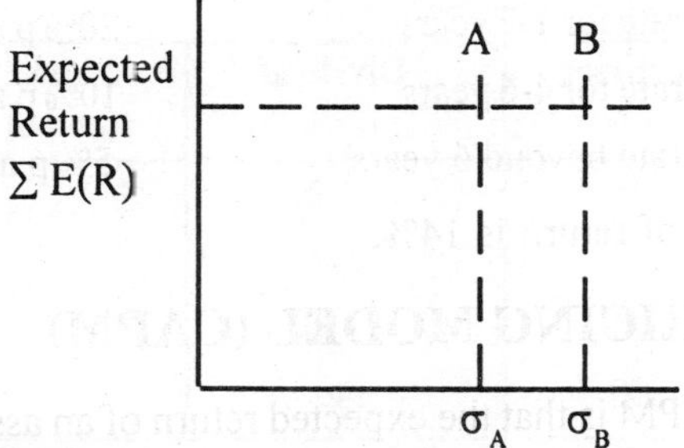

Security Market Line (SML)

The graphical version of the CAPM is called Security Market Line. It shows the relationship between beta and the required rate of return. The CAPM identifies security return net of the risk-free rate as proportional to the expected net market return, where beta serves as the constant proportionality. As a consequence of this relationship, all securities in equilibrium plot along a straight-line is called security market line (SML). It is an alternative to CML which will use beta as the independent variable and will accommodate both portfolios and individual assets.

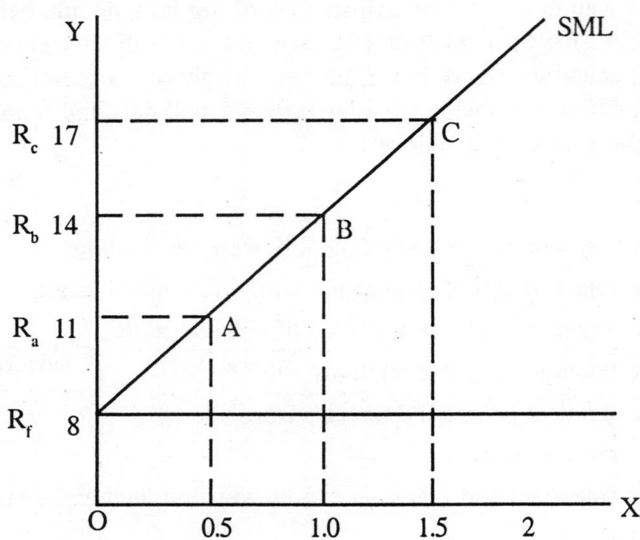

Fig. 6.1: Security Market Line

In the above figures, the required rate of return for three securities A, B and C is shown. Security 'A' is defensive security with a beta of 0.5. It's required rate of return is 11%. Security 'B' is neutral security with a beta of 1. It's required rate of return is equal to the rate of return on the market portfolio. Security 'C' is aggressive security with a beta of 1.5. Its required rate of return is 17%.

The SML has a positive slope, indicating that the expected return increases with risk (beta). The expected return of a security on the SML is determined by the riskless rate plus a systematic risk premium which is proportional to its beta.

6.7 CAPM ILLUSTRATION

Illustration 1: (CAPM)

Investment in equity shares	Initial price	Dividend	Market price (end of the year)	Beta risk factor
Cement Ltd.,	25	2	50	0.8
Steel Ltd.,	35	2	60	0.7
Liquor Ltd.,	45	2	135	0.5
Government bonds	1000	140	1005	0.99

Risk-free rate may be 14%

You are required to calculate

1. Expected return using Capital asset pricing model (CAPM)
2. Average return of the portfolio.

Solution:

(a) CAPM: $Ke = R_F + \beta (R_M - R_F)$

(1) Cement Ltd., = 14 + 0.8 (26.33 - 14)

= 14 + 0.8 (12.33)

= 14 + 9.864

= 23.86%

(2) Steel Ltd., = 14 + 0.7 (26.33 - 14)

= 22.63%

(3) Liquor Ltd., = 4 + 0.5 (26.33 - 14)

= 20.17%

(4) Govt. Bonds = 14 + 0.99 (26.33 - 14)

= 26.21%

Investment	Initial Price	Dividend	Appreciation	Dividend + Appreciation
Cement Ltd.,	25	2	25	27
Steel Ltd.,	35	2	25	27
Liquor Ltd.,	45	2	90	92
Govt. Bonds	1000	140	5	145
	1105	146		291

$$R_M = \frac{291}{1105} \times 100$$

$\therefore R_M = 26.33\%$

(b) Average Return on the Portfolio $= \dfrac{23.86 + 22.63 + 20.17 + 26.21}{4}$

$= \dfrac{92.87}{4}$

= 23.22%

Illustration 2: The following are facts available:

Risk-free rate 9%

Return of the market portfolio 18%

Beta coefficient of the shares of ABC Ltd., is 1.5

Dividend declared at the end of the year is ₹ 3 per share

Growth rate in dividend is 8%.

Compute the price at which shares of ABC Ltd., should sell.

Solution:

$K_e = R_F + \beta (R_M - R_F)$

= 9 + 1.5 (18 - 9)

= 9 + 1.5 (9)

= 9 + 13.5

= 22.5%

$$V = \frac{D_1}{ke - g}$$

$$= \frac{3}{0.225 - 0.08}$$

$$= \frac{3}{0.145}$$

= ₹ 20.69 per share

Illustration 3: The Beta Coefficient of Target Ltd., is 1.4. The company is maintaining 8% rate of growth rate in dividend and earnings. The last dividend was 4 per share. The return on Govt. securities is 10% while the return on the market portfolio is 15%. The current market price of one share of Target Ltd., is ₹ 36.

(a) What will be the equilibrium price per share of Target Ltd.,?

(b) Would you advise in purchasing share?

Solution:

$K_e = R_F + \beta (R_M - R_F)$

= 10 + 1.4 (15 - 10)

= 10 + 1.4 (5)

= 10 + 7

= 17%

D_1 = Do (1 + g)

= 4 (1 + 0.08)

= 4.32

$$V = \frac{D_1}{ke - g}$$

$$= \frac{4.32}{0.17 - 0.08}$$

= ₹ 48 per share

Comment:

Since the market price per share is ₹ 36 which is less than the intrinsic value of share, i.e., ₹ 48 per share, it is advisable to buy the shares.

Extra Practice Problem

Illustration 4: The following data pertain to the value of underlying factors of A Ltd.'s shares.

	Original	Revised
Risk-free rate	10%	8%
Market risk premium	5%	6%
BetaExpected growth rate	1.26%	1.58%
Previous dividend	₹ 2	₹ 2

(a) What is the intrinsic value of A Ltd.'s share based on the original set of values?

(b) What will it be under the revised set of values?

REVIEW QUESTIONS

Q.1. Concept Testing

(a) Intrinsic Value of Share

(b) Equity Share Valuation Model

Q.2. Explain: CAPM, CML and SML.

Q.3. 'Everybody knows PRICE but very few know VALUE'. Explain this statement with reference to valuation of equity.

CHAPTER 7

VALUE-BASED MANAGEMENT

7.1 VALUE-BASED MANAGEMENT

Creating value for shareholders is now widely accepted as the dominant corporate objective. The interest in value creation has been stimulated by several developments.

- Institutional investors, which traditionally were passive investors, have begun exerting influence on corporate managements to create value for shareholders.
- Many leading companies like General Electric, Coca-Cola, Siemens, Hindustan Unilever, Reliance Industries, and Infosys Technologies which have accorded value creation a central place in their corporate planning serve as role model for others.
- Business press is emphasizing shareholder value creation in performance rating exercises.
- Greater attention is now being paid to link top management compensation to shareholder returns.

7.2 STERN STEWART APPROACH (EVA® APPROACH)

Originally proposed by the consulting firm Stern Stewart & Co, Economic Value Added (EVA) is currently a very popular idea. *Fortune* magazine has called it "today's hottest financial idea and getting hotter" and management guru Peter Drucker referred to it as a measure of total factor productivity. Companies across a broad spectrum of industries and across a wide range of countries have joined the EVA bandwagon.

EVA is essentially the surplus left after making an appropriate charge for the capital employed in the business. It may be calculated in any of the following, apparently different but essentially equivalent, ways:

Formula (1) $EVA = NOPAT - c^* \times CAPITAL$

Formula (2) $EVA = CAPITAL\,(r - c^*)$

Formula (3) $EVA = [PAT + INT\,(1 - t)] - c^*\ CAPITAL$

Formula (4) $EVA = PAT - k_E\ EQUITY$

where EVA is the economic value added, NOPAT is the net operating profit after tax, c* is the cost of capital, CAPITAL is the economic book value of the capital employed in the firm, r is the return on capital (NOPAT/CAPITAL), PAT is the profit after tax, INT is the interest expense of the firm, t is the marginal tax rate of the firm, k_E is the cost of equity, and EQUITY is the equity employed in the firm.

To illustrate the calculation of EVA using the above formula let us look at the balance sheet and profit and loss account of Melvin Corporation given in Exhibit 7.1.

Exhibit 7.1 (A) Balance Sheet and Profit and Loss Account of Melvin Corporation

(₹ in million)

Balance Sheet as on 31.3.2010				**Profit and Loss Statement for the Year Ending on 31.03.2010**	
Liabilities		**Assets**		Net Sales	300
Equity	100	Fixed assets	140	Cost of goods sold	258
Debt	100	Net current asset	60	PBIT	42
				Interest	12
				PBT	30
				Tax (30%)	9
				PAT	21
	200		**200**		

Melvin's cost of equity is 18 percent. The interest rate on its debt is 12 percent which, given a marginal tax rate of 30 percent, translates to a post-tax cost of debt of 8.4 per cent. Since Melvin employs debt and equity in equal proportions, its weighted average cost of capital is: 0.5 × 18.0 + 0.5 × 8.4 = 13.2 per cent.

Melvin's NOPAT is: PBIT (1 – Tax rate) = 42(1 - 0.3) = ₹ 29.4 million. Given a CAPITAL of ₹ 200 million, Melvin's return on capital works out to 29.4/200 = 0.147 or 14.7 per cent.

Based on the above information, Melvin's EVA may be computed in four different, yet equivalent, ways:

EVA = NOPAT - WACC x INVESTED CAPITAL

= 29.4 - 0.132 × 200 = ₹ 3 million

EVA = (ROIC - WACC) × INVESTED CAPITAL

= (0.147 - 0.132) × 200 = ₹ 3 million

EVA = [PAT + INT (1 - 0.3)] - WACC × INVESTED CAPITAL

= [21 + 12 (1 - 0.3)] - 0.132 × 200 = ₹ 3 million

EVA = PAT – COST OF EQUITY × EQUITY

= 21 – 0.18 x 100 = ₹ 3 million

What Causes EVA to Increase? From the above analysis it is clear that EVA will rise if operating efficiency is improved, if value adding investments are made, if uneconomic activities are curtailed, and if the cost of capital is lowered. In more specific terms, EVA rises when:

"The rate of return on existing capital increases because of improvement in operating performance. This means that operating profit increases without infusion of additional capital in the business.

➢ Additional capital is invested in projects that earn a rate of return greater than the cost of capital.

➢ Capital is withdrawn from activities which earn inadequate returns.

➢ The cost of capital is lowered by altering the financing strategy.

Exhibit 7.2 presents numerical illustrations of value creating strategies.

Exhibit 7.2 (B) Numerical Illustrations of Value Creating Strategies

		Base Case
CAPITAL	:	10,000
NOPAT	:	2,000
c*	:	15%
r	:	20%

EVA = CAPITAL x (r – c*) = 10,000(0.20 - 0.15) = 500

Strategy 1: Improvement in Operating Performance

NOPAT increases from 2,000 to 2,250, due to greater operating efficiencies. This raises r to 22.5%.

As a result EVA rises to 750

EVA = CAPITAL × (r - c*) = 10,000(0.225 - 0.150) = 750

Strategy 2: Profitable Investment

A new project requiring 10,000 is expected to earn a return of 18% thereby adding 1,800 to NOPAT. This project will increase EVA, even though the consolidated return will decline to 19% (the average of 20% and 18%)

EVA = CAPITAL × (r – c*) = 20,000(0.19 – 0.15) = 800

Note that maximising EVA is more important, not maximising return on capital. Hence, the project should be accepted.

Strategy 3: Withdrawal of Unproductive Capital

1,000 of working capital can be liquidated with only a marginal decline of NOPAT. NOPAT will fall by just 50. Withdrawing this working capital would increase the rate of return to 21.67% (2,000 – 50) /(10,000 - 1,000) and EVA to 600.

EVA = 9,000 × (0.2167 – 0.150) = 600

Strategy 4: Reduction in the Cost of Capital

The capital structure of the firm is altered and this change lowers the cost of capital to 13%, without affecting anything else. As a result EVA rises from 500 to 700.

EVA = CAPITAL × (r – c*) = 10,000(0.20 – 0.13) = 700.

Link Between EVA and MVA: The market value added (MVA) is the difference between the current market value of the firm and the capital employed by the firm. For example, if the market value of a firm (the sum of the market value of its equity and debt) is 12,000 and its economic book value of capital is 10,000 the MVA is 2,000.

MVA is simply the present value of all future EVAs:

Formula 1: MVA = [Market Value of Capital Employed – Book Value of Capital Employed]

Formula 2: MVA = [Market Value of Eq. Share Capital – Book Value of Eq. Share-holders Funds]

$$MVA = \frac{EVA1}{(1+c^*)1} + \frac{EVA2}{(1+c^*)}$$

Implementing the EVA System: Implementing the EVA system involves several steps which are briefly described below:

- **Develop Top Management Commitment:** A crucial requirement of the EVA system is top management commitment. To build this commitment, the top management should be thoroughly grounded in the theory and practice of EVA.
- **Customise the Definitions of EVA:** A cross-functional team of executives should arrive at a customised definition of EVA - in terms of NOPAT, CAPITAL, and EVA calculation – that is best suited to the firm considering its informational needs and accounting system.
- **Identify EVA Centres:** A firm may be divided into EVA centres - these are responsibility centres for which individual EVAs will be calculated on a continuing basis.
- **Analyse the Drivers of EVA:** EVA must be linked to various financial and non-financial variables which drive it. An understanding of these drivers helps managers to appreciate how their actions influence value.
- **Tailor an Incentive Compensation System:** The incentive compensation system must align the interest of managers with shareholders. Ideally, it should make managers think, act, and be compensated like owners.
- **Train All the Employees:** The employees at all levels of the organisation must be trained in the basics of EVA. They must know how EVA is calculated, what EVA means, and how their actions impact on EVA.

7.3 PROBLEMS AND SOLUTION

Q. 1. The following data pertain to three division of Aura Incorporated. The company's required rate of return on invested capital is 8%.

Particulars	Division A	Division B	Division C
Sales Value (₹)	?	1 crore	?
Income (₹)	4 lakh	20 lakh	?
Average Investment (₹)	?	25 lakh	?
Sales Margin (%)	20%	?	25%
Capital Turnover (Times)	1	?	?
ROI (%)	?	?	20%
Residual Income/Economic Value Added (EVA) (₹)	?	?	1,20,000

Q.1: Solution

Division A:

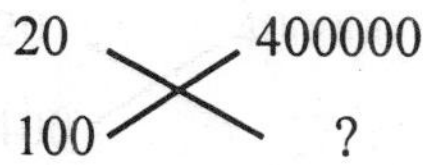

Sales Revenue = ₹ 20,00,000

$$\text{Capital Turnover} = \frac{\text{Sales}}{\text{Average Capital Employed}}$$

$$1 = \frac{20,00,000}{\text{Capital Employed}}$$

Capital Employed = ₹ 20,00,000

$$\text{RIO} = \frac{\text{Profit}}{\text{Capital Employed}} \times 100$$

$$= \frac{4,00,000}{20,00,000} \times 100$$

RIO = 20%

EVA = *NOPAT – 8% of capital employed

= 4,00,000 – 1,60,000

EVA = ₹ 2,40,000

Note: Tax is ignored.

Division B:

$$\text{Sales Margin} = \frac{\text{Profit}}{\text{Sales}} \times 100$$

$$= \frac{20,00,000}{1,00,00,000} \times 100$$

= 20%

$$\text{Capital Turnover} = \frac{\text{Sales}}{\text{Average Capital Employed}}$$

$$4 = \frac{10,00,000}{25,00,000}$$

$$= \frac{10,00,000}{25,00,000}$$

Capital = 4

$$\text{RIO} = \frac{\text{Profit}}{\text{Investment /Capital Employed}} \times 100$$

$$= \frac{20,00,000}{25,00,000} \times 100$$

= 80%

$$RI/EVA = 20,00,000 - (8\% \times 25 \text{ lakh})$$

$$= ₹\ 18 \text{ lakh}$$

Division C:

$$\text{Sales Margin} = \frac{\text{Profit}}{\text{Sales}} \times 100$$

$$25 = \frac{2,00,000}{\text{Sales}} \times 100$$

$$\text{Sales} = \frac{2,00,000}{25} \times 100$$

$$\text{Sales} = ₹\ 800000$$

$$\text{Capital Turnover} = \frac{\text{Sales}}{\text{Average Capital Employed}}$$

$$= \frac{8,00,000}{10,00,000}$$

$$\text{Capital Turnover} = 0.8$$

$$\text{RIO} = \frac{\text{Profit}}{\text{Investment}} \times 100$$

Let Profit = x

$$20 = \frac{\text{Profit}}{\text{Investment}} \times 100$$

$$\text{Investment} = 5x$$

$$= 5 \times 2,00,000$$

$$= ₹\ 10 \text{ Lakh}$$

$$= \frac{2,00,000}{10,00,000} \times 100$$

$$= 20\%$$

$$\text{EVA} = \left[\frac{8}{100} \times 5x\right]$$

$$= 1 \times - 0.4x$$

$$= 0.6x = 1,20,000$$

$$\text{Profit} = ₹\ 2,00,000$$

EVA = 2,00,000 – (8% × 10 lakh)

= ₹ 1,20,000

Q. 2. The Income Statement and Balance Sheet of Tulip Ltd. is given below:

Income Statement

Particulars	₹ (in lakh)	₹ (in lakh)
Sales	500	
Interest on Investments	10	
Profit on sale of old assets	5	
Total Income		515
Less:		
Manufacturing cost	180	
Administration Cost	60	
Selling and distribution cost	50	
Depreciation	30	
Loss on sale of an old M/C	5	325
EBIT		190
Less: Interest		20
EBT		170
Less: Tax (30%)		51
PAT		119
EPS (119 Lakh/ 5 Lakh)		₹23.82
P/E ratio		2

Balance Sheet

Liabilities	₹	Assets	₹
Equity Capital (₹ 10 share)	50	Building	80
Retained earnings	40	Machinery	70
Long term loan	60	Stock	10
Creditors	15	Debtors	12
Provisions	13	Bank	6
Total	**178**	**Total**	**178**

The cost of equity and cost of debt is 10% and 12% respectively. The company pays 30% corporate tax.

From the information given you are required to calculate the EVA. Also, calculate MVA on the basis of Market Value of equity capital.

Q.2: Solution

Earning Power ratio = Net Profit Margin × Asset T/o ratio

$$= \frac{\text{NPAT}}{\text{Sales}} \times 100 \times \frac{\text{Sales}}{\text{Total Assets}}$$

$$\text{P Ltd.,} = \frac{50{,}000}{5{,}00{,}000} \times 100 \times \frac{5{,}00{,}000}{5{,}00{,}000}$$

$$= 10\% \quad \times 1 \text{ time}$$

$$= 10\%$$

$$\text{R Ltd.,} = \frac{50{,}000}{5{,}00{,}000} \times 100 \times \frac{5{,}00{,}000}{5{,}00{,}000}$$

$$= 1\% \times 10 \text{ times} = 10\%$$

Analysis:

It is evident that the earning power of firms P and R is identical. While the firm P has higher profit margin, the firm R has higher investment turnover. Thus, the earning power is effected by two variables, viz., profit margin and investment turnover.

In this case if firm R improves its profit margin even marginally, say, from 1 per cent to 2 per cent and assuming that the sales are not affected its earning power will be doubled. Likewise, Firm P can double its earning power simply by a marginal increase in its investment turnover from 1 to 2.

Q.3. Runwall Ltd., has the following turnover ratios presented along with the corresponding industry averages:

Ratio description	Runwall Ltd.'s ratio	Industry average
Sales/Inventory	30/101 = 5 times	10 times
Sales/Receivables	5530/44 = 12 times	15 times
Sales/Fixed assets	530/98 = 5.4 times	6 times
Sales/Total assets	530/300 = 1.77 times	3 times

Financial analysis of the company is presented below in the form of a DuPont Chart. Study the chart, along with the four turnover ratios and industry averages, and comment on the major weaknesses of the company where managerial attention must be focused for the future control.

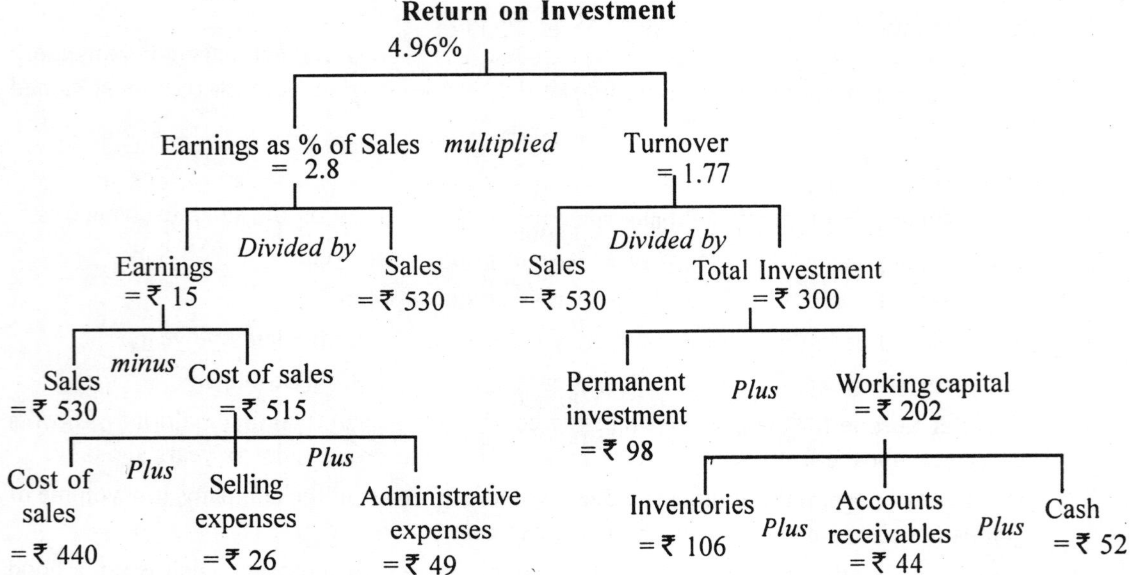

Q.3: Solution

(a) Low profit margin; indicates purchasing/production inefficiencies.

(b) Low Inventory turnover ratio indicates excess inventory. Company should come up with special scheme, adjust production to bring inventory to lower level.

(c) Assets are utilised inefficiently and or there is excess capacity.

(d) When managerial attention will be focused on above areas it will bring improvement in profit margin, Asset turnover and thereby ROI/MPS will improve.

Q.4. M/s. Sona Chandi Heera Ltd., is a Stock Exchange listed Company making good profits every year. However, the Board of Directors is very conservative and has declared dividend at fixed rate of ₹ 2 per share, when EPS is always above ₹ 25 for the last five years. The last bonus issue was made six years ago. The salary packages are also not attractive. As a result, there is high turnover of employees and low volume of company's shares on bourses. The young members of the Directors family wish to make the company more dynamic, employee-friendly and darling of the shareholders so as to make it the most valued one. What steps you would suggest to achieve these objectives?

(M.U., BMS, Oct. 2004)

Q.4. Solution

Name of the Company: M/s. Sona Chandi Heera Ltd.,

I. Facts:

(1) M/s. Sona Chandi Heera Ltd., is a stock exchange listed company.

(2) The company is making good profits every year.

(3) The Board of Directors have declared a DPS of ₹ 2 when the EPS is always above ₹ 25 for the last five years.

(4) The previous bonus issue was made six years ago.

(5) The company's salary packages are not attractive.

(6) There is a very high turnover of employees.

(7) Low volume of company's shares being traded (on bourses).

(8) Young members of the Directors family express their interest in making the company more dynamic, employee-friendly and darling of the shareholders so as to make it most valued one.

II. Observation:

(1) The company is a reputed company since its shares are listed on the stock exchange.

(2) The company has a track record of consistent profits every year.

(3) The Board of Directors adopts a conservative dividend policy.

(4) The dividend payout ratio of the company is less than 8% for the last five years.

(5) In the last five years the company has been retaining 92% of its earnings.

(6) There is a scope for bonus issue since the company has been retaining majority of profits every year for the last five years and the last bonus issue was made six years ago.

(7) Due to low image of the company and less volume of shares of the company, low volume of company's shares are traded on the stock exchanges.

(8) Due to unattractive salary packages there is high employees turnover which is not a good sign for the company's future prospects.

(9) Since the young members of the Directors family are expressing their interest in making the company most valued one there is a possibility of flow of new ideas, vision, thinking in the company.

III. Suggestions/Recommendations/Steps:

Suggestions to the management would be:

(1) Enhance dividend rate/payout ratio which is at present very low just 8% in the last five years. Since shareholders invest in a company's shares with an expectation of higher returns in the form of dividends, for e.g., 200%.

(2) Make liberal bonus issues at regular intervals (for e.g., 1:1). Bonus issue will increase the volume of shares traded and send positive signal.

(3) Revise the pay structure. Increase salary packages with incentive linked to the performance will help in reducing employees turnover.

(4) Also non-monetary incentives, employees training, motivation, employees participation in management through suggestion schemes, etc., can be used in order to reduce employee turnover.

IV. Conclusion:

The suggested action plan will help in improving the goodwill of the company, more satisfaction of the employees, value maximisation to the shareholders and bring dynamism to the management.

Practice Problem

Q. 5. The Income Statement and Balance Sheet of IHLS Company Ltd., is given below:

Income Statement

Particulars	₹ (in lakh)	₹ (in lakh)
Sales	3000	
Interest on Investments	60	
Profit on sale of old assets	30	
Total Income		3090
Less:		
Manufacturing cost	1080	
Administration cost	360	
Selling and distribution cost	300	
Depreciation	180	
Loss on sale of an old machinery and Equipment	30	1950
EBIT		1140
Less: Interest		120
EBT		1020
Less: Tax (30%)		306
PAT		714
EPS [714 lakh/30 lakh]		₹ 23.8
P/E ratio		16

Balance Sheet

Liabilities	₹	Assets	₹
Equity Capital (₹ 10 per share)	300	Building	480
Reserve and Surplus	240	Machinery & Equipments	420
Long-term Debt	360	Inventories	60
Creditors	90	Debtors	72
Provisions	78	Bank	36
Total	**1,068**	**Total**	**1,068**

The cost of equity and cost of debt is 14% and 18%, respectively. The company pays 30% corporate tax.

From the information given you are required to calculate the EVA. Also, calculate MVA on the basis of Market Value of equity capital.

Q. 6. Fill in the blanks:

The following date pertains to three divisions of Prudential Company Ltd., The company's required rate of return on invested capital is 8%.

Particulars	Division A	Division B	Division C
Sales Value (₹)	☐	12 crore	☐
Income (₹)	48 lakh	240 lakh	☐
Average Investment (₹)	☐	300 lakh	☐
Sales Margin (%)		☐	25%
Capital Turnover (Times)	20%	☐	☐
ROI (%)	2	☐	20%
Residual Income (EVA) (₹)	☐	☐	14,40,000

Q.7. Pizza Hut Ltd., has existing assets in which it has capital invested of ₹150 crore. The After Tax Operating Income is ₹20 crore and Company has a Cost of Capital of 12%. Estimate the Economic Value Added (EVA) of the firm.

Solution:

Capital Employed = 150 crore

NOPAT = 20 crore

WACC = 12%

EVA = NOPAT - (WACC x CE)

= 20 – (12% × 150)

= 20 – 18

= 2 crore

Q.8. The Income Statement and Balance Sheet of Alpha Company Ltd., are given below:

Particulars	₹ (in lakh)	₹ (in lakh)
Sales	5,000	
Interest on investments	100	
Profit on sale on old assets	50	
Total Income		5,150
Less:		
Manufacturing cost	1,800	
Administration cost	600	
Selling and distribution cost	500	
Depreciation	300	
Loss on sale of an old building	202	3,402

EBIT		1,748
Less: Interest		48
EBT		1,700
Less: Tax (30%)		510
PAT		1,190
EPS [1,190 lakh/ 50 lakh]		₹ 23.8
P/E ratio		2.5

Balance Sheet

Liabilities	(₹)	Assets	(₹)
Equity Capital (₹ 10 per share)	500	Buildings	800
Retained profits	400	Machinery	700
Term loan	600	Stock	100
Payables	150	Debtors	120
Provisions	130	Bank	60
Total	**1,780**	**Total**	**1,780**

The cost of equity and cost of debt is 14% and 8%, respectively. The company pays 30% corporate tax. Cost at debt 8% is before tax.

From the information given you are required to calculate the EVA. Also, calculate MVA on the basis of Market Value of Equity Capital.

Solution: EVA = NOPAT – (WACC × CE)

= 1,260 – (11.60% × 1,500)

= ₹ 1,086 lakhs

Calculation of NOPAT

Sales	5,000
(-) Operating Expenses	2,900
(-) Depreciation	300
EBIT	1,800
(-) Tax @ 30%	540
NOPAT	1,260

Calculation of WACC

Sources	Amt.	Proportion	Cost	WACC
1 Equity Cap.	500	33.33	14%	4.67%
2 Retained	400	26.67	14%	3.73%
3 Term Loan	600	40.00	8%	3.2%
	1,500	**100.00**		**11.60%**

Note: It is assumed that cost of debt mentioned is after tax

MVA = Market Capitalisation – Book Value of Net Worth

= 2,975 – 900

= 2,075

➢ Market Capitalisation = MPS × No. of Shares

= 59.2 × 50

= 2 975

➢ $\text{P/E Ratio} = \frac{\text{MPS}}{\text{EPS}}$

$2.5 = \frac{\text{MPS}}{23.8}$

$\therefore \text{MPS} = 2.5 \times 23.8$

$\therefore \text{MPS} = 59.2$

Q. 9. Einstien Ltd., is considering a capital project for which the following information is available.

Investment Outlay	10,000	Depreciation	Straight-line
Project Life	5 years	Tax rate	40%
Salvage Value	0	Debt Equity ratio	3:2
Annual Revenues	8,000	Cost of equity	20%
Annual costs (excluding depreciation, interest and taxes)	4,000	Cost of debt (post-tax)	8%

Calculate EVA of the project over its life.

Solution: EVA = NOPAT – (WACC × CE)

= 1,200 – (12.8% × 10,000)

= 1,200 – 1,280

= – 80

Calculation of NOPAT

Sales	8,000
(-) Operating Expenses	4,000
(-) Depreciation	2,000
EBIT	2,000
(-) Tax @ 40%	800
EBT/NOPAT	1,200

$$\text{Depreciation} = \frac{\text{Total Cost} - \text{Scrap}}{\text{Estimated Life}}$$

$$= \frac{10{,}000}{5}$$

$$= 2{,}000$$

Calculation of WACC

$$\frac{\text{Debt}}{\text{Equity}} = \frac{3}{2}$$

$$\text{Debt} = \frac{3}{5} \times 10{,}000, \qquad \therefore \text{ Equity} = \frac{2}{5} \times 10{,}000$$

$$= 6{,}000 \qquad , \qquad = 4{,}000$$

Sources	Amt.	Proportion	Cost	WACC
Debt	6,000	60%	8%	4.8
Equity	4,000	40%	20%	8
	10,000	100%		12.8

Q. 10. For B Ltd., Market rate of return (Rm) = 15%, Interest Rate of Treasury Bonds(Rf)=6.5%, Beta Factor (β)=1.20. Calculate Equity Risk Premium and Cost of Equity (ke).

Solution:

Rf = 6.5%

Rm = 15%

β = 1.20

Equity Risk Premium = Rm – R

= 15 – 6.5

= 8.5%

Cost of Equity = R + (Rm – R)

= 6.5 + 1.20 (8.5)

=16.7%

Q. 11. The following information is available of Docomo Ltd., Calculate EVA.

12% Debt capital	₹ 2,000 crore
Equity capital	₹ 500 crore
Reserves and Surplus	₹ 7,500 crore
Capital employed	₹ 10,000 crore
Risk-free rate	9%
Beta factor	1.05
Market rate of return	19%
Operating profit after tax	2,100 crore
Tax rate	30%

Q.11: Solution

EVA = NOPAT – (WACC × CE)

= 2,100 - (17.29% × 10,000)

= 2,100 – 1,729

= 371

Calculation of WACC

Sources	Amt.	Proportion	Cost	WACC
Debt	2,000	20%	8.4%	1.68
Equity	500	5%	19.5%	0.98
R&S	7,500	75%	19.5%	14.63
	10,000	100%		17.29%

Cost of Debt (kd) = I (1 – tax)

= 12 (1 - 0.3)

= 8.4%

Cost of Equity (ke) = Rf + β (Rm – R)

= 9 + 1.05 (19 – 9)

= 9 + 1.05 × 10

= 19.5%

Q. 12. Compute EVA of BPCL Ltd., for 3 years from the information given - (in ₹ lakhs)

Year	1	2	3
Average Capital Employed	3,000.00	3,500.00	4,000.00
Operating Profit before Interest	850.00	1,250.00	1,600.00
Corporate Income Taxes	80.00	70.00	120.00
Average Debt/Total Capital Employed (in%)	40.00	35.00	13.00
Beta variant	1.10	1.20	1.30
Risk-free Rate (%)	12.50	12.50	12.50
Equity Risk Premium (%)	10.00	10.00	10.00
Cost of Debt (Post tax) (%)	19.00	19.00	20.00

Q. 12: Solution

Particulars	Y_1	Y_2	Y_3
EVA=NOPAT - (WACC×CE)	=770–(3,000×21.7%) =119	= 1,180 - (3,500×22.58%) =389.7	= 1,480 - (4,000×24.79%) =488.4
(i) Calculation of NOPAT	850	1,250	1,600
EBIT			
– Tax	80	70	120
NOPAT	770	1,180	1,480

(ii) Calculation of WACC			
WACC for debt			
Proportion	40	35	13
Cost	19%	19%	20%
WACC for Equity			
Proportion (A)	7.6%	6.65	2.6
Cost	60	65	87
(B)	23.5%	24.5%	25.5%
	14.1%	15.93	22.19
(A + B) Total WACC	21.7%	22.58%	24.79%
(iii) CE (Capital Employed)	3,000	3,500	4,000

$$ke\,(Y_1) = Rf + \beta\,(Rm - R\,)$$
$$= 12.5 + 1.0\,(10)$$
$$= 12.5 + 11$$
$$= 23.5$$
$$ke\,(Y_2) = Rf + \beta\,(Rm - R\,)$$
$$= 12.50 + 1.20\,(10)$$
$$= 12.50 + 12$$
$$= 24.5$$
$$ke\,(Y_3) = Rf + \beta\,(Rm - R\,)$$
$$= 12.50 + 1.30\,(10)$$
$$= 25.5$$

Q. 13. The capital structure of BHEL Ltd., is as under:

- 80,00,000 Equity shares of ₹ 10 each = ₹ 800 lakh
- 1,00,000 12% Preference Shares of ₹ 250 each = 250 lakh
- 1,00,000 10% debentures of ₹ 500 each = 500 lakh
- 10% term loan from bank = ₹ 450 lakh

The Company's Profit and Loss Account for the year showed a balance PAT of ₹ 110 lakh, after appropriating Equity Dividend at 20%. The company is in the 40% tax bracket. Treasury bonds carry 6.5% interest and beta factor for the company may be taken at 1.5. The long-run market rate of return may be taken at 16.5%. Calculate EVA.

Q. 13: Solution

$$EVA = NOPAT - (WACC \times \text{Capital employed})$$
$$= 357 - (12.95\% \times 2{,}000)$$
$$= 357 - 259$$
$$= 98$$

Calculation of NOPAT

EAT (After dividend)	110
(+) Equity Dividend @ 20%	160
(+) Preference Dividend @ 12%	30
EAT (Before Dividend) 60%	300
(+) Tax @ 40%	200
EBT 100%	500
(+) Interest:	
Debentures	50
Loan	45
EBIT	595
(-) Tax @ 40%	238
NOPAT	357

Calculation of WACC

Sources	Amt.	Cost	Proportion	WACC
Equity Share	800	21.5	40%	8.6
12% Pref. Share	250	12%	12.5	1.5
10% Debenture	500	6%	25.00	1.5
10% Term Loan	450	6%	22.5	1.35
	2,000		100.00	12.95

➢ kd = I (1 – tax)
 = 10 (1 – 0.4)
 = 6

➢ Ke = Rf +β (Rm – R)
 = 6.5 + 1.5 (16.5 - 6.5)
 = 21.5

Q. 14. From the following information, compute EVA of TCS Ltd., (Assume 35% tax rate)

➢ Equity Share Capita l= ₹1,000 lakhs
➢ 12% Debenture = ₹500 lakhs
➢ Cost of Equity =20%
➢ Financial Leverage = 1.5 times

Q. 14: Solution

EVA = NOPAT – (WACC × CE)
 = 117 – (15.93% × 1,500)
 = 117 – 238.95
 = (121.95)

NOPAT =	EBIT =	180
	– Tax	63
	NOPAT	117

$$DFL = \frac{EBIT}{EBT}$$

$$1.5 = \frac{EBIT}{EBIT - Interest}$$

$$1.5 = \frac{EBIT}{EBT - 60}$$

1.5 (EBIT – 60) = EBIT
1.5 EBIT – 90 = 90
1.5 EBIT - EBIT = 90
EBIT = 180

Calculation of WACC

Sources	Amt.	Cost	Proportion	WACC
Equity	1000	66.67	20%	13.33
12% Debenture	500	33.33	7.8%	2.6
Capital Employed	1,500	100.00		15.93

➢ kd = I (1 – tax)
= 12 (1 – 0.35)
= 7.8%

Extra Practice Problem

Q.15. From the following information, compute EVA of Infosys Ltd., (Assume 30% tax rate)

➢ Equity Share Capital = ₹1,200 lakh
➢ 15% Debenture = ₹800 Llakh
➢ Cost of Equity =18%
➢ Financial Leverage = 2 time

Q.16. Fill in the blanks

The following data pertains to three divisions of Adidas Company Ltd., the company's required rate of return on invested capital is 8%.

Particulars	Division A	Division B	Division C
Sales Value (₹)		4 crore	
Income (₹)	16 lakh	80 lakh	
Average Investment (₹)		100 lakh	
Sales Margin (%)	20%		25%
Capital Turnover (Times)	2		
ROI (%)			20%
Residual Income (EVA)(₹)			4,80,000

Q. 17. Co. X wishes to take up the following project:

Investment	: 100	Equity Financing	: 100
Project Life	: 4 years	Depreciation	: Straight-line
Salvage Value	: Nil	Tax Rate	: 50%
Annual Revenues	: 200	Annual Costs	: 135
Cost of Equity	: 15%	(excluding depreciation, interest and taxes)	

Calculate EVA and NPV and give your recommendations for Co. X

Q. 18. Dominos & Co., has existing assets in which it has capital invested of ₹100 crore. The After Tax Operating Income is ₹15 crore and Company has a Cost of Capital of 10%. Estimate the Economic Value Added (EVA) of the firm.

Q. 19. The Income Statement and Balance Sheet of Santro Company Ltd., are given below:

Income Statement

Particulars	**₹ (in lakh)**	**₹ (in lakh)**
Sales	1,000	
Interest on investments	20	
Profit on sale on old assets	10	
Total Income		1,030
Less:		
Manufacturing cost	360	
Administration cost	120	
Selling and distribution cost	100	
Depreciation	60	
Loss on sale of an old Plant and Machinery	10	650
EBIT		380
Less: Interest		40
EBT		340
Less: Tax (30%)		102
PAT		238
EPS [238 lakh/10 lakh]		₹23.8
P/E ratio		3

Balance Sheet

Liabilities	**₹ (in lakh)**	**Assets**	**₹ (in lakh)**
Equity Capital (₹ 10 share)	100	Buildings	160
General Reserves	80	Plant & Machinery	140
Debt	120	Stock	20
Creditors	30	Receivable	24
Provisions	26	Bank	12
Total	**356**	**Total**	**356**

The cost of equity and cost of debt is 12% and 15%, respectively. The company pays 30% corporate tax.

From the information given you are required to calculate the EVA. Also, calculate MVA on the basis of Market Value of Equity Capital

Q. 20. Multiplex Ltd., is considering a capital project for which the following information is available.

Investment outlay	5,000	Depreciation	Straight-line
Project life	4 years	Tax rate	30%
Salvage value	0	Debt equity ratio	4:5
Annual revenues	6,000	Cost of equity	18%
Annual costs (excluding depreciation, interest and taxes)	3,000	Cost of debt (post-tax)	9%

Calculate EVA of the project over its life

Q. 21. The following information is available of Vodafone Ltd., Calculate EVA.

12% Debt capital	₹ 1,200 lakh
Equity capital	₹ 300 lakh
Reserves and Surplus	₹ 4,500 lakh
Capital employed	₹ 6,000 lakh
Risk-free rate	8%
Beta factor	2
Market rate of return	20%
Operating profit after tax	1,260 lakh
Tax rate	30%

Q. 22. Compute EVA of IOCL Ltd., for 3 years from the information given – (in ₹ lakh)

Year	1	2	3
Average Capital Employed	1,800.00	2,100.00	2,400.00
Operating Profit before Interest	510.00	750.00	960.00
Corporate Income Taxes	48.00	42.00	72.00
Average Debt/Total Capital Employed (in%)	60.00	40.00	20.00
Beta Variant	1.50	1.80	2.10
Risk-free Rate (%)	10.50	10.50	10.50
Equity Risk Premium (%)	8.00	8.00	8.00
Cost of Debt (Post-tax) (%)	10.00	10.00	10.00

Q. 23. The capital structure of L&T Ltd., is as under:

- 56,00,000 Equity Shares of ₹ 10 each = ₹ 560 lakh
- 1,75,000 12% Preference Shares of ₹ 100 each = 175 lakh

- 3,50,000 10% debentures of ₹ 100 each = 350 lakh
- 10% term loan from bank = ₹ 315 lakh

The Company's Profit and Loss Account for the year showed a balance PAT of ₹ 77 lakh, after appropriating Equity Dividend at 20%. The company is in the 30% tax bracket. Treasury bonds carry 7.5% interest and beta factor for the company may be taken at 1.8. The long-run market rate of return may be taken at 17.5%. Calculate EVA.

Value Added Statement

Sales	x
(-) Manufacturing Expenses (not reported as application)	(x)
(-) Administrative Expenses (not reported as application)	(x)
(-) Interest Expenses (not reported as application)	(x)
	x
(+) Other Income	x
GVA	x

Application of Gross Value Added

➤ To Employees		
Salaries, commission	x	
Wages other benefits	x	
Salaries/commission to director	x	x
➤ To Government		
Location Cess	x	
Direct Tax	x	x
➤ To Financiers		
Interest on long-term loan	x	
Dividend paid	x	x
➤ For Expansion Future Purpose		
Transfer to Reserves	x	
Retained for current year	x	x
➤ For replacement of asset		
Depreciation	x	
Transfer to Asset Replacement	x	x
	GVA →	xx

Problems and Solution

Q. 1. Prepare a Gross Value Added Statement from the following Profit and Loss Account of Strong Ltd., Show also the reconciliation between Gross Value added and profit before Taxation:

Profit and Loss Account for the year ended 31st March, 2009

Income	Notes	Amount	
		(₹ in lakh)	(₹ in lakh)
Sales			610
Other Income			25
			635
Expenditure			
Production and Operational expenses	1	465	
Administration expenses	2	19	
Interest and Other Charges	3	27	
Depreciation		14	
			525
Profit before taxes			110
Provisions for taxes			16
			94
Balance as per last Balance Sheet			7
			101
Transferred to:			
General Reserve		60	
Proposed Dividend		11	
			71
Surplus carried to Balance Sheet			30
			101

Notes:

1. Production and Operational Expenses

	(₹ in lakh)
Increase in Stock	112
Consumption of Raw Materials	185
Consumption of Stores	22
Salaries, Wages, Bonus and Other Benefits	41
Cess and Local Taxes	11
Other Manufacturing Expenses	94
	465

2. Administration expenses include *inter alia* audit fees of ₹ 4.80 lakh, salaries and commission to directors ₹ 5 lakh and provision for doubtful debts ₹ 5.20 lakh.

3. Interest and Other Charges (₹ in lakh)

Working Capital Loans from Bank	8
On Fixed loans from IDBI	12
Debentures	7
	27

Q. 1: Solution

Value Added Statement

	₹
Sales	610
(-) Manufacturing Exp. [465 - 41 - 11]	(413)
(-) Administrative Exp. [19 - 5]	(14)
(-) Interest Exp. [27 - 12 - 7]	(8)
	175
(+) Other Income	25
GVA	200

Application of Gross Value Added

	₹	₹	%
To Employees			
Salaries, Commission	41		
Wages and Other benefits			
Salaries and Commission to directors	5	46	23
To Government			
Location Cess	11		
Direct Tax	16	27	13.5
To Financiers			
Fixed loan from IDBI	12		
Interest on Debenture	7		
Dividend	11	30	15
For Expansion/Future purpose			
Transfer to Reserves	60		
Retained for current year	23	83	41.5
For replacement of asset			
Depreciation	14		
Transfer to Asset Replacement	-	14	7
		GVA 200	100

Q. 2. From the following Profit and Loss Account of Brightex Co. Ltd., prepare a gross value added statement for the year ended 31.3.2009.

Show also the reconciliation between gross value added and profit before taxation.

Income	Notes	Amount	
		(₹ 000)	(₹ 000)
Sales		6,240	
Other Income		55	6,295
Expenditure:			
Production and Operational Expenses	1	4,320	
Administration Expenses (Factory)	2	180	
Interest and Other Charges	3	624	
Depreciation		16	5,140
Profit before Taxes			1,155
Provision for Taxes			55
			1,100
Balance as per last Balance Sheet			60
Transferred to fixed assets replacement reserve		400	1,160
Dividend Paid		160	560
Surplus Carried to Balance Sheet			600

Notes:

1. Production and Operational Expenses

Consumption of raw materials	3,210
Consumption of stores	40
Local tax	8
Salaries to administrative staff	620
Other manufacturing expenses	442
	4,320

2. Administration expenses include salaries and commissions to directors 5

3. Interest and other charges include:

(a) Interest on bank overdraft (Overdraft its of temporary nature) 109

(b) Fixed Loans from ICICI: 51

(c) Working Capital loan from IFCI. 20

(d) Excise duties amount to one-tenth of total value added by manufacturing and trading activities.

Q.2: Solution

Value Added Statement

	₹
Sales	6,240
(-) Manufacturing Expenses [4,320 - 8 - 620]	(3,692)
(-) Administrative Expenses [180 - 5]	(175)
(-) Interest Expenses	-
[624 - 51]	(573)
	1,800
(+) Other Income	55
GVA	1,855

Application of Gross Value Added

	₹	₹	%
➤ To Employees			
Salaries, Commission	620		
Wages and Other benefits			
Salaries and Commission to directors	5	625	3.69
➤ To Government			
Location Cess	8		
Direct Tax	55	63	3.40
➤ To Financiers			
Fixed loan from ICICI	5		
Dividend	160	211	11.37
➤ For Expansion/Future purpose			
Retained earning for current year	(600 - 60)	540	29.11
➤ For replacement of asset			
Depreciation	16		
Transfer to Asset Replacement	400	416	22.43
	GVA →	1855	100

Notes:

(1) Indirect Taxes such as local tax and cess can also be regarded as a manufacturing expenses and will not be shown as application of gross value added system.

(2) Depreciation can be regarded as a manufacturing cost and then it should be reduced in part 1, while calculating GVA.

(3) Interest: The interest on short-term loan can be shown as application from GVA statement then short-term loan shall be reduced from part 1 of GVA.

CHAPTER 8

PROJECT FINANCING AND PROJECT APPRAISAL

8.1 TERM LOANS

Term loans are also known as term/project finance. They represent a source of debt finance which is generally repayable in more than one year but less than 10 years. The primary source of such loans are financial institutions. Commercial banks also provide term finance in a limited way. The financial institutions provide project finance for new projects as also for expansion/diversification and modernisation whereas the bulk of term loans extended by banks is in the form of working capital loan to finance the working capital requirement.

8.2 TERM LOAN PROCEDURE

The procedure associated with a term loan involves the following principal steps:

1. **Submission of Loan Application:** The borrower submits an application form that seeks comprehensive information about the project. The application form covers the following aspects:
   - **Promoter's Background** – The promoters of the company must give their detailed Biodata.
   - **Particulars of the Industrial Concern** – The products to be manufactured and the market that need to be penetrated must be stated. Also, the forecast for growth in that industry as well as their opportunities (export potential…) must be mentioned.
   - **Particulars of the Project** – Capacity, process, technical arrangements, management, location, land and buildings, plant and machinery, raw materials, effluents, labour, housing, and schedule of implementation.
   - **Cost of the Project** – The cost taking all factoring to account must be arrived at.
   - **Means of Financing** – There should be details of the debt equity ratio, the level of gearing, the capital structure, and the source of financing.
   - **Marketing and Selling Arrangement** – The project report must state if the company has appointed any wholesalers or distributors for its goods services or if it has tied-up with another company for marketing its product.
   - **Economic Considerations** – The project must be economically feasible. [i.e., Demand exceeds supply]
   - **Government Consents** – The promoters should certify that they have obtained the necessary government approvals for the project.
2. **Initial Processing of Loan Application:** When the application is received, an officer of the financial institution reviews it to ascertain whether it is complete for processing. If it is incomplete the borrower is asked to provide the required additional information. When the

application is considered complete, the financial institution prepares a 'flash report' which is essentially a summarization of the loan application. On the basis of the 'Flash Report', it is decided whether the project justifies a detailed appraisal or not.

3. **Detailed Appraisal of the Proposed Project:** The detailed appraisal of the project covers the financial, technical, economic, managerial and marketing aspects. The appraisal memorandum is a normally prepared after Marketing Project Appraisal. Based on that a decision is taken whether the project application will be accepted or not.

4. **Issue of the Letter of Sanction:** If the project is accepted, a financial letter of sanction is issued to the borrower. This communicates to the borrower the assistance sanctioned and the terms and conditions relating thereto. It includes.
   - Loan Period.
   - Security both Primary and Secondary.
   - Restrictive Covenants.
   - Repayment Schedule.

5. **Acceptance of the Terms and Conditions by the Borrowing Unit:** On receiving the letter of sanction from the financial institution, the borrowing unit convenes its board meeting at which the terms and conditions associated with the letter of sanction are accepted and an appropriate resolution is passed to that effect. The acceptance of the terms and conditions has to be conveyed to the financial institution within a stipulated period.

6. **Execution of Loan Agreement:** The financial institution, after receiving the letter of acceptance from the borrower, sends the draft of the agreement to the borrower to be executed by the authorised persons and properly stamped as per the Indian Stamp Act, 1899. The agreement, properly executed and stamped, along with other documents as required by the financial institution must be returned to it. Once the financial institution also signs the agreement, it becomes effective.

7. **Disbursement of Loans:** Periodically, the borrower is required to submit information on the physical progress of the projects, financial status of the project, arrangements made for financing the project, contributions made by the promoters, projected funds flow statement, compliance with various statutory requirements, and fulfilment of the pre-disbursement conditions. Based on the information provided by the borrower, the FI will determine the amount of term loan to be disbursed from time-to-time. Before the entire term loan is disbursed, the borrower must fully comply with all the terms and conditions of the loan agreement.

8. **Creation of Security:** The term loans (both rupee and foreign currency) and the deferred payment guarantee assistance provided by the financial institutions are secured through the first mortgage, by way of deposit of title deeds, of immovable properties and hypothecation of movable properties (in the form of guarantees by the promoters).

9. **Monitoring:** Monitoring of the project is done at the implementation stage as well as at the operational stage. During the implementation stage, the project is monitored through:
   - Regular reports, furnished by the promoters, which provide information about placement of orders, construction of buildings, procurement of plant, installation of plant and machinery, trial production, etc.

- Periodic site visits.
- Discussion with promoters, bankers, suppliers, creditors, and other connected with the project.
- Progress reports submitted by the nominee directors, and
- Audited accounts of the company.

During the operational stage, the project is monitored with the help of – (i) quarterly progress report on the project (ii) site inspection (iii) reports of nominee directors and "(iv) comparison of performance vs. promise.

The most important aspect of monitoring, of course, is the recovery of dues represented by interest and principal repayment.

Continuous monitoring helps in improving receivable management, etc.

8.3 PROJECT APPRAISAL/DUE DILIGENCE/PROJECT FEASIBILITY/ PROJECT VIABILITY/PROJECT REPORT BY FINANCIAL INSTITUTIONS

Project appraisal is the process by which a financial institution makes an independent and objective assessment of the various aspects of the investment proposition for arriving at a financing decision.

Broad aspects of appraisal

There are six broad aspects of appraisal

1. Financial feasibility
2. Technical feasibility
3. Economic feasibility
4. Management competence
5. Market appraisal
6. Environment feasibility

1. Financial Feasibility

The data required for financial feasibility analysis can be grouped as under:

- Cost of project
- Means of financing
- Cost of production and profitability
- Cashflow estimates during currency of loans
- Proforma balance sheets and revenue statement
- Cost of project – The cost of the project can be broadly classified into the following:
- Land and site development
- Building
- Plant and machinery
- Transportations, erections and commissioning

- Miscellaneous assets
- Preliminary and pre-operative expenses
- Contingency expenses
- Working capital margin

Means of Financing: There is no ideal pattern concerning means of financing for a project. The means of financing is determined by a variety of factors and considerations like magnitude of funds required, risk associated with the enterprise, nature of industry, prevailing taxation laws, etc.

The following are the sources of finance:

- Share capital
- Retained earnings
- Subsidies
- Long-term borrowing (financial institutions/banks)
- Loans from friends and relatives

Financial institutions specify certain debt equity ratios and promoters will have to raise own finance to match these ratios. A general Debt–Equity norm of up to 2 and DSCR 1.5 – 2 + is considered acceptable.

Cost of Production and Profitability

The next step is the assessment of the earning capacity of the project. The unit should be in a position to manufacture the product at a reasonable cost and sell them at a reasonable price, which would allow adequate profit margin even in a competitive market.

Cashflow Estimates

The cashflow estimates are essential to ensure availability of cash to meet the requirements of the project from time-to-time. This will indicate whether the cashflow would be adequate to meet the debt obligations and also provide sufficient margin of safety.

Proforma Balance Sheets and Revenue Statement

Proforma balance sheet and revenue statement are drawn for existing concerns going for expansions as well as for new projects. However, in the case of existing concerns going for expansion the balance sheets for the past three years are also analysed and compared, with the projections. The projected balance sheet can be drawn for the cashflow estimates and profitability projections. Various ratios are derived from the balance sheet and inferences drawn therefrom.

2. Technical Feasibility

The project needs to be examined with particular reference to the following points regarding the technical feasibility.

Location: The success of a project depends on its proper location yielding the advantages of proximity to the sources of raw material, labour, availability of power and transport facilities and market. The subsidies and other concessions available at certain specified areas are to be compared with the basic infrastructural aspects. (This lead to selection of Sanand in Gujarat for Tata 'Nano' Project.)

Land and Building: The land should necessarily be sufficient to take care of future expansions. If the land is on lease the terms and conditions of the lease are to be verified. Actual plant layout is to be studied before deciding on the size of the building.

Plant and Machinery: The important aspect to be noted in examining the list of plant and equipment is to ascertain the appropriateness of the process of technology, capacity, etc. Adequate provision for spare parts is also essential especially if the same have to be imported.

Technical Competence: The technology may be indigenous or imported through foreign collaboration. In case of indigenous technology it should be ensured that suitable technical personnel are available. For technology acquired through collaboration tie-ups the key areas to be probed are:

- The standing of the collaborators and past experiences concerning tie-up arrangements with them should be studied.
- Performance guarantee and its adequacy in relation to rated capacity of plant and machinery.

3. Economic Feasibility

The economic feasibility basically deals with the marketability of the product. Projection or forecasting of demand is no doubt a complicated matter but is of vital importance. Equally importance is to examine the sales promotion proposed by the enterprise and its adequacy. For e.g. demand exceeds supply; in power, real estate sector, and not in aviation, telecom sector.

4. Managerial Competence

The success of a business enterprise depends largely on the resourcefulness, competence and integrity of its management. However assessment of managerial competence has to be necessarily qualitative calling for understanding and judgement. The managerial requirements are the experience and capability of the principal promoters to implement and run the project. For a new entrepreneur it will always be advisable to build up a competent team of specialists in the required discipline to join hands with an entrepreneur who has the requisite organisational and managerial expertise in the implementation and operation of the project. [e.g., Manoj Tirodkar of GTL and Kalanithi Maran of Spicejet, SunTV, etc.]

5. Market Appraisal

The importance of the potential market and the need to develop a suitable marketing strategy cannot be over-emphasised. Hence efforts are made to:

- Examine the reasonableness of the demand projections.
- Assess the adequacy of the marketing infrastructure in terms of promotional effort, distribution network, transport facilities, stock levels, etc.
- Judge the knowledge, experience and competence of the key marketing personnel.
- Export potential
- Current and future market scenario/competition.

6. Environment Feasibility

It is an upcoming aspect of appraisal. Necessary approval is to be obtained from Environment Ministry.

8.4 TERMS ASSOCIATED WITH TERM LOANS (CONCEPT QUESTIONS)

(a) Maturity

The maturity period of term loans is typically longer in case of sanctions by financial institutions in the range of 6-10 years in comparison to 3-5 years of bank advances by commercial bank. However, they are rescheduled to enable corporate borrowers tide over temporary financial exigencies.

(b) Negotiated

The term loans are negotiated loans between the borrowers and the lenders. They are akin to private placement of debentures in contrast to their public offering to investors. Both the parties discuss their differences/implication and arrive at a mutually acceptable option.

(c) Security

Term loans typically represent secured borrowing. Usually assets, which are financed with the proceeds of the term loan, provide the prime security. Other assets of the firm may serve as collateral security.

Term loans are provided on the basis of the following modes of security:

Hypothecation: Under this mode of security, loans are provided against the **security of movable property**, usually inventory of goods. The goods hypothecated, however, continue to be in the **possession of the owner of these goods (i.e., the borrower)**. The rights of the lending institution (hypothecatee) depend upon the terms of contract between the borrower and the lender. Although the lender does not have physical possession of the goods, it has legal right to sell the goods to realize the outstanding loan, e.g., Car Loan, Working Capital Loan, etc.

Pledge: Pledge as a mode of security, is different from hypothecation in that in the former, unlike in the latter, the **goods which are offered as security are transferred to the physical possession of the lender.** An essential prerequisite of pledge is that the goods are in the custody of lender. The borrower who offers security is called a "pawnor" (pledgor), while the lender is called "pawnee" (pledgee). The lodging of the goods by the pledgor to the pledgee is a kind of bailment. Therefore, the pledge creates some liabilities for the lender. It must take reasonable care of goods pledged with it. In case of non-repayment of the loans, the lender enjoys the right to sell the goods and recover the dues, e.g., shares, gold etc.

Lien: The term lien refers to the right of a party to retain goods belonging to another party until a debt due to him is paid. The lien can be of two types: particular lien, and general lien. Particular lien is a right to retain goods until a claim pertaining to those goods is fully paid. On the other hand, general lien can be applied till all dues of the claimant are paid.

Mortgage: It is the **transfer of a legal/equitable interest in specific immovable property** for securing the payment of debt. The person who parts with the interest in the property is called 'mortgager' and the person in whose favour the transfer takes place is called 'mortgagee'. The instrument of transfer is called 'mortgage deed'. Mortgage is thus conveyance of interest in the mortgaged property. The mortgage interest in the property is terminated as soon as the debt is paid. [e.g., Home Loans]

Charge: Where **immovable property** of one person is, by the act of parties or by the operation of law, made security for the payment of money to another and the **transaction does not amount to mortgage,** the latter person is said to have a charge on the property and all the provisions of simple mortgage will apply on such a charge. The differences are as follows:

- ➢ A charge is not the transfer of interest in the property though it is security for payment. But mortgage is a transfer of interest in the property.
- ➢ A charge may be created by the act of parties or by the operation of law. But a mortgage can be created only by the act of parties.
- ➢ A charge need not be made in writing but a mortgage deed must be attested.
- ➢ Generally, a charge cannot be enforced against the transferee for consideration without notice.

First Charge and Second Charge

Loans are granted to borrowers against securities. Sometimes, a borrower might use the same asset for raising finance from two or more lenders. In this case the lender who has first lent to the borrower against the asset will have a right on the asset, before the second lender, in case of default. This is known as the first charge.

Only after the dues of the first lender are cleared, after selling off the asset, the second lender can claim his dues. This is known as second charge. Generally, the lender who has a second charge will price his loan higher, considering the fact that he has to bear a greater risk.

***Pari passu* charge**

In *pari passu* charge, in case of default all lenders share the right to the security in proportion to the loan amount disbursed.

Fixed and Floating Charge

Lenders lend money to borrowers against securities. A lender can have either a fixed or a floating charge on the securities. In case of a fixed charge, the lender can recover his dues from a certain predecided asset only, in case of a default by the borrower. On the other hand, a lender who has a floating charge can recover his dues from a gamut of assets. The lender who lends on a fixed charged therefore has to bear higher risk than the one lending on a floating charge. Generally, the lender who has a fixed charge will price his loan higher, considering the fact that he is to bear a greater risk.

(d) Restrictive Covenants

In order to protect their interest, financial institutions generally impose restrictive conditions on the borrowers. These are known as covenants. They are both positive (affirmative) and negative, in the sense of what the borrower should and should not do in conduct of its operations and fall into four sets as respectively related to assets-related covenants, liabilities-related covenants, cashflows-related covenants and control-related covenants.

Negative Covenants: Negative covenants state what borrowing firm should not do during the term of the loan:

- ➢ **Asset-related Covenants:** are intended to ensure the maintenance of a minimum asset base by the borrowers. Included in this set covenants are:
  - Maintenance of working capital position in terms of a minimum current ratio,
  - Restriction on creation of further charge on asset, and
  - Ban on sale of fixed assets without the lender's concurrence/approval.

- **Liability-related Covenants:** may include:
  - Restrain on the incurrence of additional debt/repayment of existing loan, say, without the concurrence/prior approval of the lender/financial institution,
  - Prohibition on disposal promoter's shareholding, buyback of shares.
- **Cashflow:** Related covenants – which are intended to restrain cash outflows of the borrowers may include.
  - Restriction on new projects/expansion without prior approval of the financial institution,
  - Limitation on dividend payment to a certain amount/rate.
  - Ceiling on director fees, managerial salary and perks.
- **Control-related Covenants:** Aim at ensuring competent management for the borrowers. This set of covenants may include:
  - Broadbasing of board of directors and finalisation of management set-up in consultation with the financial institution,
  - Effective organisational changes and appointment of suitable professional staff, and
  - Appointment of nominee directors to represent the financial institutions and safeguard their interests.
- **Positive Covenants:** In addition to the foregoing negative covenants, certain positive/affirmative covenants stating what the borrowing firm should do during the term of a loan are also included in a loan agreement. They provide for:
  - Furnishing of periodical reports/financial statements to the lenders,
  - Maintenance of a minimum level of working capital,
  - Creation of sinking fund for redemption of debt, and
  - Maintenance of certain net worth.

(e) Margin Money

Margin money is one of the important factors, which is evaluated by the financial institutions while considering the project for financial assistance.

When borrower/owner introduces the margin money amount in the project, then financial institution undertakes disbursement of term loan. The quantum of margin money (for e.g., 25%, 50%) depends on the creditworthiness of the borrower and nature of security for e.g., 30% margin money in case of housing loan from reputed builders.

(f) Fixed and Floating Rates

Floating rate as opposed to fixed rates vary over the tenor of the loan. These variations are linked to changes in an underlying benchmark rate. Thus, a borrower with a floating rate loan for three years could end up paying 9 per cent in the first year, 10 per cent in the second and 8 per cent in the third.

Loan floating interest rates are offered at lower rates as compared to fixed rates, as the borrower bears the risk of fluctuations. The choice ultimately depends on the borrower's perception on the movement in the interest rates in the loan period. 90% of loan sanctioned is on floating rates. In year 2009, SBI has launched 8% fixed rate for 1st year and 8.5% for 2nd and 3rd year and thereafter floating rate depending upon PLR/Base rate for housing/car loan. This is combination, i.e., initially fixed and later fluctuating.

(g) Moratorium

Financial institutions may allow for a delay in the payment of the first principal instalment to the borrowers. The period between the sanction of the loan and the first principal instalment repayment is known as moratorium. The bank studies profitability statement and cashflow projections prepared by borrowing unit and arrives at a conclusion regarding as to the length of moratorium period. Projects like Bandra-Worli sea link, Metro Rail, etc., takes years to complete and hence loan will have requisite moratorium period.

(h) Reschedulement

In the event of a borrower not being able to pay their instalments as per the repayment schedule, financial institutions may restructure the repayment schedule of the borrowers to prevent the term loan from turning bad. In case of increase in interest rates, to avoid increase in instalment borrower may request increase in loan period. Also, temporary change in market conditions can result into borrower unable to pay and hence request for reschedulement (e.g., Kingfisher Airlines).

(i) Interest

- **Penal:** financial institutions levy a penal interest on the borrowers who default on interest payment in spite of having the ability to pay.
- **Rebate:** financial institutions may grant a rebate in the interest payment to borrowers who are willing to pay but do not have the ability to pay. (e.g., Farmers in case of drought/flood).
- **Waiver:** financial institutions may also waiver off some part of the interest payment to borrowers who are not in a sound financial position (e.g., SSI, Farmers...)
- **Prepayment Penalty:** It is charged if the loan is repaid earlier than scheduled. This is done to discourage early payment. This is because lender will lose his future income, i.e., interest, [for e.g., Housing loan 2.5% prepayment penalty].

(j) Sensitivity Analysis

One measure which expresses risk in more precise term is sensitivity analysis. It provides information as to how sensitive the estimated project parameters, namely, the expected cashflow, the discount rate and the project life are to be estimation errors. The analysis of these lines is important as the future is always uncertain and there will always be estimation errors. Sensitivity analysis takes care of estimation errors by using a number of possible outcomes in evaluating a project. The method adopted under sensitivity analysis is to evaluate a project using a number of estimated cashflows to provide to the decisionmaker an insight into the variability of the outcomes.

Sensitivity analysis provides different cashflow estimates under three assumptions: (i) the worst (i.e., the most pessimistic), (ii) the expected (i.e., the most likely), and (iii) the best (i.e., the most optimistic) outcomes associated with the project. The ultimate decision is based on assessment and acceptability of risks involved.

(k) Verification and Validation Security

Once a charge has been created on an asset, the borrower can register the charge with the registrar of companies. Thus, the asset is open for verification to any lender who may or may not want to place a charge on the asset.

(i) Financial Ratios used for Appraisal of Term Loan Proposal

1. Interest Coverage Ratio $= \dfrac{\text{PBIT}}{\text{Interest}}$ = x times

2. Interest and (P) Loan Repayment Coverage Ratio $= \dfrac{\text{PBIT}}{\text{Int.} + \text{(P) Inst}}$ = x times

3. Debt Service Coverage Ratio $= \dfrac{\text{PBIT} + \text{Depr} - \text{Tax}}{\text{Int.} + \text{(P) Inst}}$ = x times

4. Debt Equity Ratio $= \dfrac{\text{Dept}}{\text{Equity}}$ = x

5. ROI $= \dfrac{\text{PBIT}}{\text{Cap. Emp.}} \times 100$ = x %

(m) Credit rating

The banks evaluate the borrower depending on the risk involved in the financing to them. "Lower the risk, Lower the interest and higher the risk, higher the rate of interest."

For e.g., RIL will get loan at lower rate of interest as compared to DLF, since it has higher credit rating.

The aggregate marks and the credit eating are as under:

Exhibit 1

Credit Risk code	Scoring Band
AAA + : Prime	90 % and above
AAA : Excellent	80% and above but < 90%
AA : Good	60% and above but < 80%
A : Satisfactory	40% and above but < 60%
B : Risk prone	Below 40%
C : High risk	Doubtful asset
D : Highest risk	On verge of insolvency

The credit score is frequently revised by credit rating agencies based on changes in financial standing, information system, financial discipline, market condition, etc., of the borrower.

NEWS ARTICLE

Listed Defaulters May Be Named. ***(Economic Times, 14 June, '10)***

High-level Panel On Fin Mkts Feels Naming Erring Co's will Improve Transparency.

Dheeraj Tiwari and Rohini Singh, NEW DELHI.

A COMMITTEE comprising senior government officials and financial regulators has proposed mandatory disclosure of loan defaults by listed companies, a move aimed at protecting shareholders interest and boosting investors confidence. This will promote transparency and strengthen corporate governance. The proposal was discussed at the May 24 meeting of the High-level Coordination Committee on Financial Markets, said a senior finance ministry official. Market regulator Securities and Exchange Board of India (SEBI) will examine the practical aspects of the proposal.

SEBI may consider making changes in the listing norms so that whenever a company defaults on any payment obligation, it would trigger a public announcement, the official said, requesting anonymity. The meeting of the coordination committee was chaired by Reserve Bank of India (RBI) governor, D. Subbarao. Finance secretary Ashok Chawla, department of financial services secretary, R. Gopalan, chief economic advisor, Kaushik Basu, SEBI chairman, CB Bhave, Insurance Regulatory & Development Authority (IRDA) chairman, J Hari Narayan and senior officials of the Pension Fund Regulatory & Development Authority (PFRDA) attended the meeting.

At present, information on loan defaults is available only to the lenders, RBI and credit information companies such as CIBIL. As per the current practice, banks disclose a list of defaulters to RBI on a quarterly basis. A copy of this report is forwarded to SEBI and CIBIL.

Globally, there were a number of corporate loan defaults in 2009, after some of the world's largest economies were hit by the worst financial crisis since 1930s. India also felt the tremors of the crisis, leading to a few high-profile default cases. Also knowing that they have to disclose loan default their best not to default on loan obligations. This will help financial/banking sector, by reducing bad debts/ NPA, etc. Also, lenders can then avoid loan application from defaulter.

SBI Likely To Fix Base Rate At Around 7.75% ***(Economic Times, 28 June, '10)***

The central bank introduced the base rate model from July 1 to replace the existing benchmark prime lending rate (BPLR) model with a view to bring in more transparency in the way banks lend. At present, banks charge much lower rates to high-rated corporate borrowers, but demand a higher rate from the common man.

However, banks are worried that corporate customers, seeking short-term loans, may approach alternative sources for funding, as no bank will be allowed to lend below its base rate.

The effective rate, which a customer will have to pay on loans, will comprise tenure premium, channel specific transaction charges and risk premium of loans above the base rate

Most of the public sector banks are likely to track SBIs base rate while arriving at their own rates, which could be between 7% and 7.5%.

On the other side, private and foreign sector lenders are expected to go for 6-7.5% to attract corporate borrowers seeking short-term loans.

Recently, SBI chairman OP Bhatt had said the banks base rate will be calculated in line with its cost of deposits.

According to RBI guidelines, banks are free to take any parameter to calculate their base rate and are allowed to try different methodologies till December.

There is a huge premium lenders are charging for fixed rate loans. Do you think the era of fixed rate loans is over? ***(Economic Times, 28 June, '10)***

Fixed rate loans are costlier because the lender, in order to avoid a maturity and interest rate mismatch, has to borrow long-term fixed rate money, which always costs more than floating rate funds. Since fixed rates are costlier than floating rate loans, most borrowers prefer floating rate loans as people don't expect interest rates to remain high for ever. If someone takes a fixed rate loan, he is stuck at that rate for life and would not get the benefit of falling rates in future.

Keki Mistry, CEO & Chairman, HDFC

8.5 PROBLEMS AND SOLUTION

Q. 1. The following data is available in respect of Vijay Textiles Ltd.:

(i) The company as incorporated in 1975 with the promoters having experience of more than 35 years in the textile field and is brand leader in micro yarn.

(ii) The company proposes to borrow the term loan under TUFS (Technology Up-gradation Funds Scheme.)

(iii) The present installed capacity is 10 machines or 6,000 TPA or polyster texturised yarn.

(iv) The additional investment will increase the installed capacity by 3,600 TPA.

(v) The present and proposed set up is at Silvassa a backward area and enjoys income tax holiday for 5 years. Tax rate is 40%.

(vi) ICICI, IDBI and SBI financed the present unit.

(vii) The project will result into economies of scale, reduced cost of production, higher production due to yarn speed being faster due to latest generation machine, best quality due to the modernised machine.

(viii) The expected ROI of the project is 18%.

(ix) Depreciation for project is ₹400 lakh every year.

(x) The cost of proposed project and the means of finance are as follows:

Proposed Project	**₹ In lakh**
Cost of Project	
Land and Site Development	27
Factory Building	155
Plant and Machinery	1,604
Electrical Installation	24
Misc. Fixed Assets	10
Preoperative Expenses	20
Contingencies	67
Margin Money For Working Capital	93
Total	**2,000**
Means of Finance	
Promoters Funds	
Additional Equity Share Capital	300
Internal Cash Accrual	500
Term Loan	1,200
Total	**2,000**

(xi) The term lending institution has interest rate of 13% for similar risk project and the term loan is repayable in 5 years with installment and interest repayable at the end of each year.

General Manager of the term lending institution has requested you to:

(a) Prepare Flash Report from the point of view of the term lending institution.

(b) Evaluate the project for profitability in the next 5 years.

(c) Calculate the debt service coverage ratio for the term loan.

(MU, BMS, April 2002)

Q. 1: Solution

(a) Flash Report

Name of Borrower: Vijay Textile Ltd.,

Term Loan Amount: ₹ 1200 lakh

Rate of Interest: 13% p.a.

1. Financial Feasibility

(a) The Company will enjoy Income Tax holiday for 5 years.

(b) The expected ROI of the project is 18%

(c) The total project cost is ₹1200 lakh

∴ Debt – Equity Ratio is 1.5 (1,200/800)

2. Technical Feasibility

(a) The Company proposes to borrow the Term Loan under TUFS

(b) The expansion will result into higher production and best quality due to latest generation machines.

(c) The proposed expansion is at Silvasa a backward area.

3. Economic Feasibility

(a) The installed capacity will increase from 6,000 TPA to 9,600 TPA.

(b) The project will result into economies of scale.

4. Management Competence

The promoters are having more than 35 years of experience in the textile field.

5. Market Appraisal

(a) The Company is a brand leader in micro yarn.

(b) ICICI, IDBI and SBI have financed the present unit.

(b) Loan Amortization Schedule

Equal principal Installment Method

Year	P (o/s) at beg.	(P) Install Int.	@ 13%	Loan Inst.	P (o/s) end
1	1,200	240	156.0	396.0	960
2	960	240	124.8	364.8	720
3	720	240	93.6	333.6	480
4	480	240	62.4	302.4	240
5	240	240	31.2	271.2	–

$$\text{ROI} = \frac{\text{EBIT}}{\text{TA}} \times 100$$

$$\therefore \text{EBIT} = \frac{\text{ROI}}{100} \times \text{TA}$$

$$= \frac{18}{100} \times 2{,}000$$

$$= ₹\ 360 \text{ lakh}$$

Revenue Statement for year ended ______

Particulars	1	2	3	4	5
EBIT	360	360	360	360	360
Interest	156	124.8	93.6	62.4	31.2
EBT	204	235.2	266.4	297.6	328.8
(-) Tax	-	-	-	-	-
EAT	204	235.2	266.4	297.6	328.8

(c) DSCR

Particulars	1	2	3	4	5
DSCR $\frac{\text{EBIT + Dep} - \text{T}}{\text{I + (P) Inst. (time)}}$	$\frac{360 + 400 - 0}{396}$ = 1.91	$\frac{760}{364.8}$ = 2.08	$\frac{760}{333.6}$ = 2.28	$\frac{760}{302.4}$ = 2.51	$\frac{760}{271.2}$ = 2.80
Overall DSCR	$\frac{1.91 + 2.08 + 2.28 + 2.51 + 2.80}{5}$ = 2.32 times				

Note: Tax holiday for 1st Five Years.

Q. 2. You are approached by a financial institution to appraise the following project:

Name of the Borrowers: Anju Devi Chemicals Private Limited

Proposed loan is taken to set up a chemical unit for processing industrial waste into a marketable product XYZ. The product has a demand for 50,000 litres. The processing costs include variable cost of ₹ 5 per litre and fixed cost (excluding depreciation) ₹ 30,000 per year. Advertising expenses are also expected to be ₹ 20,000 per year.

XYZ can be sold at ₹ 10 per litre. Raw Material (Industrial waste) is available at rupee one per litre. The capital cost of chemical unit is ₹ 7,50,000.

The company has applied for a loan of ₹ 6,00,000 for a term of 10 years and that is over the life of the asset. The promoters of the company are young, dynamic and highly qualified people but are doing the venture for the first time. The promoters are unable to provide any collateral security for the loan and expect personal guarantee of their parents.

They have thought of this project after market research. The said research has stated in the risk factors about invasion of Malaysia in chemical market and drastic reduction in selling price of similar products.

The above unit is an SSI unit and its average tax rate is 20%. Interest rate is 12% p.a.

Loan is repayable equally in 10 annual installments along with interest at the end of each year. You are required to:

(i) Give the cashflow generated by the above project for the first 3 years only.
(ii) Calculate the Debt Service Coverage Ratio for the above 3 years.
(iii) Prepare the flash report presenting the above information to the financial institution.

(MU, BMS, April 2003)

Q. 2: Solution

(iii) Flash Report

Name of the Borrower: Anju Devi Chemicals Private Limited

Term Loan Amount: ₹ 6,00,000

Rate of Interest: 12% p.a.

1. Financial Feasibility

(a) The promoters are unable to provide any collateral security except personal guarantee of parents.
(b) The above units is an SSI unit and will enjoy benefits including lower tax rate 20%
(c) Project Cost ₹ 7,50,000. Hence, Debt Equity ratio is 4. (6,00,000/1,50,000)

2. Technical Feasibility

The proposed loan is taken to set up a chemical unit for processing industrial waste into a marketable product XYZ.

3. Economic Feasibility

The product has a demand for 50,000 litres.

4. Management Competence

The promoters of the Company are young, dynamic and highly qualified but are doing the venture for the first time.

5. Market Appraisal

(a) The promoters have undertaken the project after doing market research.
(b) The research stated in the risk factor about invasion of Malaysia in chemical market and drastic reducing in selling price.

(i) Loan Amortization Schedule

Equal Principal installment Method

Year	P (o/s) at beg.	(P) Install Int.	@ 13%	Loan Inst.	P (o/s) end
1	6,00,000	72,000	60,000	1,32,000	5,40,000
2	5,40,000	64,800	60,000	1,24,800	4,80,000
3	4,80,000	57,600	60,000	1,17,600	4,20,000

Revenue/cashflow Statement for the first 3 years only

Particulars	Year 1	Year 2	Year 3
Sales (50,000 × 10)	5,00,000	5,00,000	5,00,000
(-) Variable Cost			
Raw Mat. = 50,000			
Other VC 2,50,000	3,00,000	3,00,000	3,00,000
Contribution	2,00,000	2,00,000	2,00,000
(-) Fixed cost			
Advtg. 20,000			
Other fixed 30,000	50,000	50,000	50,000
EBDIT	1,50,000	1,50,000	1,50,000
(-)Depreciation (750000 ÷ 10)	75,000	75,000	75,000
EBIT	75,000	75,000	75,000
(-) Interest	72,000	64,800	57,600
EBT	3,000	10,200	17,400
(-) Tax @ 20%	600	2,040	3,480
EAT	2,400	8,160	75,000
(+) Depreciation	75,000	75,000	13,920
CASHFLOW generated	77,400	83,160	88,920
ii) DSCR			
$\frac{\text{EBIT + D – Tax}}{\text{I + P. Inst. (time)}}$	$\frac{75,000 + 75,000 - 600}{72,000 + 62,000}$	$\frac{75,000 + 75,000 - 2,040}{1,24,800}$	$\frac{75,000 + 75,000 - 3,480}{1,17,600}$
	=1.11	= 1.19	= 1.25

Q. 3. Calculate the important ratios for granting term loans and give your recommendations from the following information:

₹ in lakh

Year	I	II	III
Profit Before Interest and Tax Rate 40%	60.00	80.00	100.00

Loan is repayable in equal principal installments at the end of the each of the 3 years along with interest. Loan amount ₹420 lakh @ 12% p.a.

Capital investment in the project: ₹600 lakh depreciable equally over 3 years.

(MU, BMS, April 2003)

Q. 3: Solution

Loan Amortization Schedule
Equal Principle installment method

Year	P (o/s) at beg.	(P) Install Int.	@ 13%	Loan Inst.	P (o/s) end
1	420	50.4	140	190.4	280
2	280	33.6	140	173.6	140
3	140	16.8	140	156.8	NIL

Revenue Statement for the year ended _______

Particulars	Year 1	Year 2	Year 3
EBDIT	260	280	300
(-) Depreciation	200	200	200
EBIT (given)	60	80	100
(-) Interest	50.4	33.6	16.8
EBT	9.6	46.4	83.2
(-) Tax @ 40%	3.84	18.56	33.28
EAT	5.76	27.84	49.92
1. Int. Coverage Ratio $= \frac{\text{EBIT}}{\text{Int.}}$	$= \frac{60}{50.4} = 1.195$	$= \frac{80}{33.6} = 2.38$	$= \frac{100}{16.8} = 5.95$
2. Int. and (P) Loan repay cov. Ratio $= \frac{\text{EBIT}}{\text{I. + P. Inst.}}$ (times)	$= \frac{60}{190.4}$ $= 0.32$	$= \frac{80}{173.6}$ $= 0.46$	$= \frac{100}{156.8}$ $= 0.64$
3. Debt Service coverage Ratio (DSCR) $= \frac{\text{EBIT + D. – Tax}}{\text{I + (P) Inst.}}$ (times)	$= \frac{60 + 200 - 3.84}{190.4}$ $= 1.355$	$= \frac{80 + 200 - 18.56}{173.6}$ $= 1.51$	$= \frac{100 + 200 - 33.28}{156.8}$ $= 1.70$
Overall DSCR	$= \frac{1.34 + 1.51 - 1.70}{3} = 1.52$ times		

Recommendation:

If other parameters of project appraisal are satisfactory, the financial institution is advised to **sanction term loan** of ₹ 420 lakh @ 12% p.a., since company satisfies the standard ratios.

Q. 4. Prepare an amortization schedule from the following information, assuming that the amount payable is an equated annual installment.

Amount borrowed	₹ 2,40,000	Annuity rate = 4.111
Compound annual interest	12%; Repayment period	6 years

(MU, PGDFM, May 2003)

Q. 4: Solution

Loan Amortization Schedule
Equal Annual Loan Instalment Method

Year	P (o/s) at beg.	(P) Install Int.	@ 13%	Loan Inst.	P (o/s) end
1	2,40,000	28,800	29,580	58,380	2,10,420
2	2,10,420	25,250	33,130	58,380	1,77,290
3	1,77,290	21,275	37,105	58,380	1,40,185
4	1,40,185	16,822	41,558	58,380	98,627
5	98,627	11,835	46,545	58,380	52,082
6	52,082	*6,298	52,082	58,380	–

$$\text{Equal loan instalment} = \frac{\text{Loan Amount}}{\text{Annuity Rate}}$$

$$= \frac{2,40,000}{4.111}$$

$$= ₹\ 58,380 \text{ (Approx.)}$$

Q. 5. Mr. Chawathe, General Manager of FICOM, a Financial Institution, was in relaxed mood. Just thought of having a walk around, went out, grabbed peanuts to munch. As he was about to throw the wrapping paper in a dust bin, he noticed something! The paper was part of an old flash report of FICOM's appraisal process. Only partial data was visible. GM could make out that this was the report of Chemexperts Ltd of Nasik, a manufacturer of bulk drugs and whose directors were IIT Gold Medallist. Total loan sanctioned was ₹ 1,200 lakh @ 13% rate of interest on reducing balance, against the total cost of the project at ₹ 1,850 lakh. Principal amount to be repaid in 24 equal quarterly instalments. Loan sanctioned against the security of Plant and Machinery, Collateral security of RBI Bond and Personal Guarantee of the directors. You are required to list any eight items of the flash report.

(MU, BMS, Oct. 2006)

Q. 5: Solution

Flash Report

Name of the Borrower	:	Chemexperts Ltd.,
Loan Amount	:	₹ 1,200 lakh
Rate of Interest	:	13%
Term Loan Period	:	6 years

1. Financial Feasibility

(a) Project Cost ₹ 1,850 lakh.

(b) Hence, Debt Equity ratio is 1.85 (1,200 ÷ 650)

(c) Principal amount to be repaid in 24 equal quarterly installments.

(d) Loan sanctioned against the prime security of plant and machinery.

(e) Collateral security is RBI bonds and personal guarantee of the directors.

2. Technical Feasibility

(a) The project is located at Nasik, Maharashtra.

(b) The project is for manufacture of BULK DRUGS.

3. Economic Feasibility

4. Management Competence

The directors are IIT Gold medalists.

5. Market Appraisal

Q. 6. A company wants to start a new project. The cost of the project is ₹ 400 crore. Out of which 75% is for capital assets. The capital asset is depreciated over a period of 3 years at the rate of $33\frac{1}{3}$ %. The expected sales turnover is ₹ 600 crore. The variable cost is 50%, fixed cost is 5% excluding depreciation and interest.

The company has resources to the extent of 50% of cost of project. The company has never defaulted in the previous borrowing.

The rate of interest to be charged is 12% p.a. The company has to pay 6 installments half-yearly along with the interest. The company wants to borrow from financial institutions around ₹ 240 crore. The balance finance above ₹210 crore is available from the bank at 14% p.a.

You are required to find out the profitability of the project and the terms and conditions laid down for various appraisals of projects. Tax rate applicable to company is 40%. Prepare a project report.

Q. 6: Solution

W.N.1. Capital Asset/Fixed Asset $= 400 \times \frac{75}{100} =$ ₹ 300 crore

W.N.2. Dep. p.a. $= 300 \times 33\frac{1}{3}$ = ₹100 crore

W.N.3. Project cost = ₹ 400 crore

Loan from financial institutions

₹ 240 crore

➤ Own funds

- reqd = ₹ 160 crore
- available = ₹ 200 crore

(50% × 400)

Note: The company is advised to take own funds only to extent reqd, in order to under-take 'Trading on Equity.'

Loan Amortisation Schedule Equal principal instalment Method

Year	P (o/s) at beg.	(P) Install Int.	@ 13%	Loan Inst.	P (o/s) end
1 → I	240	14.7 / 12 { 26.7	40	54.7	200
→ II	200		40	52	160
2 → I	160	9.6 / 7.2 { 16.8	40	49.6	120
→ II	120		40	47.2	80
3 → I	80	4.8 / 2.4 { 7.2	40	44.8	40
→ II	40		40	42.4	–

W.N. 4. Interest for the year 1; 1st half

$$= 30 \times \frac{14}{100} \times \frac{6}{12} = 2.1$$

$$= 210 \times \frac{12}{100} \times \frac{6}{12} = 12.6$$

$$= 14.7$$

Profitability/Revenue Statement for year ended ______

Particulars	1	2	3
Sales	600	600	600
(-) V.C @ (50%)	300	300	300
Contribution	300	300	300
(-) Fixed Cost (5% × 600)	30	30	30
PBDIT	270	270	270
(-) Dep.	100	100	100
PBIT	170	170	170
(-) Interest	26.7	16.8	7.2
PBT	143.3	153.2	162.8
(-) Tax 40%	57.32	61.28	65.12
PAT	85.98	91.92	97.68
DSCR			
$\frac{\text{PBIT} + \text{D} - \text{Tax}}{\text{I} + \text{P. Inst.}}$	= 1.99	= 2.16	= 2.35

Project Report

Name of the borrower: ______ Ltd.,

Term Loan Amt : ₹ 240 crore

Rate of Interest : 12%/14%.

Loan Period : 3 years

1. Financial Feasibility

(a) The cost of the project is ₹ 400 crore. Hence debt equity ratio is 1.50. (240/160)

(b) Own funds available are more than required by ₹ 40 crore. (200 – 160)

(c) The company has never defaulted in the previous borrowing. It indicates good credit standing.

(d) Profitability ratios and DSCR are satisfactory.

2. Technical Feasibility

3. Economic Feasibility

4. Management Competence

An established company wants to start a new project.

5. Market Appraisal

Q. 7. (a) Mr. Anil Sane a fresh MBA wishes to start a manufacturing unit from his ancestral factory premises. He has ₹ 1,05,200 in his bank account. His parents have promised to gift him ₹ 3,50,000.

He has estimated the project cost at ₹ 18,00,000 of which machinery will be ₹ 15,25,000 and the remaining amount will be for furniture and fittings. The bank finance is available to the extent of 80% of the project cost. He expects first year's sales at ₹ 40,00,000 with annual increase of 20% every year over previous year. The cost of sales will be 80% of sales. The rate of interest on loan will be 10% on reducing balance method. The loan is repayable @ ₹ 3,00,000 at the end of every year. He charges depreciation @ 20% on his fixed assets under straight-line and his other overheads for three years are ₹2,40,000, ₹3,00,000 and ₹3,60,000 per year, respectively. You are required to prepare the projected Profit and Loss account and Projected Balance Sheet for the first 3 years of operation to be presented to the bankers, assuming that the first year is also a full year of 12 months activities and rate of income tax is flat @30%.

(b) Also find out any five plus points of the above loan proposal from banker's point of view.

(MU, BMS, April 2006)

Q. 7: Solution

(a)

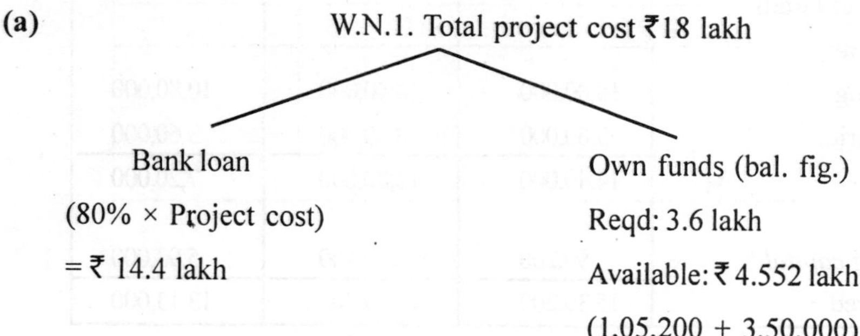

Note: The Company is advised to take bank loan to full extent, in order to undertake 'Trading on Equity'.

Loan Amortisation Schedule Equal Principal Installment Method

Year	Principal @ beg.	Int. @ 10%	Principal inst.	Loan inst.	P (o/s) at end
1	14,40,000	1,44,000	3,00,000	4,44,000	11,40,000
2	11,40,000	1,14,000	3,00,000	4,14,000	8,40,000
3	8,40,000	84,000	3,00,000	3,84,000	5,40,000

Projected Profit and Loss A/c Income Statement for year ended ______

Particulars	1	2	3
Sales	40,00,000	48,00,000	57,60,000
(-) Cost of Sales (80%)	32,00,000	38,40,000	46,08,000
Gross Profit	8,00,000	9,60,000	11,52,000
(-) Overheads	2,40,000	3,00,000	3,60,000
PBDIT	5,60,000	6,60,000	7,92,000
(-) Depric. (20% × 18L)	3,60,000	3,60,000	3,60,000
PBIT	2,00,000	3,00,000	4,32,000
(-) Interest	1,44,000	11,40,000	84,000
PBT	56,000	1,86,000	3,48,000
(-) Tax 30%	16,800	55,800	1,04,400
PAT	39,200	1,30,200	2,43,600

Projected Balance Sheet as on

Particulars	Year 1	Year 2	Year 3
1. Sources of Funds			
A. Owner's Funds			
Capital	3,60,000	3,99,200	5,29,400
+ Profit	39,200	1,30,200	2,43,600
A]	3,99,200	5,29,400	7,73,000
B. Borrowed Funds			
Bank Loan B]	11,40,000	8,40,000	5,40,000
Capital Employed → (A + B)	15,39,200	13,69,400	13,13,000
2. Application of Funds			
A. Fixed Asset			
Opening	18,00,000	14,40,000	10,80,000
(-) Depric.	3,60,000	3,60,000	3,60,000
A]	14,40,000	10,80,000	7,20,000
B. Working capital *	99,200	2,89,400	5,93,000
Capital Employed	15,39,200	13,69,400	13,13,000

Note: Working capital is taken as balance figure.

(b) Five positive points from Banker's point of view

1. Financial Feasibility

(a) Ancestral factory premises, No gestation time. No charge on factory premises, i.e., greater quality of security for loan.

(b) Own funds available ₹ 4,55,200 is more than required amount of ₹ 3,60,000 by ₹ 95,200. Also, no burden of repayment.

(c) Projected increase in sales by 20%

(d) High profitability ratios/DSCR and interest coverage ratio, indicating Debt servicing capability.

2. Management Competence

The promoter is a fresh MBA, i.e., young qualified promoter.

Q. 8. You are a Chief Manager of a branch of a leading Private Sector Bank. In the first week of March 2010, the management of the bank wishes to disburse maximum loans as huge amount of deposits are lying idle. The Credit Appraisal Department of your branch has shortlisted three loan proposals. On the basis of the following summarized information, you are required to help the management to select the best possible proposal by listing the merits and demerits of each project separately –

Particulars	Project A	Project B	Project C
Cost of Project	120	150	100
Loan required	100	110	80
Rate of Interest	12%	12%	11%
Depreciation (on cost of project)	15%	10%	20%
Average yearly Net Profit before tax	35	50	30
Rate of Tax	30%	30%	30%
Repayment period in years	6	5	7
Security Offered	Machinery	Land and Building	Bank Deposits

(MU, BMS, April 2010)

Q. 8: Solution

Important Ratios

	Project A	Project B	Project C
1. Debt Equity ratio			
$= \frac{\text{Debt.}}{\text{Equity}}$	$= \frac{100}{20} = 5$	$\frac{110}{40} = 2.75$	$\frac{80}{20} = 4$
Rank	III	I	II
2. Return on Inv.			
$= \frac{\text{PBIT}}{\text{Cap E}} \times 100$	$= \frac{35 + 12}{120} \times 100$	$= \frac{50 + 13.2}{150} \times 100$	$= \frac{30 + 8.8}{100} \times 100$
	= 39.17%	= 42.13%	= 38.8%
Rank	II	I	III

3. Interest Coverage ratio			
$= \frac{\text{PBIT}}{\text{Int.}}$	$\frac{35 + 12}{12}$	$\frac{50 + 13.2}{13.2}$	$\frac{30 + 8.8}{8.8}$
	= 3.92 times	4.79 times	4.41 times
Rank	III	I	II
4. DSCR			
$\frac{\text{PBIT + Debt − Tax}}{\text{Int + (P) Inst}}$	$= \frac{47 + 18 - 10.5}{12 + 16.67}$	$= \frac{63.2 + 15 - 15}{13.2 + 22}$	$\frac{38.8 + 20 - 9}{8.8 + 11.43}$
	$= \frac{54.5}{28.67}$	$= \frac{63.2}{35.2}$	$= \frac{49.8}{20.23}$
	= 1.9 times	= 1.80 times	= 2.46 times
Rank	II	III	I

Notes: 1. Ratios are calculated for the first year.

2. It is assumed that loan is paid in equal principal installment.

Project A

Merits

1. Reasonably high ROI, i.e., 39.17%.
2. DSCR 1.9 times higher than standard 1.5.
3. Satisfactory interest coverage ratio 3.92 times.

Demerits

1. High Debt Equity ratio, i.e., 5
2. Machinery as security which is subject to reduction in value over the years due to depreciation.

Project B

Merits

1. Lowest debt equity ratio amongst three companies, i.e., 2.75 times.
2. Highest ROI amongst three companies, i.e., 42.13%.
3. Highest interest coverage ratio amongst three companies, i.e., 4.79 times.
4. DSCR 1.8 times higher than standard 1.5.
5. Land and Building offered as security which is generally subject to appreciation over the years.

Demerits

1. Debt equity ratio even though lowest amongst three companies is higher than the standard 2.

Project C

Merits

1. Reasonably high ROI, i.e., 38.8%.
2. Reasonably high interest coverage ratio 4.41 times.
3. Highest DSCR amongst three companies, i.e., 2.46 times.
4. Bank deposit as security is the best possible security as it can be very easily converted into money in case of default and is not subject to fluctuations in value.

Demerits

(a) High debt equity ratio, i.e., 4.

(b) Longest repayment period, i.e., 7 years amongst three companies.

Conclusion

Based on the above merits and demerits of each project my recommendation is to select Project B. Second best choice is Project C because of high quality of security.

Q.9. Complete the following income statement of Uninor Ltd., for the year ended 31 March.

Income Statement of Uninor Ltd.,

Particulars	31st March, 2004 ₹	31st March, 2005 ₹	31st March, 2006 ₹	31st March, 2007 ₹	31st March, 2008 ₹	31st March, 2009 ₹
Sales	50,00,000	60,00,000	70,00,000	?	?	?
Less: Cost of Sales	30,00,000	36,00,000	42,00,000	?	?	?
Gross Margin	**20,00,000**	**24,00,000**	**28,00,000**	**?**	**?**	**?**
Less: **Operating Expenses**						
(A) Management Expenses	3,00,000	3,20,000	3,40,000	?	?	?
(B) Sales Expenses	5,00,000	6,00,000	7,00,000	?	?	?
(C) Finance Expenses (Interest on Debentures)	3,00,000	3,00,000	3,00,000	?	?	?
Total Expenses (A+B+C)	**11,00,000**	**12,20,000**	**13,40,000**	**?**	**?**	**?**
Net Profit before Tax and Depreciation	9,00,000	11,80,000	14,60,000	?	?	?
Less: Depreciation	5,00,000	4,00,000	3,20,000	?	?	?
Net Profit before Tax	4,00,000	7,80,000	11,40,000	?	?	?
Less: Tax @50%	2,00,000	3,90,000	5,70,000	?	?	?
Net Profit after Tax	**2,00,000**	**3,90,000**	**5,70,000**	**?**	**?**	**?**

Additional Information:

1. Percentage of gross margin will remain the same for the year ended 31st March, 07, 31st March, 08 and 31st March, 09.
2. Variable Management Expenses are 2% of sales.
3. Sales expenses are 10% of sales.
4. 10% debentures are to be redeemed in 3 annual equal instalments commencing from 31 March, 07.

Additions to the fixed assets will be made on 1st April, 06 amounting to ₹ 12,20,000 and rate of depreciation will remain the same, i.e., 20% p.a. on W.D.V. Calculate DSCR.

Q. 9: Solution

Income Statement of Uninor Ltd., for year ended 31st March

Particulars	31st March, 2004 ₹	31st March, 2005 ₹	31st March, 2006 ₹	31st March, 2007 ₹	31st March, 2008 ₹	31st March, 2009 ₹
Sales	50,00,000	60,00,000	70,00,000	80,00,000	90,00,000	1,00,00,000
Less: Cost of Sales	30,00,000	36,00,000	42,00,000	48,00,000	54,00,000	60,00,000
Gross Margin	**20,00,000**	**24,00,000**	**28,00,000**	**32,00,000**	**36,00,000**	**40,00,000**
Less: **Operating Expenses**						
(A) Management Expenses	3,00,000	3,20,000	3,40,000	3,60,000	3,80,000	4,00,000
(B) Sales Expenses	5,00,000	6,00,000	7,00,000	8,00,000	9,00,000	10,00,000
(C) Finance Expenses (Interest on Debentures)	3,00,000	3,00,000	3,00,000	3,00,000	2,00,000	1,00,000
Total Expenses (A+B+C)	**11,00,000**	**12,20,000**	**13,40,000**	**14,60,000**	**14,80,000**	**15,00,000**
Net Profit before Tax and Depric.	9,00,000	11,80,000	14,60,000	17,40,000	21,20,000	25,00,000
Less: Depreciation	5,00,000	4,00,000	3,20,000	5,00,000	4,00,000	3,20,000
Net Profit before Tax	4,00,000	7,80,000	11,40,000	12,40,000	17,20,000	21,80,000
Less: Tax @50%	2,00,000	3,90,000	5,70,000	6,20,000	8,60,000	10,90,000
Net Profit after Tax	**2,00,000**	**3,90,000**	**5,70,000**	**6,20,000**	**8,60,000**	**10,90,000**

$$\text{DSCR} = \frac{\text{PBIT} + \text{Depr} - \text{Tax}}{\text{Int.} + \text{(P)Inst.}}$$

$$2007 = \frac{1{,}540 + 500 - 620}{1{,}300} = 1.09$$

$$2008 = \frac{1{,}920 + 400 - 860}{1{,}200} = 1.22$$

$$2009 = \frac{2{,}280 + 320 - 1090}{1{,}100} = 1.37$$

Note: In the absence of information, it is assured that sales increases by ₹10,00,000 every year.

Workings:

1. Management Expenses:

Particulars	2004 ₹	2005 ₹	2006 ₹	2007 ₹	2008 ₹	2009 ₹
Variable	1,00,000	1,20,000	1,40,000	1,60,000	1,80,000	2,00,000
Fixed *	2,00,000	2,00,000	2,00,000	2,00,000	2,00,000	2,00,000
Total	**3,00,000**	**3,20,000**	**3,40,000**	**3,60,000**	**3,80,000**	**4,00,000**

* bal. figure

2. Interest on Debentures:

		₹
Year Ending 2007:	3,00,000 × 3/3	=3,00,000
Year Ending 2008:	3,00,000 × 2/3	=2,00,000
Year Ending 2009:	3,00,000 × 1/3	= 1,00,000

3. Fixed Assets:

Calculation at depreciation

Particulars	₹
1 – 4 – 2005 WDV @ 100%	16,00,000
Less: Depreciation @ 20% WDV	3,20,000
1 – 4 – 2006 WDV @ 80%	12,80,000
Add: Addition on 1-4-06	12,20,000
1 – 4 – 2006 WDV	25,00,000
Depreciation for 2006 – 07	5,00,000
Depreciation for 2007 – 08	4,00,000
Depreciation for 2008 – 09	3,20,000

Q.10. Mr. Anil Kumar is carrying out retail business in electronic items. After observing trade practices, he has decided to start a small-scale manufacturing unit to produce electrical fittings. His Balance Sheet as on 31-3-2007, before starting manufacturing activities, is as under:

Liabilities	₹	**Assets**	
Capital	5,55,500	Furniture	40,000
		Computer	60,000
		Investments	1,50,000
		Fixed deposits with bank	2,00,000
		Cash and Bank balance	1,05,500
	5,55,500		**5,55,500**

In order to carry-out new activity he will take factory premises on a rental basis "@ ₹ 10,000 p.m. from 1.9.2007 and from 1.4.2008 the rent will be ₹ 15,000 p.m. He is confident of setting up manufacturing unit by 30.8.2007 and start manufacturing and selling from 1st September, 2007.

The cost of machineries will be ₹ 10,00,000 for which he will be approaching Bank of Baroda for term loan of ₹ 8,00,000, balance being his own contribution. The loan repayment will start from 1.4.2008, in the quarterly instalment of ₹ 50,000 payable on 1st April, 1st July, 1st October, and 1st January every year.

He will have no income in financial year 2007-08 till setting up of the unit, i.e., up to 30-8-2007. Thereafter he expects his sales to be ₹ 80,000 p.m. from 1-9-2007 to 31-3-2008 and afterwards every year ₹ 18,00,000 with yearly increment of 10% over the previous year.

His cost structure will remain more or less unchanged up to 31-3-2010 and cost break up on sales will be: Direct ost @ 40%, Office Overheads 20%, Selling and Distribution 5%, Depreciation will be charged on all fixed assets @ 10% under W.D.V. (full year's depreciation even if the assets are used for a part of the year) and interest for first year ending 31-3-2008 will be ₹ 59,000 and thereafter it will be at ₹ 70,000, ₹ 54,000 and ₹ 43,000 respectively for subsequent years.

You are required to prepare Projected Statement of Profit and Loss for the financial years 2007-08, 2008-09 and 2009-10. Calculate Interest coverage ratio.

Q. 10: Solution

Projected Profit and Loss Statement **(All figures in ₹)**

Particulars	**2007-08**	**2008-09**	**2009-10**
Sales	5,60,000	18,00,000	19,80,000
Less: **Expenses:**			
Direct Cost (40% Sales)	2,24,000	7,20,000	7,92,000
Office Overheads (20% Sales)	1,12,000	3,60,000	3,96,000
Selling and Distribution Overheads (5% Sales)	28,000	90,000	99,000
Factory Rent	70,000	1,80,000	1,80,000
PBDIT	**1,26,000**	**4,50,000**	**5,13,000**
Less: **Depreciation on:**			
Furniture	4,000	3,600	3,240
Computer	6,000	5,400	4,860
Machinery	1,00,000	90,000	81,000
PBIT	**16,000**	**3,51,000**	**4,23,900**
Less: Interest on Term Loan	59,000	70,000	54,000
NPBT	**(43,000)**	**2,81,000**	**3,69,900**

Working Notes:

1. Factory Rent

01/09/2007 to 31/03/2008 (7 months) @ ₹ 10,000 p.m. = ₹70,000

01/04/2008 to 31/03/2009 and 01/04/2009 to 31/03/2010 (12 months) @ ₹15,000 p.m. = ₹1,80,000 p.a.

2. Sales

01/09/2007 to 31/03/2008 (7 months) @ ₹ 80,000 p.m. = ₹5,60,000

01/04/2008 to 31/03/2009 = ₹18,00,000

01/04/2009 to 31/03/2010 = ₹18,00,000 + 10% = ₹19,80,000

3. Cost Break-up

Direct Cost 40% × Sales

Office Overheads 20% × Sales

S and D Overheads 5% × Sales

4. Depreciation on all fixed assets

@ 10% WDV Method

Particulars	Furniture	Computer	Machinery
WDV/Cost	40,000	60,000	10,00,000
Depreciation 07-08	4,000	6,0001	.,00,000
WDV	36,000	54,000	9,00,000
Depreciation 08-09	3,600	5,400	90,000
WDV	32,400	48,600	8,10,000
Depreciation 09-10	3,240	4,860	81,000

$$\text{Interest Coverage Ratio} = \frac{\text{PBIT}}{\text{Int}}$$

$$\text{Year 1} = \frac{16,000}{59,000} = 0.27 \text{ times}$$

$$\text{Year 2} = \frac{3,51,000}{70,000} = 5.01 \text{ times}$$

$$\text{Year 3} = \frac{4,23,000}{54,000} = 7.85 \text{ times}$$

Extra Practice Problems

Q. 11. Prepare an amortization schedule from the following information, assuming that the amount is an equated annual instalment. Amount borrowed = ₹12,00,000, compound Annual Interest = @10%. Repayment period = 10 years. Annuity factor @10% for the 10 years is 6.145.

Q. 12. Prepare an amortization schedule from the following information, assuming that the principal amount is repayable equally along with interest payable on unpaid loans.

Amount Borrowed	₹9,50,000
Annual Interest	@10%
Repayment Period	5 years

Q. 13. Prepare an amortization schedule from the following information, assuming that the principal amount is repayable equally along with interest payable on outstanding loans.

Amount Borrowed	₹6,00,000
Annual Interest	@11%
Repayment Period	6 years

Q. 14. Prepare an amortization schedule from the following information, Amount to be borrowed is ₹ 4,00,000. It will carry an interest rate of 14% p.a. on reducing balance basis. Term of loan is 5 years. One year moratorium on principal will be available after which, it will be payable in eight equal half-yearly instalments.

Q. 15. Calculate the important ratios for granting term loans and give your recommendations from the following information

Year	**I**	**II**	**III (₹ in lakh)**
Profit before Interest and Tax	50.00	60.00	70.00
Interest on Term Loan @12%	36.00	24.00	12.00
Tax Rate 35%			

Loan is repayable in equal instalments at the end of each of the 3 years along with interest. Investment in project: ₹ 500 lakh. Depreciation for the project is ₹150 lakh every year. List out the other considerations to be borne in mind while assessing term loan proposal.

Q. 16. Calculate the important ratios for granting term loans and give your recommendations from the given projections:-

(₹ in millions)

Year	**2010**	**2011**	**2012**	**2013**	**2014**
EBIT	560	630	700	735	805

Additional Information:

1. Tax Rate @ 30%
2. Principal amount of loan is repayable equally along with interest payable on outstanding loans at the end of each year.
3. Loan amount in consideration ₹ 1,750 million at the rate of 9% p.a.
4. Repayment tenure 5 years.
5. Total Capital Investment: ₹ 2,500 million depreciable equally over 5 years.

CHAPTER 9 SHORT-TERM AND LONG-TERM SOURCES OF FINANCE

Finance is the lifeblood of an organization can exist without it. Finance is required because receipts do not match expenditure, inflows do not match outflows. Sources of finance are categorized in three ways:

1. According to the period, i.e., short, medium and long-term
2. According to the ownership, i.e., owners fund and borrowed funds
3. According to the generation, i.e., internal and external sources

9.1 SHORT-TERM SOURCES OF FINANCE

Short-terms finances are required primarily to meet working capital requirements. The focus is on maintaining liquidity at a reasonable cost. The various sources of short-term finance are:

1. Trade Credit: This is the credit extended by suppliers of material and other resources.

2. Cash Credits/Overdrafts: Under this arrangement the borrower can borrow up to a fixed limit and repay it as and when he desires. Interest is charged only running balance and not on the sanctioned amount. A minimal charge is payable for availing this facility.

3. Loans Repayable in One Year: They are either credited to the current of the borrower or given to him in cash. A fixed rate of interest is charged and the loan amount is repayable on demand or in periodical instalments.

4. Purchase/Discount of Bills: A bill may be discounted with the bank and when it matures on a future date the bank collects the amount from the party who had excepted the bill. When a bank is short of funds it can sell or rediscount the bill on the other hand the bank with surplus funds would invest in bill. However, with discount rate at 10-11 per cent for 90-day paper, bill discounting is an expensive sources of short-term funds.

5. Letter of Credit: A letter of credit (L/C) is an instrument issued by a bank on behalf of an importer, whereby the bank agrees to honour the draft drawn on the importer provided certain conditions are satisfied. Through the letter of credit arrangement, the credit of the importer is substituted by the credit of the bank. Hence, it virtually eliminates the risk of the exporter when he sells to an unknown importer in a foreign country. When an L/C is opened by the bank in favour of the customer it takes the responsibility of honouring the obligation in case the customer fails to do so. In this case even though the customer provides the credit the risk is borne by the bank.

6. Inter-corporate Deposits: A deposit made by one company with another, normally for a period of up to 6 months is referred to as an inter-corporate deposit. Such deposit are usually of three types:

(a) **Call Deposits:** In theory, a call deposit is withdrawable by the lender on giving a days notice. In practice, however, the lender has to wait for at least three days.

(b) **Three-months Deposits:** More popular in practice, these deposits are taken by borrowers to tide over a short-term cash inadequacy that may be caused due to one or more of the following factors: disruption in production, excessive imports of raw material, tax payment delay in collection, dividend payment, and unplanned capital expenditure.

(c) **Six-months Deposits:** Normally, lending companies do not extend deposits beyond this timeframe. Such deposits are usually made with first-class borrowers.

As inter-corporate deposits represent unsecured borrowing, the lending company must satisfy itself about the creditworthiness of the borrowing firm.

Characteristics of the Inter-corporate Deposit Market:

(a) **Lack of Regulation:** The lack of legal hassles and bureaucratic red tapism makes an inter-corporate deposit transaction very convenient.

(b) **Secrecy:** Brokers are discreet about their lists of borrowers and lenders.

(c) **Importance of Personal Contacts:** Lending decisions in the inter-corporate deposit markets are based on personal contacts and market information which may sometime lack reliability.

7. Short-term Loan From Financial Institution: The Life Insurance Corporation of India, The General Insurance Corporation of India and The Unit Trust of India provide short-term loans to manufacturing companies with an excellent track record.

Features:

(a) They are totally unsecured.

(b) The loan is given for the period of one year and can be renewed for two consecutive years, provided the original eligibility criteria are satisfied.

(c) After a loan is repaid, the company has to wait for at least six months before availing of a fresh loan.

(d) The loans carry a higher interest rate. However, there is a rebate of 1% for prompt payment.

8. Commercial Paper (CP): Large firms who are financially strong issue commercial paper. It represents a short-term unsecured promissory note issued by firms of high credit rating.

Its important features include:

1. Maturity ranges from 90-180 days.
2. It is sold at a discount from its face value and redeemed at its face value. Thus the implicit interest rate is a function of size of the discount and the period of maturity.
3. CPs are either directly placed with investors or sold though dealers/merchant bankers. Usually bought by investors who keep it till the maturity and hence there is no well-developed secondary market.

Who can issue CP?

Highly rated listed companies, primary dealers and All-India financial institutions have been permitted to raise short-term resources.

Eligibility of Issuing CP

Minimum tangible net worth as per latest audited balance sheet is ₹ 5 crore.

Company has been sanctioned working capital limit by bank(s) or all-India financial institution(s), and the company is classified as a standard asset by the financing bank(s) institution(s)

Minimum Credit Rating required from recognised credit rating agencies

Maturity period of CP

The CP can be issued for maturities between 15 days to one year from the date of its issue.

Minimum amount of investment and denomination of CP

The minimum amount required to be invested by a single investor is at least ₹ 5 lakh. It is issued in denominations of ₹ 5 lakh or multiples thereof.

9. Factoring: Factoring is a financial transaction whereby a business sells its accounts receivables at discount to a factor. The three parties directly are: the seller, debtor, and the factor. The seller is owed money (usually for worked performed or goods sold) by the second party, the debtor. The seller then sells the debtor's accounts at a discount to the third party, the factor. The debtor then directly pays the factor the full value of invoice.

Factoring differs from a bank loan in three main ways. First, the emphasis is on the value of the receivables, not the firm's creditworthiness. Secondly, factoring is not a loan it is the purchased of an asset (the receivable). Finally, a bank loan involves two parties, whereas factoring involves three.

Features of Factoring Arrangement:

(a) The factor selects the account of the client that would be bought by it.

(b) The factor assumes responsibility for collecting the debt of accounts handled by it.

(c) The factor advance money to the client against not-yet-collected and not-yet-due debts. Typically the amount advanced is 70-80% of the face value of the debt and carries an interest rate, which may be equal to or marginally higher than the lending rate of commercial banks.

(d) Factoring may be on a recourse basis or non-recourse basis (full credit risk). (Presently, in India it is done only on a recourse basis)

Forfaiting is similar to factoring. It is the purchasing of an exporter's receivables (the amount importers owe the exporter) at a discount by paying cash. The forfaiter, the purchaser of the receivables), becomes the entity to whom the importer is obliged to pay its debt. By purchasing these receivables which are usually guaranteed by the importer's bank the forfaiter frees the exporter from credit and from the risk of not receiving payment from the importer who purchased the goods on credit.

9.2 SOURCES OF LONG-TERM FINANCE

Introduction

As you are aware of finance is the lifeblood of business. It is of vital significance for modern business which requires huge capital. Funds required for a business may be classified as long-term and short-term. You have learnt about short-term finance in the previous Part. Finance is required for a long period also. It is required for purchasing fixed assets like land and building, machinery, etc. Even a portion of working capital, which is required to meet day-to-day expenses, is of a permanent nature. To

finance if we require long-term capital. The amount of long-term capital depends upon the scale of business and nature of business. In this lesson, you will learn about various sources of long-term finance and the advantages and disadvantages of each source.

Long-term Finance - Its Meaning and Purpose

A business requires funds to purchase fixed assets like land and building, plant and machinery, furniture, etc. These assets may be regarded as the foundation of a business. The capital required for these assets is called fixed capital. A part of the working capital is also of a permanent nature. Funds required for this part of the working capital and for fixed capital is called long-term finance.

Purpose of Long-term Finance:

Long-term finance is required for the following purposes:

1. **To Finance Fixed Assets:** Business requires fixed assets like machines, building, furniture, etc. Finance required to buy these assets is for a long period, because such assets can be used for a long period and are not for resale.
2. **To Finance the Permanent Part of Working Capital:** Business is a continuing activity. It must have a certain amount of working capital which would be needed again and again. This part of working capital is of a fixed or permanent nature. This requirement is also met through long-term funds.
3. **To Finance Growth and Expansion of Business:** Expansion of business requires investment of a huge amount of capital permanently or for a long period.

9.3 FACTORS DETERMINING LONG-TERM FINANCIAL REQUIREMENTS

The amount required to meet the long-term capital needs of a company depends upon many factors. These are:

(a) **Nature of Business:** The nature and character of a business determines the amount of fixed capital. A manufacturing company requires land, building, machines, etc. So, it has to invest a large amount of capital for a long period. But a trading concern dealing in, say, washing machines will require a smaller amount of long-term fund because it does not have to buy building or machines.

(b) **Nature of Goods Produced:** If a business is engaged in manufacturing small and simple articles it will require a smaller amount of fixed capital as compared to one manufacturing heavy machines or heavy consumer items like cars, refrigerators, etc., which will require more fixed capital.

(c) **Technology Used:** In heavy industries like steel/cement the fixed capital investment is larger than in the case of a business producing plastic jars using simple technology or producing goods using labour-intensive technique or service sector companies.

9.4 SOURCES OF LONG-TERM FINANCE

The main sources of long-term finance are as follows:

1. Shares

These are issued to the general public. These may be of two types: (i) Equity, and (ii) Preference. The holders of shares are the owners of the business.

2. **Debentures:** These are also issued to the general public. The holders of debentures are the creditors of the company.

3. **Retained Earnings:** The Company may not distribute the whole of its profits among its shareholders. It may retain a part of the profits and utilize it as capital.

4. **Public Deposits:** General public also like to deposit their savings with a popular and well-established company which can pay interest periodically and pay back the deposit when due.

5. **Term Loans from Banks:** Many industrial development banks, cooperative banks and commercial banks grant medium-term loans for a period of three to five years.

6. **Loan from Financial Institutions:** There are many specialised financial institutions established by the Central and State Governments which give long-term loans at reasonable rate of interest. Some of these institutions are: Industrial Finance Corporation of India (IFCI), Industrial Development Bank of India (IDBI), Industrial Credit and Investment Corporation of India (ICICI), Unit Trust of India (UTI), State Finance Corporations, etc.

7. **American Depository Receipts (ADR):** ADR is a stock, which trades in United States but represents a specified number of shares in a foreign corporation. Indian companies having capital demands that are more than the availability of finance at home can issue 'ADR'.

8. **Global Depository Receipts (GDR):** GDRs are essentially instrument created by overseas depository bank that are authorised by issuing companies in India to issue instrument outside the country.

9. **Lease Financing:** In the recent years, the lease financing has emerged as one of the most important sources of long-term financing. Under the leasing arrangement the company acquires the right to use the asset from lessor without holding the title to it.

10. **Hire Purchase:** In case of hire purchase transaction, the asset is delivered by the owner to company on the agreement that company pays the agreed amount in periodical instalments.

11. **Venture Capital:** Venture capital is money provided by professional institutions who invest along side management in young, rapidly growing companies that have the potential to develop into significant economic companies.

12. **External Commercial Borrowing (ECB):** The guiding principles of ECB policy is government desire of maintaining prudent limits for total external borrowing and at the same time giving flexibility to corporates.

13. **Euro Bond and Foreign Bond:** A company can raise fund by issuing Euro bond and foreign bond to investors in other countries.

14. **Government Subsidies:** Government subsidies are the concessions and incentives given by government to lower the commodity price in public interest.

15. **Securitization:** Securitization is a structured finance process that distributes risk by aggregating assets in a pool (often by selling assets to a special purpose entity), then issuing new securities backed by the assets and their cashflows. The securities are sold to investors who share the risk and reward from those assets.

In Text Question 9.1

A. Fill in the blanks with appropriate words given within brackets against each sentence.

1. Long-term finance is required for _______________ (Fixed Assets/Current Assets)
2. Long-term sources of finance are also required for_______________ of working capital (whole/permanent part)
3. Investment in machines require _________ (Short-term finance/long-term finance)
4. Fixed capital requirement is more in __________ business (manufacturing/trading).

B. Name the long-term source of finance in the following cases:

1. A part of profits of the company that is used as capital.
2. Savings of the public invested in companies for safety and interest earning.
3. Available to a company as ownership capital.
4. Long-term loans from the public.

1. Shares

Issue of shares is the main source of long-term finance. Shares are issued by joint stock companies to the public. A company divides its capital into units of a definite face value, say of ₹ 10 each or ₹ 100 each. Each unit is called a share. A person holding shares is called a shareholder.

Characteristics of shares:

The main characteristics of shares are following:

1. It is a unit of capital of the company.
2. Each share is of a definite face value.
3. A share certificate is issued to a shareholder indicating the number of shares and the face value amount.
4. Each share has a distinct number.
5. The face value of a share indicates the interest of a person in the company and the extent of his liability.
6. Shares are transferable units.

Investors are of different habits and temperaments. Some want to take lesser risk and are interested in a regular income. There are others who may take greater risk in anticipation of huge profits in future. In order to tap the savings of different types of people, a company may issue different types of shares. These are:

- Preference shares, and
- Equity shares.

Preference Shares: Preference shares are the shares which carry preferential rights over the equity shares. These rights are: (a) receiving dividends at a fixed rate, (b) priority in getting back the capital in case the company is wound up or after fixed period. Investments in these shares are relatively safe, and a preference shareholder also gets dividend regularly.

Equity Shares: Equity shares are shares which do not enjoy any preferential right in the matter of payment of dividend or repayment of capital. The equity shareholder gets dividend only after the payment of dividends to the preference shares. There is no fixed rate of dividend for equity shareholders. The rate of dividend depends upon the surplus profits. In case of winding up of a company, the equity share capital is refunded only after refunding the preference share capital. Equity shareholders have the right to take part in the management of the company. However, equity shares also carry more risk. They have the potential of high returns.

Following are the merits and demerits of equity shares:

(a) Merits

(A) To the shareholders:

1. In case there are good profits, the company pays dividend to the equity shareholders at a higher rate.
2. The value of equity shares, i.e., price goes up in the stock market with the increase in profits of the concern.
3. Equity shares can be easily sold in the stock market.
4. Equity shareholders have greater say in the management of a company as they are conferred voting rights by the Articles of Association.

(B) To the Management:

1. Acompany can raise fixed capital by issuing equity shares without creating any charge on its fixed assets.
2. The capital raised by issuing equity shares is not required to be paid back during the lifetime of the company. It will be paid back only if the company is wound up.
3. There is no liability on the company regarding payment of dividend on equity shares. The company may declare dividends only if there are enough profits.
4. If a company raises more capital by issuing equity shares, it leads to greater confidence among the investors, lenders and creditors.

(b) Demerits:

(A) To the Shareholders:

1. **Uncertainly about Payment of Dividend:** Equity shareholders get dividend only when the company is earning sufficient profits and the Board of Directors declare dividend. If there are preference shareholders, equity shareholders get dividend only after payment of dividend to the preference shareholders.
2. **Speculative:** Often there is speculation on the prices of equity shares. This is particularly so in times of boom and doom. In bull market price of equity shares generally rise more than the fundamentals of the company deserve and vice versa.
3. **Danger of Overcapitalisation:** In case the management miscalculates the long-term financial requirements, it may raise more funds than required by issuing shares. This may amount to overcapitalization which in turn leads to low value of shares in the stockmarket.
4. **Ownership in Name Only:** Holding of equity shares in a company makes the holder one of the owners of the company. Such shareholders enjoy voting rights. They manage and control the company. But then it is all in theory. In practice, a handful of persons, (i.e., promoters) control the votes and manage the company. Moreover, the decision to declare dividend rests with the Board of Directors.

5. **Higher Risk:** Equity shareholders bear a very high degree of risk. In case of losses they do not get dividend. In case of winding up of a company, they are the very last to get refund of the money invested. Equity shares actually swim and sink with the company.

(B) To the Management

1. **No Trading on Equity:** Trading on equity means ability of a company to raise funds through preference shares, debentures and bank loans, etc. On such funds the company has to pay at a fixed rate. This enables equity shareholders to enjoy a higher rate of return when profits are large. The major part of the profit earned is paid to the equity shareholders because borrowed funds carry only a fixed rate of interest. But if a company has only equity shares and does not have either preference shares, debentures or loans, it cannot have the advantage of trading on equity.
2. **Conflict of Interests:** As the equity shareholders carry voting rights, groups are formed to corner the votes and grab the control of the company. There develops conflict of interests which is harmful for the smooth functioning of a company (e.g., Ranbaxy Ltd.,)

Difference Between Preference Shares and Equity Shares: We have learnt the meaning and the feature of preference and equity shares. Now we can differentiate between the two.

Basic of Difference	Preference Shares	Equity Shares
1. Choice	It is not compulsory to issue these shares	It is compulsory to issue the shares.
2. Payment of dividend	Dividend is paid on these shares in preference to the equity shares.	Dividend is paid on these shares only after paying dividend on preference shares.
3. Return of capital	In case of winding up of a company the capital is refunded in preference over the equity shares	Capital of these shares is refunded in case of winding up of the company after refund of preference share capital.
4. Risk/return potential	Generally low	Generally high

Various Options for issuing Equity shares

1. Public offer *(Domestic)*
   - IPO
   - FPO
   - IDR

   (International)
   - ADR, GDR
2. Pvt. Offer/Pvt. Placement
   - Preferential Allotment
   - Qualified Institutional placement.
   - Warrants
   - ESOP
   - Sweat Equity

- Issue of shares for consideration other than cash (for e.g., merger, acquisition, etc.)
- Rights Issue
- Bonus Issue

3. Others (in both Public and Pvt. offer)
   - Convertible Preference Shares
   - Convertible debentures/bonds

In Text Question 9.2

A. Following are the characteristics either of equity shares or of preference shares. Put the appropriate characteristics against:

(a) Equity shares, and (b) preference shares:

(i) No fixed rate of dividend.

(ii) Carry maximum risk.

(iii) Priority regarding payment of dividend and repayment of capital.

(iv) Provides scope for trading on equity.

B. Following are the merits and demerits of equity shares. Classify them as:

(a) Merits to shareholders, (b) Demerits to shareholders, (c) Merits to management, (d) Demerits to management.

(i) In case of good profits, company pays higher dividend

(ii) Benefit of trading on equity will not be available

(iii) It helps in creating more confidence among the investors and creditors

(iv) No certainty of payment of dividends.

2. Debenture

Whenever a company wants to borrow a large amount of fund for a long but fixed period, it can borrow from the general public by issuing loan certificates called debentures. The total amount to be borrowed is divided into units of fixed amount say of ₹ 100 each. These units are called debentures. These are offered to the public to subscribe in the same manner as is done in the case of shares. A debenture is issued under the common seal of the company. It is a written acknowledgement of money borrowed. It specifies the terms and conditions, such as rate of interest, time of repayment, security offered, etc.

Characteristics of Debentures

Following are the characteristics of debentures:

(i) Debentureholders are the creditors of the company. They are entitled to periodic payment of interest at a fixed rate.

(ii) Debentures are repayable after a fixed period of time, say five years or seven years as per agreed terms.

(iii) Debentureholders do not carry voting rights.

(iv) Ordinarily, debentures are secured. In case the company fails to pay interest on debentures or repay the principal amount, the debentureholders can recover it from the sale of the assets of the company.

Types of Debentures:

Debentures may be classified as:

(a) Redeemable Debentures and Irredeemable Debentures

(b) Convertible Debentures and Non-convertible Debentures.

Redeemable Debentures:

These are debentures repayable on a predetermined date or at any time prior to their maturity, provided the company so desires and gives a notice to that effect.

Irredeemable Debentures:

These are also called perpetual debentures. A company is not bound to repay the amount during its lifetime. If the issuing company fails to pay the interest, it has to redeem such debentures.

Convertible Debentures:

The holders of these debentures are given the option to convert their debentures into equity shares at a time and in a ratio as decided by the company.

Non-convertible Debentures:

These debentures cannot be converted into shares.

Merits of Debentures:

Following are some of the advantages of debentures:

1. Raising Funds without Allowing Control Over the Company: Debentureholders have no right either to vote or take part in the management of the company.

2. Reliable Source of Long-term Finance: Since debentures are ordinarily issued for a fixed period, the company can make the best use of the money. It helps long-term planning.

3. Tax Benefits: Interest paid on debentures is treated as an expense and is charged to the profits of the company. The company thus saves income tax.

4. Investors' Safety: Debentures are mostly secured. On winding up of the company, they are repayable before any payment is made to the shareholders. Interest on debentures is payable irrespective of profit or loss.

Demerits:

1. As the interest on debentures has to be paid every year whether there are profits or not, it becomes burdensome in case the company incurs losses.

2. Usually the debentures are secured. The company creates a charge on its assets in favour of debentureholders. So, a company which does not own enough fixed assets cannot borrow money by issuing debentures. Moreover, the assets of the company once mortgaged cannot be used for further borrowing.

3. Debenture-finance enables a company to trade on equity. But too much of such finance leaves little for shareholders, as most of the profits may be required to pay interest on debentures. This brings frustration in the minds of shareholders and the value of shares may fall in the securities markets.

4. Burdensome in times of depression: During depression the profits of the company decline. It may be difficult to pay interest on debentures. As interest goes on accumulating, it may lead to the closure of the company. Until now you have learnt about issue of shares and debentures as two main sources of raising long-term finance. You have also learnt about the merits and demerits of the two. Now, let us make a comparative study of shares and debentures for raising long-term capital.

Basis	Shares	Debentures
1. Status	Shareholders are the owners of the company. They provide ownership capital which is not refundable.	Debentureholders are the creditors of the company. They provide loans generally for a fixed period. Such loans are to be paid back.
2. Nature of return on investment	Shareholders get dividends. The amount is not fixed. It depends on the profit of the company. Hence only those persons invest in shares who are ready to take risk.	Interest is paid on debentures on a fixed rate. Interest is payable even if the company is running at a loss. So, it is good investment for those who do not want to take high risk.
3. Rights.	Shareholders are the real owners of the company. They have the right to vote and frame the objectives and policies of the company.	Debentureholders do not have the right to attend meetings of the company. So they have no say in the management of the company.
4. Security	No security is required to issue shares.	Generally, debentures are secured. Therefore sufficient fixed assets are required when debentures are to be issued.
5. Order of repayment	Shareholders take the maximum risk because their capital will be paid back only after repaying the loan of debenture holders .	Debentureholders have the priority of repayment over shareholders.

In Text Question 9.3

A. Write True or False:

1. Debentureholders are the creditors of the company.
2. Debentureholders have the right to vote in the meetings of the company.
3. Interest at a fixed rate is paid on debentures.
4. Debentures carry more risk than shares.
5. Debentures are generally redeemable after a fixed period.

B. Match the following.

1. Convertible debenture.	(i) Holders have the right to recover their money from the ale of assets of the company
2. Secured debentures	(ii) Deducted from the profits of the company.
3. Interest on debentures	(iii) Permanent liability on the company.
4. Irredeemable Debentures exchange	(iv) The holders of such debentures are given the option to them for shares.

C. Following sentences relate to either shares or debentures. Put tick (√) mark in the correct box given in the table below:

(i) They provide ownership capital.

(ii) Return on these is called interest.

(iii) Return on these is called dividend.

(iv) Holders enjoy voting rights.

(v) Holders are the creditors of the company.

	(i)	(ii)	(iii)	(iv)	(v)
1. Shares					
2. Debentures					

3. Retained Earnings

Like an individual, companies also set aside a part of their profits to meet future requirements of capital. Companies keep these savings in various accounts such as General Reserve, Debenture Redemption Reserve and Dividend Equalisation Reserve, etc. These reserves can be used to meet long-term financial requirements. The portion of the profits which is not distributed among the shareholders but is retained and is used in business is called retained earnings or ploughing back of profits. As per Indian Companies Act, companies are required to transfer a part of their profits in reserves. The amount so kept in reserve may be used to buy fixed assets. This is called internal financing.

Merits:

Following are the benefits of retained earnings:

1. Cheap Source of Capital: No expenses are incurred when capital is available from this source. There is no obligation on the part of the company either to pay interest or pay back the money. It can safely be used for expansion and modernisation of business.

2. Financial Stability: A company which has enough reserves can face ups and downs in business. Such companies can continue with their business even in depression, thus building up its goodwill.

3. Benefits to the Shareholders: Shareholders may get dividend out of reserves even if the company does not earn enough profit. Due to reserves, there is capital appreciation, i.e., the value of shares go up in the share market .

Limitation:

Following are the limitations of Retained Earnings:

1. Huge Profit: This method of financing is possible only when there are huge profits and that too for many years.

2. Dissatisfaction Among Shareholders: When funds accumulate in reserves, bonus shares are issued to the shareholders to capitalise such funds. Hence, the company has to pay more dividends. By retained earnings the real capital does not increase while the liability increases. In case bonus shares are not issued, it may create a situation of undercapitalisation because the rate of dividend will be much higher as compared to other companies.

3. Fear of Monopoly: Through ploughing back of profits, companies increase their financial strength. Companies may throw out their competitors from the market and monopolise their position.

4. Mismanagement of Funds: Capital accumulated through retained earnings encourages management to spend carelessly.

In Text Question 9.4

Which of the following statements are right and which are wrong?

1. Retained earning is the portion of profit which is not distributed among shareholders as dividend.
2. A company can create reserves even if it is running at a loss.
3. Heavy expenses are incurred to raise capital through retained earnings.
4. Retained earnings are useful for shareholders because it brings stability in the rate of dividend and leads to capital appreciation.
5. Retained earning means ploughing back of profits.

4. Public Deposits

It is a very old source of finance in India. When modern banks were not there, people used to deposit their savings with business concerns of good repute. Even today it is a very popular and convenient method of raising medium-term finance. The period for which business undertakings accept public deposits ranges from six months to three years.

Procedure to Raise Funds Through Public Deposits: An undertaking which wants to raise funds through public deposits advertises in the newspapers. The advertisement highlights the achievements and future prospects of the undertaking and invites the investors to deposit their savings with it. It declares the rate of interest which may vary depending upon the period for which money is deposited. It also declares the time and mode of payment of interest and the repayment of deposits. A depositor may get his money back before the date of repayment of deposits for which he will have to give notice in advance.

Features:

1. These deposits are not secured.
2. They are available for a period ranging from 6 months to 3 years.
3. They carry a fixed rate of interest.
4. They do not require complicated legal formalities as are required in the case of shares or debentures. Keeping in view the malpractices of certain companies, such as not paying interest for years together and not refunding the money, the Government has framed certain rules and regulations regarding inviting public to deposit their savings and accepting them.

Rules governing public deposits

Following are the main rules governing public deposits:

1. Deposits should not be made for less than six months or more than three years.
2. Public is invited to deposit their savings through an advertisement in the press. This advertisement should contain all relevant information about the company.
3. Maximum rate of interest is fixed by the Reserve Bank of India.
4. Maximum rate of brokerage is also fixed by the Reserve Bank of India.
5. The amount of deposit should not exceed 25% of the paid-up capital and general reserves.

6. The company is required to maintain Register of Depositors containing all particulars as to public deposits.
7. In case the interest payable to any depositor exceeds ₹ 10,000 p.a., the company is required to deduct income tax at source.

Advantages:

Following are the advantages of public deposits:

1. Simple and Easy: The method of borrowing money through public deposit is very simple. It does not require many legal formalities. It has to be advertised in the newspapers and a receipt is to be issued.

2. No Charge on Assets: Public deposits are not secured. They do not have any charge on the fixed assets of the company.

3. Economical: Expenses incurred on borrowing through public deposits is much less than expenses of other sources like shares and debentures.

4. Flexibility: Public deposits bring flexibility in the structure of the capital of the company. These can be raised when needed and refunded when not required.

Disadvantages:

Following are the disadvantages of public deposits:

1. Uncertainty: A concern should be of high repute and have a high credit rating to attract public to deposit their savings. There may be sudden withdrawals of deposits which may create financial problems.

2. Insecurity: Public deposits do not have any charge on the assets of the concern. It may not always be safe to deposit savings with companies particularly those which are not very sound.

3. Lack of attraction for professional investors: As the rate of return is low and there is no capital appreciation, the professional investors do not appreciate this mode of investment.

4. Uneconomical: The rate of interest paid on public deposits may be low but then there are other expenses like commission and brokerage which make it uneconomical.

5. Hindrance to Growth of Capital Market: If more and more money is deposited with the companies in this form there will be less investment in securities. Hence, the capital market will not grow. This will deprive both the companies and the investors of the benefits of good securities.

6. Over Capitalisation: As it is an easy, convenient and cheaper source of raising money, companies may raise more money than is required. In that case it may not be able to make the best use of the funds or may indulge in speculative activities.

In Text Question 9.5

A. Tick the correct part of the statements:

1. Public deposits are secured/unsecured.
2. Public deposits involve/do not involve any charge on the assets of the company.
3. Advertisement is required/not required for inviting public deposit.
4. Public deposits can be/cannot be for more than three years.

B. Write yes or no against the following statements:

(i) The system of public deposits is economical.

(ii) Public deposits are secured.

(iii) Rate of interest on public deposits is not fixed.

(iv) Public deposits help in the growth of a sound capital market in the country.

(v) Public deposit is a method which has become popular only recently.

5. Borrowing from Commercial Banks

Traditionally, commercial banks in India do not grant long-term loans. They grant loans only for short period not extending one year. But recently they have started giving loans for a long period. Commercial banks give term loans, i.e., for more than one year. The period of repayment of short-term loan is extended at intervals and in some cases loan is given directly for a long period. Commercial banks provide long-term finance to small-scale units in the priority sector.

Merits of long-term borrowings from commercial banks:

The merits of long-term borrowing from banks are as follows:

1. It is a flexible source of finance as loans can be repaid when the need is met.
2. Finance is available for a definite period, hence, it is not a permanent burden.
3. Banks keep the financial operations of their clients secret.
4. Less time and cost is involved as compared to issue of shares, debentures, etc.
5. Banks do not interfere in the internal affairs of the borrowing concern, hence the management retains the control of the company.
6. Loans can be paid back in easy instalments.
7. In case of small-scale industries and industries in villages and backward areas, the interest charged is low.

Demerits:

Following are the demerits of borrowing from commercial banks:

1. Banks require personal guarantee or pledge of assets and business cannot raise further loans on these assets.
2. In case the short-term loans are extended again and again, there is always uncertainty about this continuity.
3. Too many formalities are to be fulfilled for getting term loans from banks. These formalities make the borrowings from banks time-consuming and inconvenient.

In Text Question 9.6

Write 'True' if the statement is correct and 'False' if the statement is incorrect:

(a) Commercial banks do not grant long-term loans.

(b) Short-term loans granted by commercial banks can become long-term loans.

(c) Commercial banks charge high rate of interest while giving loans to small-scale industries and industrial units set up in villages.

(d) No guarantee or pledge of assets is to be made while borrowing from commercial banks.

6. Loan from Financial Institutions:

There are many specialised financial institutions established by the Central and State Governments which give long-term loans at reasonable rate of interest. Some of these institutions are: Industrial Finance Corporation of India (IFCI), Industrial Development Bank of India (IDBI), Industrial Credit and Investment Corporation of India (ICICI), Unit Trust of India (UTI), State Finance Corporations, etc.

What You Have Learnt?

Capital is the lifeblood of business. A business requires capital to purchase its fixed assets, which is called long-term finance. The factors that determine the long-term requirements of capital are:

(i) Nature of business,

(ii) Size of business,

(iii) Kinds of goods produced, and

(iv) Technology used.

The main sources of raising long-term finance are:

(i) Shares,

(ii) Debentures,

(iii) Public deposits,

(iv) Retained earnings,

(v) Loans from financial institutions, and

(vi) Term loans from banks.

Share is a unit of capital of a company of a definite face value. Share indicates certain rights of its holder and the extent of his liability.

Shares are mainly of two types:

(i) Equity shares and

(ii) Preference shares.

Preference shares are the shares which carry preferential rights of receiving dividend and repayment of capital (in case the company is wound up) over other shares.

Equity shares are shares which do not carry any preferential right. Holders of these shares are the real owners of the company. They get dividends only when dividend on preference shares has been paid.

Issue of debenture is a source of borrowed capital. A debenture is a written acknowledgement of debt by a company. Debentureholders are the creditors of the company. They do not enjoy any voting rights. They are secured. Debentures may be:

(a) redeemable or irredeemable, and (b) convertible or non-convertible.

Public deposits channelise savings into business. They are unsecured. They bear fixed rate of interest. Deposits generally are for one year to three years. An advertisement is required for inviting public deposits.

Retained earning is a portion of profit, earned by an enterprise, set aside to finance its activities. It is also called ploughing back of profit or internal financing.

Commercial banks traditionally give loans for a short period. But recently they have started giving term loans both by extending the short-term loans and also directly for a long period.

Terminal Questions

1. Why does business need long-term finance? Explain in brief.
2. Give the advantages of equity shares to: (a) the management and to (b) the shareholders.
3. Differentiate between:

   (a) Equity shares and preference shares (b) Shares and Debentures
4. State the meaning of Debenture. Give the merits and demerits of debentures as a source of long-term finance.
5. Define Retained Earnings. What are the limitations of Retained Earning as a source of finance?
6. Briefly explain the meaning of Public Deposits. State the government rules and regulations regarding Public Deposits.
7. List out the various advantages and disadvantages of long-term loans from commercial banks.
8. The management of an engineering company has decided to double its manufacturing capacity. Suggest, giving arguments, whether it should issue shares or debentures?

Answers to in Text Questions

9.1 A. 1. Fixed Assets 2. Permanent 3. Long-term finance 4. Manufacturing

9.2 B. 1. Retained earnings 2. Public Deposits 3. Shares 4. Debentures

9.2 A (a) Equity Shares (i), (ii)

(b) Preference Shares (iii), (iv)

B (i) (a), (ii) (d), (iii) (c), (iv) (b)

9.3 (A) 1. True 2. False 3. True 4. False 5. True

(B) (1) (iv), (2) (i), (3) (ii), (4) (iii)

9.4 1. Right 2. Wrong 3. Wrong 4. Right 5. Right

9.5 (A) 1. Unsecured 2. Do not involve 3. Required 4. Cannot be

(B) (i) Yes, (ii) No, (iii) No, (iv) No, (v) No.

9.6 (a) False (b) True (c) False (d) False

7. American Depository Receipts (ADRs)

Definition: An ADR is a certificate issued by an American bank, which represents a foreign stock share, held on deposit. Since the bank holds the stock, it is equivalent to trading the foreign stock.

Origin and Nature: Introduced to the financial markets in 1927, an American Depository Receipt (ADR) is a stock, which trades in the United States but represents a specified number of shares in a foreign corporation. ADRs are bought and sold in American markets just like regular shares, and are issues/sponsored in the US by a bank or brokerage house. ADRs were introduced as a result of the difficulty buying shares in other countries, which trade at different prices and currency values. For this reason the US banks simply purchase a large lot of shares from the company, bundle the shares into groups and reissue them on the NYSE, AMEX, or NASDAQ.

Why do companies use ADRs?

1. Companies may have capital demands that are more than the availability of financing at home. It gives more US exposure and allows them to enter the US equity markets.
2. Increasing the size of the market for its shares that may increase or stabilize the share price.
3. They also enhance the image of the company's products or services.
4. For those companies who are truly global, it allows buyers of the company's products and services to also invest in the company.

The following are a few Indian companies whose ADRs are being traded in the American Exchanges: Infosys, Reliance, Dr. Reddy's Laboratories, etc.

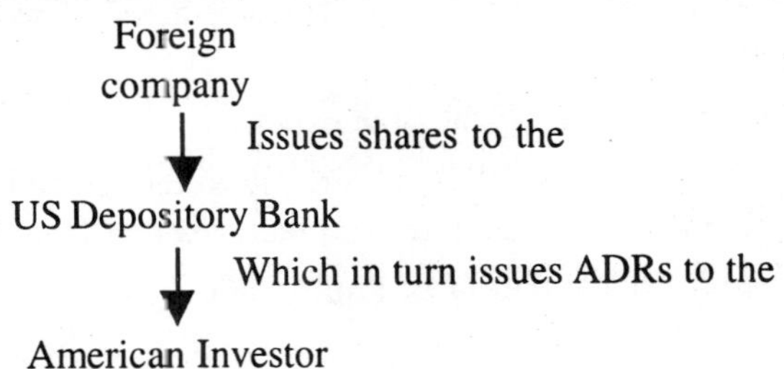

Benefits of ADRs to investors:

- Abundant selection.
- Easier than buying foreign shares
- Entitled to the same information disclosure as holders of the underlying security.
- All notices and reports are issued in English language.
- All issuers must report by US standards.
- Denominated in US dollars.

8. Global Depository Receipts (GDRs)

Nature and Definition: Global Depository Receipts (GDRs) are essentially instruments created by overseas depository bank that are authorized by issuing companies in India to issue outside the country. GDRs are issued to non-resident investors against the shares of the issuing companies held with the nominated domestic custodian banks. They are negotiable certificates that usually represent a company's publicly trade equity and are denominated in US dollars. They are listed in a European Stock Exchange often Luxembourg, but London is also used. For all good purposes, GDRs can be treated as direct investment in the issuing companies.

Advantages of GDR for the Issuer: The share price of the company may stabilize because of the widening of the market. The image of the issuer is also enhanced in the global market. Euro issues cost less than domestic rights issue. Companies making Euro issue may have understanding with depository bank resulting in certain voting pattern. The Indian company does not bear any foreign exchange risk since the securities are denominated in the rupees. On the other hand, it receives the proceeds of Euro issue in foreign currency. Euro-issues are easier to administer since dealings are with a single shareholder, the custodian depository bank.

Advantages to the Investor: In regard to the investor, they enjoy the benefits of international diversification while avoiding long delays in settlement and transfer of shares, confusing trade and tax practices. GDRs are quoted in dollars and dividends are paid in dollar, free of foreign exchange risk. They enable the foreign investor to avoid restriction on purchase and holding of individual company's shares. GDRs are quite as liquid as the underlying shares and they can be exchanged for shares. A GDR is tradable both in Europe and America.

9. Lease Financing

1. Lease: A contract of lease may be defined as "A contract whereby the owner of an asset (lessor) grants to the another party (lessee) the exclusive right to use the asset usually for an agreed period of time in return for the payment of rent".

Important features here are:

(a) Owner and user are different.

(b) Depreciation claim is not with the user (lessee) as he is not the owner. Lessor (owner) claims the depreciation.

(c) Lease (rent) payment is a tax-deductible expense.

(d) In most transactions, asset is delivered directly to the lessee by the manufacturer/supplier. Lessor makes payment to the supplier and receives rent from lessee in future periods.

(e) Lease funded assets do not alter Debt Equity ratio.

2. Types of Leases:

Distinction between Operating Lease and Finance Lease

1. Operating Lease	2. Finance Lease
1. In an operating lease all the risks and rewards incidental to ownership are not transferred by the lessee to the lessor.	1. In a finance lease the lessor transfers all the risks and rewards incidental to the ownership of the asset to the lessee.
2. Operating lease is cancelable by either party during the lease period.	2. Finance lease is non-cancellable and it involves payment of lease rentals over an obligatory non-cancellable lease period.
3. In an operating lease the lessor does not relay on only a single lessee for recovery of his investment since the lease periods are shorter such as even an hour, a day, a week, or a month and so on. The lessor is ultimately interested in the residual value of the asset.	3. In a finance lease the lessor is only a financer and usually not interested in the asset.
4. An operating lease is termed as a 'Service Lease'	4. Finance lease is also termed as 'full-payout leases'.
5. In an operating lease the cost of asset is not fully amortised during the primary lease cancellable) period.	5. The finance lease enables the lessor to recover his investment in the asset lease plus to derive a profit.
6. Operating lease being shorter than the expected economic life of the asset no such option of purchase of the asset by the lessee exists there.	6. In a finance lease the lessee has the option to purchase the asset at a price on a date the option becomes exercisable or at the end of the lease agreement period.
7. An operating lease is generally for a period shorter than the economic life of the leased asset.	7. In a finance lease the lease term is for the major part of the economic life of the asset.

8. In an operating lease the lessor other than financing the cost of leased asset, also provides such as repairs, maintenance and technical advice.	8. In a finance lease the lessee is responsible for the repairs and maintenance, insurance and risk of obsolescence of the asset leased.
9. In an operating lease the lessor bears the risk of obsolescence of the asset leased.	9. In a finance lease the lessee has to bear the risk of obsolescence of the asset leased.
10. **Examples:** Aircrafts, buildings, heavy machinery, railway, buses, etc.	10. **Examples:** Hiring a cab, chartering of Air crafts, hiring of cranes, etc.

3. Leveraged Lease: Under leveraged leses there are three parties. The lessor, the lessee and the financial institution/bank who lends a major cost of the asset leased. The lessor contributes 20% to 50% of the cost and the lender contributes 50% to 80% of the cost of the asset. The periodic lease rental is being appropriately divided between the lender and the lessor.

4. Sale and Leaseback: In case of sale and lease back as the name suggest, the firm sells an asset that it already owns to another firm/party and (hires) gets its own leaseback from the buyer which is usually a financial institution or a leasing company.

5. Direct Lease: In case of direct lease the lessee acquires the equipment directly from the manufacturer or arrange the desired equipment to be purchased by the leasing company.

6. Cross-border Lease/International Lease: A cross-border lease is also known as an international lease or a transnational lease. In this case lessee and the lessor are domiciled in different countries. It is an agreement between the nationals of two countries.

7. Triple Net Lease: In case of triple net lease one is obligated to pay the following typical executory costs in addition to and separate from the basic lease rental payments. Such additional executory costs are:

(i) Sales Tax

(ii) Property Tax

(iii) Repairs

(iv) Parts and Accessories

(v) Insurance

(vi) Maintenance and Servicing

8. Master Lease: Master leases are structure for lessees who either will be leasing several pieces of equipment to be received over a period of time or leasing equipment that will require frequent substitution.

10. Hire Purchase

In case of hire purchase transaction, the goods are delivered by the owner to another person on the agreement that such person pays the agreed amount in the periodical instalment.

Important features here are:

(a) Ownership of the asset is transferred to the buyer only on payment of the last instalment.

(b) Buyer claims depreciation on the asset.

Lease	Hire Purchase
• Lessor claims depreciation • On completion of contract residual (salvage) value goes to lessor. • In absence of specific agreement otherwise, asset is to be returned to the lessor after the lease period. • Lease payment is fully deductible for tax.	• Buyer claim depreciation • On completion of contract residual (salvage) value goes to buyer. • Asset is conclusively purchased by the buyer at the end of the agreement period. • Only interest portion of EMI/ hire value is tax deductible.

11. Venture Capital

Venture capital is the money provided by professionals who invest alongside management in young, rapidly growing companies that have the potential to develop into significant economic contributors. Venture capital is an important source of equity for start-up companies.

Venture Capitalists Generally: Finance new and rapidly growing companies.

- ➢ Purchase equity securities
- ➢ Assist in the development of new product or services
- ➢ Add value to the company through active participation
- ➢ Take higher risk with the expectation of higher rewards
- ➢ Have a long-term orientation

When considering an investment, venture capitalists carefully screen the technical and business merits of the proposed company. Venture capitalists only invest in a small percentage of the businesses they review and have a long-term perspective. They also actively work with the company's management, especially with contact and strategy formulation. Companies such as Digital Equipment Corporation, Apple, Federal Express, Compaq, Sun Microsystems, Intel, Microsoft and Gentech are famous examples of companies that received venture capital early in their development period.

In India, these funds are governed by the Securities and Exchange Board of India (SEBI) guidelines. According to this, venture capital fund means a fund established in the form of the company or trust, which raises monies through loans, donations, and issue of securities or units as the case may be, and makes or proposes to make investments in accordance with these regulations.

The basic principle underlying venture capital is invest in high-risk projects with the anticipation of high returns. These funds are then invested in several fledgeing enterprises, which require funding, but unable to access it through the conventional sources such as bank and financial institutions. Typically first generation entrepreneurs start such enterprises. Such enterprises generally do not have any major collateral to offer as security, hence banks and financial institutions are averse to funding them. Venture capital funding may be by way of investment in the equity of the new enterprises or a combination of debt and equity, though equity is the most preferred route.

Since most of the venture finance is through this route are in new areas (worldwide venture capital follows "hot industries" like infotech, electronic and biotechnology), the probability of success is very low. All projects financed have a potentially high return. Some projects fail and some give moderate returns. The investment, however, is a long- term risk capital as such projects normally take 3 to 7 years to generate substantial returns. Venture capitalists give "more than money" to the venture and seek to add value to the investee unit by active participation in its management. They monitor and evaluate project on a continuous basis.

To conclude, a venture financier is one who funds a start up company, in most cases promoted by a first generation technocrat promoter with equity. A venture capitalist is not a lender, but an equity partner. He is driven by maximization: wealth maximization. Venture capitalists are sources of expertise for the companies they finance. Exit is preferably through listing on stock exchanges. This method has been extremely successful in USA, and venture funds have been credited with the success of technology companies in Silicon valley.

12. External Commercial Borrowings (ECB)

External commercial borrowings are one of the modes for sourcing of funds for corporates. The Government of India has come out with guidelines for approval of external commercial borrowings. These guidelines reflect the government's desire of maintaining prudent limits for total external borrowings and at the same time give flexibility to corporates. The guiding principles of ECB policy are keep borrowing maturities long, costs low, and encourage infrastructure and export sector financing which are crucial for overall growth of the economy.

Applicants will be free to raise ECB from any internationally recognised source like banks, export credit agencies, suppliers of equipment, foreign collaborations, foreign equityholders, international capital markets, etc.

13. Eurobonds and Foreign Bonds

A company can raise funds by issuing Euro bonds and foreign bonds to investors in other countries. Euro bonds are bonds sold outside the country in whose currency they are denominated. They are issued directly by the borrowers to the investors. Euro bond market is a free market without any regulation. It is a self-regulated market. Both fixed rate and floating rate Euro bonds are issued by the borrowers. A foreign bond is different from Euro bond. It is issued by a company in a domestic market of a foreign market. It is denominated by the currency of the country where it is issued and is subject to the laws and regulations of that country.

14. Government Subsidies

Government subsidies are the concessions and incentives given by Central or State Government or both. A subsidy is the converse of an indirect tax, while indirect tax raises the price of the taxed commodity a subsidy is expected to lower the commodity price.

Forms of subsidies:

1. Cash subsidies, e.g., export, fertilizer, food, etc.
2. Interest or credit subsidies
3. Tax subsidies
4. Equity subsidies, e.g., investment in equity share

Viability Gap Funding (VGF) e.g. Mumbai Metro Project.

15. Securitization

Securitization is a **structured finance** process that distributes risk by aggregating **assets** in a pool (often by selling assets to a **special purpose entity**), then issuing new securities backed by the assets and their cashflows. The securities are sold to investors who share the risk and reward from those assets.

Securitization is similar to a sale of a profitable business ("spinning off") into a separate entity. The previous owner trades its ownership of that unit, and all the profit and loss that might come in the future, for present cash. The buyers invest in the success and/or failure of the unit, and receive a premium (usually in the form of **interest**) for doing so. In most securitized investment structures, the investors' rights to receive cashflows are divided into **"tranches"**: senior tranche investors lower their risk of default in return for lower interest payments, while junior tranche investors assume a higher risk in return for higher interest.

Securitization is designed to reduce the risk of bankruptcy and thereby obtain lower interest rates from potential lenders. A credit derivative is also sometimes used to change the credit quality of the underlying portfolio so that it will be acceptable to the final investors. As a portfolio risk backed by amortizing cashflows and unlike general corporate debt the credit quality of securitized debt is non-stationary due to changes in volatility that are time- and structure-dependent. If the transaction is properly structured and the pool performs as expected, the credit risk of all tranches of structured debt improves; if improperly structured, the affected tranches will experience dramatic credit deterioration and loss.

Securitisation has evolved from its tentative beginnings in the late 1970s to a vital funding source with an estimated outstanding of $10.24 trillion in the United States and $2.25 trillion in Europe as of the 2nd quarter of 2008. In 2007, ABS issuance amounted to $3,455 billion in the US and $652 billion in Europe.

Bonds backed by an isolated pool of cashflows are generally referred to as Asset-backed securities (ABS). ABS can be subdivided into a number of common classes:

- **Mortgage-backed Securities (MBS):** Backed by lenders' accounts receivable under mortgage loans secured by real estate.
- **Residential Mortgage-backed Securities (RMBS):** Backed by mortgages on houses and condominiums; often originated by government-sponsored enterprises in the United States.
- **Commercial Mortgage-backed Securities (CMBS):** Backed by mortgages on commercial real estate such as hotels, office buildings and shopping malls.
- Credit card ABS
- Student loan ABS

Whole business securitization (WBS): Backed by an entire operating business. WBS arrangements first appeared in the United Kingdom in the 1990s, and became common in various commonwealth legal systems where senior creditors of an insolvent business effectively gain the right to control the company.

9.5 MOTIVES FOR SECURITISATION

Advantages to Issuer

- **Reduces Funding Costs:** Through securitisation, a company rated BB but with AAA worthy cashflow would be able to borrow at possibly AAA rates. This is the number one reason to securitize a cashflow and can have a tremendous impact on borrowing costs. The difference between BB debt and AAA debt can be multiple hundreds of basis points. For example, Moody's downgraded Ford Motor Credit's rating in January 2002, but senior automobile backed securities, issued by Ford Motor Credit in January 2002 and April 2002, continue to be rated AAA because of the strength of the underlying collateral and other credit enhancements.

- **Reduces Asset-liability Mismatch:** "Depending on the structure chosen, Securitisation can offer perfect matched funding by eliminating funding exposure in terms of both duration and pricing basis". Essentially, in most banks and finance companies, the liability book or the funding is from borrowings. This often comes at a high cost. Securitisation allows such banks and finance companies to create a self-funded asset book.
- **Lower Capital Requirements:** Some firms, due to legal, regulatory, or other reasons, have a limit or range that their leverage is allowed to be. By securitizing some of their assets, which qualifies as a sale for accounting purposes, these firms will be able to lessen the equity on their balance sheets while maintaining the "earning power" of the asset.
- **Locking-in Profits:** For a given block of business, the total profits have not yet emerged and thus remain uncertain. Once the block has been securitized, the level of profits has now been locked-in for that company, thus the risk of profit not emerging, or the benefit of super-profits, has now been passed on.
- **Transfer Risks (credit, liquidity, prepayment, reinvestment, asset concentration):** Securitisation makes it possible to transfer risks from an entity that does not want to bear it, to the one that does. Two good examples of this are catastrophe bonds and entertainment securitisations. Similarly, by securitizing a block of business (thereby locking-in a degree of profits), the company has effectively freed up its balance to go out and write more profitable business.
- **Off Balance Sheet:** Derivatives of many types have in the past been referred to as "off-balance-sheet". This term implies that the use of derivatives has no balance sheet impact. While there are differences among the various accounting standards internationally, there is a general trend towards the requirement to record derivatives at fair value on the balance sheet.
- **Earnings:** Securitisation makes it possible to record an earnings bounce without any real addition to the firm. When a securitisation takes place, there often is a "true sale" that takes place between the originator (the parent company) and the SPE. This sale has to be for the market value of the underlying assets for the "true sale" to stick and thus this sale is reflected on the parent company's balance sheet, which will boost earnings for that quarter by the amount of the sale. While not illegal in any respect, this does distort the true earnings of the parent company.
- **Admissibility:** Future cashflows may not get full credit in a company's accounts (life insurance companies, for example, may not always get full credit for future surpluses in their regulatory balance sheet), and a securitisation effectively turns an admissible future surplus flow into an admissible immediate cash asset.
- **Liquidity:** Future cashflows may simply be balance sheet items which currently are not available for spending, whereas once the book has been securitized, the cash would be available for immediate spending or investment. This also creates a reinvestment book which may well be at better rates.

Disadvantages to Issuer

- **May reduce Portfolio Quality:** If the AAA risks, for example, are being securitized out, this would leave a materially worse quality of residual risk.
- **Costs:** Securitisations are expensive due to management and system costs, legal fees, underwriting fees, rating fees and ongoing administration. An allowance for unforeseen costs is usually essential in securitisations, especially if it is a typical securitisation.

- **Size Limitations:** Securitisations often require large-scale structuring, and thus may not be cost-efficient for small and medium transactions.
- **Risks:** Since securitisation is a structured transaction, it may include par structures as well as credit enhancements that are subject to risks of impairment, such as prepayment, as well as credit loss, especially for structures where there are some retained strips.

Advantages to Investors

Opportunity to potentially earn a higher rate of return (on a risk-adjusted basis)

- **Opportunity to Invest in a Specific Pool of High Quality Credit-enhanced Assets:** Due to the stringent requirements for corporations (for example) to attain high ratings, there is a dearth of highly rated entities that exist. Securitisations, however, allow for the creation of large quantities of AAA, AA or A rated bonds, and risk- averse institutional investors, or investors that are required to invest in only highly rated assets, have access to a larger pool of investment options.
- **Portfolio Diversification:** Depending on the securitisation, hedge funds as well as other institutional investors tend to like investing in bonds created through securitisations because they may be uncorrelated to their other bonds and securities.
- **Isolation of Credit Risk from the Parent Entity:** Since the assets that are securitized are isolated (at least in theory) from the assets of the originating entity, under securitisation it may be possible for the securitisation to receive a higher credit rating than the "parent", because the underlying risks are different. For example, a small bank may be considered more risky than the mortgage loans it makes to its customers; were the mortgage loans to remain with the bank, the borrowers may effectively be paying higher interest (or, just as likely, the bank would be paying higher interest to its creditors, and hence less profitable).

Risks to Investors

Liquidity Risk

- **Credit/default:** Default risk is generally accepted as a borrower's inability to meet interest payment obligations on time. For ABS, default may occur when maintenance obligations on the underlying collateral are not sufficiently met as detailed in its prospectus. A key indicator of a particular security's default risk is its credit rating. Different tranches within the ABS are rated differently, with senior classes of most issues receiving the highest rating, and subordinated classes receiving correspondingly lower credit ratings.

However, the credit crisis of 2007-2008 has exposed a potential flaw in the securitisation process. Loan originators retain no residual risk for the loans they make, but collect substantial fees on loan issuance and securitisation, which do not encourage improvement of underwriting standards.

Event Risk

- **Prepayment/reinvestment/early Amortization:** The majority of revolving ABS are subject to some degree of early amortization risk. The risk stems from specific early amortization events or payout events that cause the security to be paid-off prematurely. Typically, payout events include insufficient payments from the underlying borrowers, insufficient excess Fixed Income Sectors: Asset-backed securities spread, a rise in the default rate on the underlying loans above a specified level, a decrease in credit enhancements below a specific level, and bankruptcy on the part of the sponsor or servicer.

- **Currency Interest Rate Fluctuations:** Like all fixed income securities, the prices of fixed rate ABS move in response to changes in interest rates. Fluctuations in interest rates affect floating rate. ABS prices less than fixed rate securities, as the index against which the ABS rate adjusts will reflect interest rate changes in the economy. Furthermore, interest rate changes may affect the prepayment rates on underlying loans that back some types of ABS, which can affect yields. Home equity loans tend to be the most sensitive to changes in interest rates, while auto loans, student loans, and credit cards are generally less sensitive to interest rates.

Contractual agreements

- **Moral Hazard:** Investors usually rely on the deal manager to price the securitisations' underlying assets. If the manager earns fees based on performance, there may be a temptation to mark up the prices of the portfolio assets. Conflicts of interest can also arise with senior note holders when the manager has a claim on the deal's excess spread.
- **Servicer Risk:** The transfer or collection of payments may be delayed or reduced if the servicer becomes insolvent. This risk is mitigated by having a back-up servicer involved in the transaction.

Summary: Securitization is the process of taking an illiquid asset, or group of assets, and through financial engineering, transforming them into a security.

A typical example of securitization is a mortgage-backed security (MBS), which is a type of asset-backed security that is secured by a collection of mortgages. The process works as follows:

First, a regulated and authorized financial institution originates numerous mortgages, which are secured by claims against the various properties the mortgagors purchase. Then, all of the individual mortgages are bundled together into a mortgage pool, which is held in trust as the collateral for an MBS. The MBS can be issued by a third-party financial company, such a large investment banking firm, or by the same bank that originated the mortgages in the first place.

REVIEW QUESTIONS

Q.1. Concept Testing.

(a) Any three Short-term Sources of Finance.

(b) Any three Long-term Sources of Finance.

(c) Any two modern Long-term Sources of Finance.

(d) Inter-corporate deposit.

(e) Merits and Demerits of Equity Share Capital.

(f) Types of Debentures.

(g) ADR.

(h) Venture Capital.

Q.2. Differentiate Equity Shares and Preference Share Capital.

Q.3. What is Securitisation? Explain motives/Advantages of Securitisation.

❑❑❑

CHAPTER 10 CREDIT RATING

10.1 CREDIT RATING

Introduction

Credit rating may be defined as an expression, through use of symbols, of opinion about the quality of credit of the issuer of debt securities with reference to a particular instrument. Credit rating is a symbolic indicator of the current opinion on the relative capability of the corporate entity to timely service debts and obligations, with reference to the instrument rated by credit rating agency. Credit rating is a simple and easy to understand symbolic indicator of the opinion of a credit rating agency about the risk involved in a borrowing programme of an issuer with reference to the capability of the issuer to repay the debt as per terms of the issue. Such rating, which is expressed in symbols, is subject to an upward or downward change, as the situation changes.

Definition

Credit rating is an expression through the use of alpha-numeric symbols of the opinion about Credit Quality of the issuer of securities with reference to a particular instrument. In credit rating what is rated is the debt instrument and not the issuer company. Credit rating pre-estimates the repayment capacity of the debtor/borrower as well as payment of periodical interest on it. Credit rating has become necessary in view of the increasing number of cases of default in the payment of interest and repayment of principal amount borrowed by the companies by way of term loan, Commercial Papers, fixed deposits and debentures.

Importance of Credit Rating

The globalization of the financial markets has also served to expand the role of credit ratings whose assessments on sovereign and corporate entities have been increasingly used as benchmarks by regulators and investors. Credit ratings have become a universal phenomenon throughout the capital markets, relied upon by investors, issuers and regulators alike. Credit rating agencies play a critical role in capital markets, guiding the asset allocation of institutional investors as private capital moves freely around the world in search of the best trade-off between risk and return. Companies also try their best to service debt as per agreement to maintain/improve its credit rating.

Basic Objective of Credit Rating

The basic objective of credit rating is to provide an opinion on the relative credit risk associated with the instrument being rated.

10.2 INSTRUMENTS ELIGIBLE FOR CREDIT RATING

The term credit rating refers to evaluation of debt instruments. Debt instruments include both long-term instruments like bonds and debentures, and short-term obligations like Commercial Paper. Apart from these, fixed deposits, certificates of deposits, inter-corporate deposits, structured obligations, municipal debt, infrastructure bond, asset-backed securities, mutual funds, etc., are also rated.

Determinants of Rating

The default-risk assessment and quality rating assigned to an issue are primarily determined by three factors:

1. The company's ability to pay,
2. The strength of the security owner's claim on the issue, and
3. The economic significance of the industry and marketplace of the issuer.

Benefits of Credit Rating

Rating serves as a useful tool for different constituents of the capital market namely investors, issuers of debt instruments, financial intermediaries, business enterprises, regulators, etc. These benefits are described below:

Benefits of Credit Rating to Investors:

1. **Quick Investment Decisions:** Based on the credit rating assigned to various instruments investor can take quick decisions about the investment to be made in various instruments without undertaking detailed fundamental analysis of a company.
2. **Safeguards Against Bankruptcy:** An instrument with high credit rating gives an assurance to the investors of safety of their investment and the interest or return on their investments with least risk of bankruptcy.
3. **Risk Recognition:** Credit rating provides rating symbols which carry information in easily recognizable manner for the benefit of investors to perceive risk involved in investment.
4. **Choice of Investment:** Investors can make choice of various instruments depending upon their own risk profile, deploying investible funds and diversification plan.
5. **Credibility of Issuer:** The rating symbol assigned to a debt instrument gives an idea about the credibility of the issuer company which enhances confidence of investors.
6. **Independent Investment Decisions:** Investors need not depend upon the advice of financial intermediaries such as, the stockbrokers, the portfolio managers, or financial consultants as the rating symbol assigned to a particular instrument suggests the creditworthiness of the instrument and indicates the degree of risk involved in it.
7. **Rating Surveillance:** Investors benefit from the credit rating agency's ongoing surveillance of the rated instruments of different companies. This helps them to change their investment decision on the basis of change of credit rating.

Benefits of Credit Rating to Issuer Company

1. **Lower Cost of Borrowing:** A company, whose debt instruments is highly rated, will be in a position to reduce the cost of borrowing by quoting lesser interest rate on fixed deposits or debentures or bonds because of lower credit risk. (for e.g., RIL, Bharti Airtel, etc.)

2. **Lower Cost of Issue:** A company with higher rated instrument is able to attract the investors with least efforts and raise the required funds with minimum cost of public issues and thus control expenses on media coverage, conferences and other marketing expenditures.
3. **Create Better Brand Image:** Companies with higher rated instruments due to their own image and can use credit rating as a marketing tool to create better image in dealing with its customers, lenders and other creditors.
4. **Growth:** Due to better image created through higher credit rating the company can mobilize funds from the public and institutional lenders like banks and financial institutions for its growth plans to undertake expansion of their existing operations or new projects.
5. **Wider Audience:** A company having very good rating for its debt instrument can approach investors in different strata of the society for resource mobilization using the press media.
6. **Self-discipline:** Rating encourages the companies to match with the existing sound practices and to come out with more disclosures about their accounting system, financial reporting and management pattern, etc.

Criticisms on Credit Rating Agencies

1. Credit rating agencies do not downgrade companies promptly enough as soon as the credit quality deteriorates, resulting into slower response from investors.
2. Rating agencies have been criticised for having too familiar a relationship with company management, possibly opening themselves to undue influence or the vulnerability of being misled. (for e.g., Enron, Citibank, Satyam enjoyed high rating for a considerable period of time that war warranted by their performance/ fundamentals).
3. Credit rating agencies have made errors of judgement in assigning high rating to products which have subsequently been downgraded.
4. Lowering of a credit rating by rating agencies can create a vicious cycle, as not only the interest rates for that company would go up, but other contracts with financial institutions may be affected adversely, causing an increase in expenses and ensuring decrease in creditworthiness.
5. Credit rating agencies are for profit entities their incentives may be affected.
6. Conflicts of interest often arise because the rating agencies are paid by the companies issuing the securities, so how can they play the role of a regulator?

What credit rating is not... (misconceptions clarified)

1. Credit rating agencies rate the aforesaid debt instruments of companies. They do not rate the companies, but their individual debt securities. The rating is specific to the instrument and it is not the rating of the issuer.
2. A rating reflects default risk only, not the price risk associated with changes in the level or shape of the yield curve.
3. It is important to emphasise that credit ratings are not recommendations to invest. They do not take into account many aspects, which influence an investment decision.
4. Credit rating agencies do not, evaluate the reasonableness of the issue price, possibilities of earning capital gains or take into account the liquidity position in the secondary market.

5. Ratings also do not take into account the risk of prepayment by the issuer, or interest rate risk or exchange rate risks. Although these are often related to the credit risk, the rating essentially is an opinion on the relative quality of the credit risk.
6. Credit ratings are opinions only. It has to be noted that there is no privacy of contract between an investor and a rating agency and the investor is not protected by the opinion of the rating agency.
7. Ratings are not a guarantee against loss. They are simply opinions, based on analysis of the risk of default which helps in making decisions based on particular preference of risk and return.
8. There is no compulsion on the corporate sector to obtain or publicise the credit rating except for certain instruments.
9. Credit ratings are not recommendations to buy or sell or hold a specified rated security nor are they offered as guarantees or protections against default.

10.3 CREDIT RATING AGENCIES (CRAs)

The credit rating agencies (CARs) regularly analyse the financial position of corporations and assign and revise the ratings for their securities. Credit rating agencies (CRAs) are an integral part of the modern capital markets. CRA have been providing opinions on the creditworthiness of issuers of securities and other financial instruments. Credit rating is only a risk evaluation of a Fee Based Services assignment undertaken by the Credit rating agencies. The most dominating factor is the reputation and analytical credibility of the credit rating agency. Credit rating agencies continuously monitors the corporate and the rating is monitored till the life of the instrument. If necessary, the rating is changed, upwards or downwards. In other words, a rating is valid during the life of the instrument unless it is changed. Credit rating agencies maintain absolute independence from market participants to provide unbiased opinions. The ratings are a result of collective judgement of committee members. The Credit rating agencies, thus assist and form an integral part of a broader programme of financial disintermediation and broadening and deepening of the debt market. The credit rating agencies operating in India are registered with the Reserve Bank of India.

Functions of a Credit Rating Agencies

1. **Assists Investors:** It assists investors, both individual as well as institutional, in making well-informed investment decisions.
2. **Ensures Adequate Disclosures:** Credit rating agencies ensures that adequate information is disclosed to it and after assessing all the risks involved it decides on a credit symbol.
3. **Easy Understanding:** The credit rating symbols are easily understandable to the investors based on which they can take well, informed investment decision. "Triple A" indicates highest safety and "D" indicates default which is easily understandable.
4. **Low Cost Funds:** High credit rating indicates low risk which means companies with high credit rating can raise the required funds at lower rates of returns.
5. **Constant Monitoring:** Once the rating has been assigned the credit rating agencies constantly monitors the degree of risk exposure of the firm and accordingly based on it, it can upgrade or even downgrade the assigned credit rating symbols.

6. **Credit Quality Information:** Credit rating agencies informs the investors regarding the credit quality of the company which the investors are not aware of and thus facilitates in promotion of the public issues of the companies.

Important Credit Rating Agencies

Some of the important credit rating agencies in India are as follows:

1. Credit Rating and Information Services of India Limited (CRISIL)
2. Investment Information and Credit Rating Agency of India Limited (ICRA)
3. Credit Analysis and Research Limited (CARE)
4. Duff and Phelps Credit Rating of India (Pvt.) Ltd.,
5. Onida Individual Credit Rating Agency Ltd., (ONICRA)

1. Credit Rating and Information Services of India Limited (CRISIL):

CRISIL is the first rating agency to be set up in India. CRISIL is India's leadings Ratings, Research, Risk and Policy Advisory Company. This was set up by ICICI and UTI in 1988. Standard & Poors acquired 9.68% shareholding in CRISIL, in 1996-97. Other shareholders include: Asian Development Bank (ADB), LIC, State Bank of India and HDFC, etc. The CRISIL is the world's fourth largest rating agency. Leveraging these crore strengths CRISIL delivery includes.

(a) Make capital markets function better.

(b) Help clients mitigate and manage their business and financial risks.

(c) Help shape public policy, of the government/companies.

The activities of CRISIL are as under:

1. To provide credit rating service in respect of:
   (a) Ratings of corporate debt issuances.
   (b) Ratings of banks, non-banking finance companies.
   (c) Ratings of borrowing programmes of governments and government bodies.
   (d) Ratings of structured finance instruments.
   (e) Ratings of microfinance institutions.
2. To provide analytical tools for management of risks such as market risk, credit and operational risk and valuation services.
3. To undertake research on economy, industry and company performance and publish such reports.
4. To provide corporate as well as market advisory services to corporate and non-corporate clients.

CRISIL's core values include Analytical Rigour, Independence, Integrity, Innovation and Commitment. Through the years, CRISIL has continued to innovate and play the role of a pioneer in the development of the Indian debt market. CRISIL rates long-term instruments such as debentures/bonds and preference shares, structured obligations (including asset-backed securities) and fixed deposits; it also rates short-term instruments such as Commercial Paper programmes and short-term deposits. As part of bank loan ratings, CRISIL also rates credit facilities extended to borrowers by banks. All it gives CRISIL a unique place in terms of experience in understanding the extent of credit enhancement arising from such structures. CRISIL's market share is around 75%.

CRISIL Credit Rating Symbols

Investment Grades	Debentures	Fixed Deposits
1. Highest Safety	AAA	FAAA
2. High Safety	AA	FAA
3. Adequate Safety	A	FA
4. Moderate Safety	BBB	FBBB
5. Inadequate Safety	BB	FBB
6. High Risk	B	FB
7. Substantial Risk	C	FC
8. Default	D	FD

Rating Process

- CRISIL receives the completed application form along with the rating fee
- CRISIL's representatives visit the company
- CRISIL's analysts have a short discussion with the management of the company
- CRISIL prepares a rating report, assigns a rating and sends the copy of the report to company and NSIC

2. *Investment Information and Credit Rating Agency of India Limited (ICRA)*

ICRA was promoted by IFCI in 1991 to meet the requirements of the companies based in north India. Along with IFCI, State Bank of India, Unit Trust of India, PNB and LIC were the other promoters of the company. The International Credit Rating Agency, Moody's Investors Service is ICRA's largest shareholder. Today, ICRA and its subsidiaries together form the ICRA Group of Companies. ICRA is a Public Limited Company, with its shares listed on the Bombay Stock Exchange and the National Stock Exchange. ICRA has dedicated teams for monetary, fiscal, industry and sector research, and a panel of advisors to enhance their inhouse capabilities and research base to enable to maintain the highest standards of quality and credibility. ICRA provides range of services like Rating Services, Grading Services, Information Services, Research and Publications, Industry and Sector Analysis, Customised Research, Rating Profile, Management Consulting Services, Software Development, Online Software and Knowledge Process Outsourcing, etc.

ICRA Credit Rating Symbols

Investment Grades	Debentures/Bonds	Fixed Deposits	Commercial Paper
1. Highest Safety	LAAA	MAAA	A-1
2. High Safety	LAA	MAA	A-2
3. Adequate Safety	LA	MA	A-3
4. Moderate Safety	LBBB	–	–
5. Inadequate Safety	LBB	MB	–
6. Risk Prone	LB	MC	A-4
7. Substantial Risk	LC	–	–
8. Default	LD	MD	A-5

ICRA has been providing investors with independent, professional and reliable rating opinions on debt instruments since 1991. Based on the feedback received from the market and to extend its rating coverage to corporate entities who do not have firm or immediate debt issue plans, ICRA has launched the Issuer Rating services in India.

The Benefits

For lenders/investors, ICRA issuer ratings would

- Provide an objective, independent and reliable opinion on credit quality,
- Facilitate an informed investment decision,
- Assist in risk pricing and capital allocation, and
- Facilitate portfolio management and monitoring.

For the rated entities, ICRA issuer ratings may help to

- Improve the comfort level with prospective/existing lenders/investors,
- Negotiate terms based on their inherent credit quality,
- Reduce the time involved in loan approvals, and
- Access a broader investor base.

3. Credit Analysis & Research Ltd., (CARE)

CARE is a credit rating and information services company promoted by IDBI jointly with investment institutions, banks and finance companies. The company commenced its operations in October 1993.

The functions of CARE Ltd., are as under:

1. To undertake credit rating of all types of debt instruments, both short-term and long-term.
2. To make available information on any company, industry or sector required by a business enterprise.
3. To undertake equity research study of listed or to be listed companies on the major stock exchanges.

Credit Analysis & Research Ltd., (CARE Ratings) is a full service rating company that offers a wide range of rating and grading services across sectors since its inception in April 1993. CARE is recognised by Securities and Exchange Board of India (SEBI), Government of India (GoI), Reserve Bank of India (RBI), etc. The ratings division of CARE has over a decade long of experience in rating debt instruments/enterprise ratings covering the full spectrum of universe comprising:

(a) Industrial Companies,

(b) Service Companies,

(c) Infrastructure Companies,

(d) Banks and Financial Institutions (FIs),

(e) Non-banking Finance Companies (NBFCs),

(f) Public Sector Undertakings (PSUs),

(g) State Government Undertakings, and

(h) Structured Finance Transactions.

In addition to debt ratings CARE Ratings has experience in providing the following specialized grading/rating services:

(a) IPO grading,

(b) Mutual Fund Credit Quality Ratings,

(c) Insurance Claims Paying Ability Ratings,

(d) Issuer Ratings.

CARE Ratings is well equipped to rate all types of debt instruments like Commercial Paper, Fixed Deposit, Bonds, Debentures, Hybrid Instruments, Structured Obligations, Preference Shares, Loans, Asset Backed Securities (ABS), Residential Mortgage, etc. CARE Ratings services has been recognized by statutory authorities and other agencies in India which include Securities and Exchange Board of India (SEBI), Reserve Bank of India (RBI), Director General, Shipping and Ministry of Petroleum and Natural Gas (MoPNG), Government of India (GoI), National Housing Bank (NHB), National Bank for Agriculture and Rural development (NABARD), National Small-scale Industries Commission (NSIC).

4. Duff & Phelps Credit Rating India Private Ltd., (DCR)

DCR India or Duff & Phelps Credit Rating India Private Ltd., is one of the top credit rating agencies in India. Duff & Phelps Credit Rating India Private Ltd., (DCR India) has played an important role in rating India's FOREX debt obligations. This credit rating company was set-up in 1996. It was promoted by JM Financial and Alliance Group jointly with international rating agency Duff & Phelps. Duff & Phelps was founded in 1932 to provide high quality investment research services focused on the utility industry. Over the decades, it has evolved into a diversified financial services firm that provides financial advisory, investment banking, credit rating and investment management services. The investment management and credit rating businesses were acquired by Virtus Investment Partners and Fitch, respectively.

The activities of Duff & Phelps Credit Rating India Private Ltd., are as under:

(a) To undertake credit rating of debt instruments including rating of Commercial Papers.

(b) To evaluate company performance and give rating to them, and

(c) To provide country rating.

5. Onida Individual Credit Rating Agency Ltd., (ONICRA)

This agency rates the creditworthiness corporation/individual borrowers. This agency rates the risk attached with the transaction entered into with an individual. This type of credit rating has applications in credit cards, housing finance, leasing/hire purchase, personal loans, etc.

10.4 RATING METHODOLOGY

Process of Credit Rating

Credit rating is an interactive process which involves a number of steps on the basis of assessment on which rating is assigned.

Flow Chart of Rating Process

Different Rating Agencies have different processes for rating an instrument. Generally followed rating process is used by the credit rating agencies.

1. Mandate 2. Assign rating team	Activity 1 and 2 Initial stage
3. Receive initial information 4. Meeting and visits 5. Analysis and presentation of report	Activity 1 to 5 Fact finding and Analysis; conduct basic research
6. Preview meeting 7. Rating meeting 8. Assign rating	Rating finalisation Fresh Inputs
9. Communicating rating and the rationale 10. Acceptance 11. Surveillance	Request for review Non-acceptance

The rating process commences at the request of the prospective issuer and on receipt of information as may be available with such issuer. A team of analysts takes up the work of collection of data and information from the books and records of the concern and interacts with its executives. The team also relies on the inhouse research and database and other secondary sources considered reliable by the rating agency. On completion of the analysis, a rating report is submitted to the rating committee followed by presentation of key rating issues by the rating team. The ratings are assigned by the rating committee. The rating agency ensures strict confidentiality of the information collected from the issuers during the rating process.

Role of SEBI with Respect to Credit Rating

In India, credit rating business is regulated by SEBI. Four credit rating agencies recognized by SEBI have been operating in India. As per the SEBI regulations, credit rating is nothing but a Fee Based Services opinion regarding securities expressed in the form of standard symbol or in any other standardized form assigned by a credit rating agency. Now, Securities and Exchange Board of India (SEBI) has decided to enforce mandatory rating of all debt are statutorily required to be rated. A credit rating agency has to inform SEBI about new rating instruments or symbols introduced by it.

News Article

HAPPY TIDINGS SET TELECOM STOCKS AFIRE *Economic Times*

It was a Good Friday for the markets as a flurry of Good News and upgrades set telecom stocks soaring while sugar cost found a sweet note to end the week on Powerful promises.

HAPPY TIDINGS SET TELECOM STOCKS AFIRE

Our Bureau MUMBAI/NEW DELHI

SHARES of wireless telecom service-providers such as Bharti Airtel and Idea Cellular led the market rally on Friday, heartened by rating and price target upgrades by investment bank Credit Suisse. Investors cheered the upgrades, as it has come when most fund managers and analysts are still pessimistic about the industry's growth prospects due to sharp cuts in tariffs and concern over rising debt.

Credit Suisse, in a report dated July 8, upgraded its rating on Bharti to outperform from neutral and price target to ₹ 360 from 320, driving up its stock by 9.7% to ₹ 308.10 on Friday. News that Singapore Telecommunications, South East Asia's largest telecom firm, bought around 16 lakh shares in Bharti through the open market also boosted sentiment.

Idea Cellular's rating was upgraded to 'outperform' from 'underperform' and price target was raised to ₹ 75 from ₹ 50 at Credit Suisse. The investment bank also upgraded its rating on Reliance Communications (RCOM) to neutral from underperform and price target to ₹ 185 from ₹ 150.

Idea Cellular surged 13.3% to ₹ 67, and Tata Teleservices shot up 5.5% to ₹ 23 on Friday. RCOM was flat in a rising Mumbai market, moving up 3% to ₹ 193.

"We believe that concerns on competition, regulation, 3G auction fee and RIL's entry have been overstated", Credit Suisse analysts said in a report called "The night is darkest before the dawn".

"With improved outlook for mobile businesses, we raise our FY11 (2010-11) EPS estimate for Idea and RCOM by 7% and 100%, respectively", the report said.

The investment bank cut its earnings per share estimate for Bharti by 6% in 2010-11 to factor in the "value destruction" from the acquisition of African mobile operator Zain.

In August 2011 credit rating Agency 'standard and poors' downgraded USA credit rating from AAA to AA+.

This had effect on capital markets across the world.

India faces downgrade, 12 June 2012 *Economic Times* by S&P

Germany	AAA
USA	AA+
China	AA-
Brazil	BBB+
Ireland	BBB
Spain	BBB
India	BBB- with negative outlook
Greece	CCC

CHAPTER 11

PROSPECTUS FOR ISSUE OF SHARES

11.1 PROSPECTUS

According to Companies Act 1956, Section 2 (36), "A prospectus is any document described or issued as a prospectus and includes any notice, circular, advertisement or other document inviting deposits from the public or inviting offers from the public for the subscription or purchase of any shares or debentures of a body corporate".

In simple words, any document inviting deposits from the public or inviting offers from the public for the subscription of shares or debentures of a company is a prospectus.

Vetting by SEBI/Stock Exchanges

(a) A company cannot come out with public issues unless draft prospectus is filed with SEBI.

(b) A company cannot file prospectus directly with SEBI. It has to be filed through a merchant banker. After the preparation of prospectus, the merchant banker along with the due diligence certificate and other compliances sends the same to SEBI for vetting.

(c) SEBI on receiving the same, scrutinizes it and may suggest changes within 21 days of receipt of prospectus. (Earlier, the situation was that the company was required to obtain Acknowledgement Card from SEBI).

11.2 CONTENTS OF A PROSPECTUS

Prospectus is an invitation to the public for the subscription or purchase of any shares or debentures of a corporate body. It can be a notice, circular, or and other document. Prospectus usually contains risk factors, issue highlights and details of the company such as general information, term and particulars of the issue, etc.

The format of the prospectus (with respect to the revisions made by SEBI in 2000) requires it to be divided into three parts. Contents and format of the cover pages are also specified. Important details such as risk factors and issue highlights such as name of issuer company and regd. office, size of issue, issue opening date, credit rating, etc., must be mentioned on the cover pages.

In the first part brief particulars are to be given about matters like:

1. General Information; E.g,. Name and address of the registered office of the company.
   (a) Disclaimer clause taking no responsibility for statements other than those made in the prospectus.
   (b) Name of stock exchange where application for listing is made
   (c) Minimum subscription clause.
   (d) Issue schedule, i.e., date of opening, closing, earliest closing
   (e) Name and address of the auditors, lead manager, registrars, etc.

(f) Credit rating

(g) Name and addresses of the trustees of the debenture trust deed, in case of debentures

2. Capital Structure of the Company

(a) Authorized, issued, subscribed and paid-up capital

(b) Size of the present issue, giving separately reservation for preferential allotment to promotion and others.

3. Term of the Present Issue

(a) Terms of payment

(b) How to apply (using the application form, on the basis of the study of the prospectus and mode of payment, disclosure for stock invests, Application Supported By Blocked Amount (ASBA) etc.)

(c) Refund orders, utilization of issue proceeds.

4. Particulars of the Issue

(a) Object(s) of the issue

(b) Project cost

(c) Means of financing (Promoters' condition)

(d) Appraisal

5. Company Management and Project

(a) History and main objects and present business of the company

(b) Promoters and their background

(c) Key managerial personnel

(d) Location of the project

(e) Technology, collaborations, capacity, future prospects, etc.

(f) Stock market data, if any of last three years.

6. Management Discussion and Analysis of Financial Condition and Results of Operation.

7. Financial Information of Group Companies

8. Promise vs. Performance of Earlier Issues

9. Internal and External Risk Factors

Part II requires the company to give detailed information. This part is divided into three subpart.

(a) General information regarding directors, lead manager, etc.

(b) Financial information including ratios, etc.

(c) Statutory information like details about minimum subscription, underwriting, revaluation, etc.

Part III gives the explanation of terms used in Parts I and II

Concept Testing

(A) Dating of Prospectus (Section 55)

A prospectus issued by or in relation to an intended company must be dated and that date is, unless the contrary is proved, taken as date of publication of the prospectus.

(B) Signing of Prospectus

In case the prospectus is issued by an intended company it has to be signed by the proposed directors of the companies, the prospectus has to be signed by every person who is named therein as director of the company or by his agent authorized in writing.

(C) Objectives of Registration of Prospectus

(a) To keep an authenticated record of the terms and conditions of issues of shares or debentures.

(b) To pinpoint the responsibility of the persons issuing the prospectus for the statements made by them in the prospectus.

(D) The Issue of a Prospectus is not Necessary in the Following Cases

(a) Where an offer is made in connection with a bonafied invitation to a person to enter into an underwriting agreement with respect to the shares to the shares of debentures.

(b) Where the shares or debentures are not offered to the public. This will be the case when the promoters are confident of raising capital through private sources and contacts.

(c) Where the shares or debentures are offered to the existing members or debenture-holder of the company.

(d) Where the shares or debentures offered are uniform in all respects with shares or debentures previously issued and quoted on a recognized stock exchange.

(E) Types of Prospectuses

1. **Letter of Offer or Prospectus:** prospectus is a document inviting the public to subscribe its securities, i.e., share or debentures of the company.
2. **Letter of Rights:** When a company makes a rights issue, it sends a "Letters of Rights" to its existing equity shareholders indicating the number of new shares they are entitled.
3. **Statement in Lieu of Prospectus:** The Companies Act, 1956 SCHEDULE III and IV lay down the form of statement in lieu of prospectus. A company is required to issue a statement in lieu of prospectus when it is covered under the provision of Section 44(2) (b) or Section 70 of the Companies Act 1956.
4. **Shelf Prospectus:** A prospectus which the company has got vetted from SEBI for a series of issues which the company proposes to come out in the near future within a stipulated time period. This avoids repeated preparation of the prospectus and getting it approved from the regulatory authorities time and again.
5. **Draft Prospectus:** A company intending to come out with a public issue prepares a draft prospectus and files it through a merchant banker with SEBI.
6. **Red Herring Prospectus:** A red herring prospectus is a prospectus which does not have complete particulars of the price of the securities offered. The BRLM conducts due diligence of the issuer during the preparation of a red herring prospectus. The red herring prospectus is filed with SEBI and later it is filed with ROC. A red herring prospectus is used in case of a book building, where the face value is indicated but the issue price is left open for the bidders to bid on the basis of the indicated price band.

JAYPEE INFRATECH LIMITED

[illegible]

Registered and Corporate Office: [illegible]

Telephone: [illegible] Facsimile: [illegible]

Contact Person and Compliance Officer: [illegible]

PROMOTER OF THE COMPANY: JAIPRAKASH ASSOCIATES LIMITED

PUBLIC ISSUE OF [●] EQUITY SHARES OF FACE VALUE OF RS. 10 EACH ("EQUITY SHARES") OF JAYPEE INFRATECH LIMITED (THE "COMPANY" OR THE "ISSUER") FOR CASH AT A PRICE OF RS. [●] PER EQUITY SHARE (INCLUDING A SHARE PREMIUM OF RS. [●] PER EQUITY SHARE) AGGREGATING RS. [●] MILLION (THE "ISSUE") CONSISTING OF A FRESH ISSUE OF UP TO [●] EQUITY SHARES BY THE COMPANY AT THE ISSUE PRICE AGGREGATING UP TO RS. [illegible] MILLION ("FRESH ISSUE") AND AN OFFER FOR SALE OF [illegible] EQUITY SHARES ("OFFER FOR SALE") BY JAIPRAKASH ASSOCIATES LIMITED (THE "SELLING SHAREHOLDER"). THE ISSUE INCLUDES A RESERVATION OF UP TO [●] EQUITY SHARES FOR THE ELIGIBLE SHAREHOLDERS (AS DEFINED HEREINBELOW, AND SUCH PORTION, THE "SHAREHOLDERS RESERVATION PORTION"). THE ISSUE LESS THE SHAREHOLDERS RESERVATION PORTION IS REFERRED TO AS THE "NET ISSUE". THE ISSUE WILL CONSTITUTE [●]% OF THE FULLY DILUTED POST-ISSUE PAID-UP CAPITAL OF THE COMPANY AND THE NET ISSUE WILL CONSTITUTE [●]% OF THE FULLY DILUTED POST-ISSUE PAID-UP CAPITAL OF THE COMPANY.

THE PRICE BAND, RETAIL DISCOUNT AND THE MINIMUM BID LOT WILL BE DECIDED BY THE COMPANY AND THE SELLING SHAREHOLDER IN CONSULTATION WITH THE BOOK RUNNING LEAD MANAGERS AND ADVERTISED AT LEAST TWO WORKING DAYS PRIOR TO THE BID/ISSUE OPENING DATE.

[illegible]

[illegible]

[illegible]

RISKS IN RELATION TO FIRST ISSUE

[illegible]

GENERAL RISKS

[illegible]

IPO GRADING

[illegible]

ISSUER'S ABSOLUTE RESPONSIBILITY

[illegible]

LISTING

[illegible]

BOOK RUNNING LEAD MANAGERS

Morgan Stanley	BofA Merrill Lynch	AXIS BANK	ENAM	ICICI Securities
Morgan Stanley India Company Private Limited [illegible]	DSP Merrill Lynch Limited [illegible]	Axis Bank Limited [illegible]	Enam Securities Private Limited [illegible]	ICICI Securities Limited [illegible]
IDFC CAPITAL	JM FINANCIAL	kotak		**REGISTRAR TO THE ISSUE** KARVY
IDFC Capital Limited [illegible]	JM Financial Consultants Private Limited [illegible]	Kotak Mahindra Capital Company Limited [illegible]	SBI Capital Markets Limited [illegible]	Karvy Computershare Private Limited [illegible]

BID/ISSUE PROGRAMME

BIDDING/ISSUE OPENS ON THURSDAY, APRIL 29, 2010	BIDDING/ISSUE CLOSES ON TUESDAY, MAY 4, 2010

[illegible]

JP INFRATECH

TABLE OF CONTENTS

❑❑❑

CHAPTER 12 UNDERWRITING

12.1 UNDERWRITING

When a company offers shares to the public, it would like to ensure success of the issue. A company with a view to protecting subscription by members of the public and with a view to enabling it to get the requisite amount of share capital, will enter into an agreement with financial institutions, whereby the financial institutions undertake to subscribe or find someone else to subscribe to a certain number of all of the shares which are not taken up by the public. This undertaking by the financial institution is called underwriting. In consideration of the risk they are paid a commission or fees, even if actually they are not required to take up even a single share. Sometimes, underwriters, finding that they have undertaken too heavy responsibility or liability to be borne by them, underwrite, in turn, with other underwriters so as to get rid of their liability or a portion of their underwriting. This is called sub-underwriting.

Underwriting Contracts may be of Three Types

- **Pure or open underwriting** is an agreement whereby the underwriter agrees to subscribe to only that portion of the shares not taken up by the public.
- **Firm underwriting** is an agreement under which the underwriter or underwriters agree to take up stipulated shares or debentures irrespective of the fact whether they are subscribed to by the public or not and makes payment before issue opens.
- **Partial underwriting underwriting** a portion of the issue of shares or debentures. Often, instead of one party underwriting the entire issue, different parties may underwrite different portions, together making up the whole or the company may get only a portion of the issue underwritten.

As per the listing requirement, every underwriter-broker has to obtain the permission of the stock exchange of which he is a member in order to act as an underwriter-broker for any public issue.

The Securities and the Exchange Board of India (SEBI) has waived the earlier stipulation of compulsory underwriting of all public issues. Underwriting has now been made a voluntary proposition. That is, it has now become the promoters/issue manager's option whether or not to get the proposed public issue underwritten partly or fully. Therefore, in Indian context open or partial underwriting is popular. But after debacle of IPO of Emmar MGF Ltd., and Wokhardth Hospital Ltd., in 2008 SEBI is of the view that FIRM writing should be made compulsory.

CHAPTER 13

MERCHANT BANKING

13.1 MERCHANT BANKER

A merchant banker could be defined as "**An organization that acts as an intermediary between the issuers and the ultimate purchaser of securities in the primary market**".

Merchant banker has been defined under the securities and exchange board of India (Merchant banker) Rules, 1992 as "any person who is engaged in the business of Issue Management either by making arrangement regarding selling, buying or subscribing to securities as manager, consultant advisor or rendering corporate advisory service in relation to such Issue Management".

A merchant banker is an institution that helps companies to raise capital. It is an organization that underwrites corporate securities, provides advisory service to its clients.

What is Merchant Banking/Investment Banking?

Merchant bankers' facilitates the issue process and their activities are termed as 'merchant banking'. Essentially, merchant banking is what merchant bankers do.

Classification of Merchant Banking

- **Fee-based Merchant Banking:** These banks do not take Balance Sheet Position, i.e., these are only a service provider or in other words these are channel between two or more parties that comply each others requirements, (e.g., Public Issue, QIP).
- **Fund-based Merchant Banking:** These banks take Balance Sheet Position. They initially provide funds to the client from their own resources in exchange of securities (Bonds, debentures, equity...) and thereafter sell the same to others. These banks function mostly when funds requirement by client is urgent, (e.g., Bought out deal).

Functions and Services of Merchant Banks

1. **Consultancy Services:** Offers valuable Consultancy Services to their clients on financial, managerial, technical, marketing and many other problems.
2. **Government Consent:** Help their clients in completing lengthy legal formalities for securing government consent or license for setting up a new venture or for expansion or modernization of business.
3. **Project Planning and Feasibility Study:** Collect necessary information about the project and prepares project report with the help of their expert staff.
4. **Raising Financial Resources:** Prepare financial plans on behalf of their clients and conduct negotiations with financial institution and get loans approved on favourable terms and conditions. Also helps in identifying strategic investor.

5. **Issue Management:** Manages capital issues on behalf of their clients and provide finance to them. This includes preparation and issue of prospectus, appointment of bankers, underwriting arrangement, press publicity, etc.

6. **Portfolio Management:** Offer advise to their clients on investment in Government securities, shares, mutual funds, etc. Undertake purchase and sale of securities and management of individual investment portfolio of investors.

7. **Advice on Expansion Programme:** Assistance is offered in framing and executing expansion and diversification programmes.

8. **Loan Syndication:** Foreign currency loans have to be arranged from Indian financing agencies and/or foreign finance institution. Merchant bankers help in coordinating above, drafting agreements, etc. Eg., Loan Syndication in case of TATA Steel takeover of Corus and Bharti Airtel takeover of ZAIN Telecom.

9. **Corporate Restructuring:** Offer professional expertise in identifying the sellers/buyers, handling the negotiations, processing the documents, etc., when a company plans to acquire a new company or when a group wants to disinvest and sell one of the units.

10. **Revival Packages for Sick Units:** Provide for rehabilitation of sick units. Participate in negotiation with BIFR and consortium meetings of banks and financial institutions. Merchant banker also ensures compliance with various regulatory guidelines.

11. **Miscellaneous Services:**
    - Arrangement of finance for working capital needs of business units.
    - Arrangement of lease finance.
    - Assistance in securing foreign collaborations/expansion.
    - Help in framing capital structure and financial plan.
    - Recruitment, selection and placement of managerial and technical staff, etc.

SEBI has laid down following authorised activities of merchant bankers:

- Issue management.
- Corporate advisor.
- Underwriting.
- Portfolio management services.
- Managers, consultants or advisers.

Discuss the Role of a Merchant Banker in the following:

- **Instrument Designing and Pricing:** A cardinal principle of corporate finance is to maintain a proper proportion between public issue and loan capital to increase the rate of return on capital employed. It is always a wise step to keep the quantum of share capital higher than the loaned funds. The debt-equity ratio has to be considered for this purpose for having a balanced mixture of owned and loaned capital. Expert advise should be obtained from the auditors/financial controller/legal advisers and stockbrokers of the company. The norms fixed for this purpose by the stock exchange/controller of capital issues should also be taken into account. The proportion of various types of funds has, therefore be in optimum mix. Merchant banker has to do valuation of shares, etc., and then decide the issue price range.

➢ **Rights Issue:** The merchant banker work would also relate to advise to the companies on any rights issue. They may advise on the documents needed, size of rights issues, the need for underwriting, terms (price) and other necessary actions with regard to the issue of rights shares.

13.2 REGULATORY FRAMEWORK FOR MERCHANT BANKING

The following are the SEBI guidelines for merchant bankers

1. **Authorisation:** Any person or body proposing to engage in the business of merchant banking would need authorization by the Securities and Exchange Board of India (SEBI) in their prescribed format. This will also apply to those presently engaged in merchant banking activity, including as managers, consultants, or advisers to issues.
2. **Authorised Activities:**
   (a) Issue of management, which will inter alia consist of preparation of prospectus and other information relating to the issues, determining financing structure, tie-up of financers and final allotment and/or refund of subscription.
   (b) Corporate advisory services relating to the issue
   (c) Underwriting
   (d) Portfolio management services
   (e) Managers, consultant or adviser in the issue
3. **Authorisation Criteria:** All merchant bankers are expected to perform with high standards of integrity and fairness in all their dealings. A code of conduct for merchant bankers will be prescribed by SEBI. Within this context, SEBI's authorization criteria would take into account mainly the following:
   (a) Professional competence
   (b) Personnel, their adequacy and quality, and other infrastructure
   (c) Capital adequacy
   (d) Past track record, experience, general reputation and fairness in all their transactions.
4. **Terms of autorisation:**
   (a) All merchant bankers, including the existing ones, must obtain the authorization from SEBI.
   (b) All merchant bankers must have a minimum net worth of ₹10 crore.
   (c) The authorization will be for a initial period of three years.
   (d) SEBI may collect from the merchant bankers an initial authorization fee, an annual fee and a renewal fee.
   (e) All issues must be managed by at least one authorised banker functioning as the sole or lead manager.
   (f) The specific responsibilities of each lead manager must be submitted to SEBI prior to the issue.
   (g) While directors, promoters and every person who authorises the issue of prospectus shall bear full responsibility for the contents of the prospectus, merchant banker shall exercise due diligence independently verifying the contents of prospectus and reasonableness of the views expressed therein.

(h) Lead managers/merchant bankers would be responsible for ensuring timely refunds and allotment of securities to the investors.

(i) The involvement of merchant banker in an issue should continue at least till completion of essential follow-up steps, which will include the listing of the instrument, and dispatch of certificates (in physical/demat form).

(j) The merchant banker shall make available to SEBI such information, documents, returns and reports as may be prescribed and called for.

(k) SEBI shall prepare and prescribe a code of conduct for merchant bankers which they should adhere to.

(l) SEBI may suspend/cancel the authorization of merchant bankers for suitable duration in case of violations of the guidelines.

Regulations with respect to the CODE OF CONDUCT to be followed by Merchant Bankers

A merchant banker will be deemed to be guilty of misconduct or unprofessional conduct if he violates intentionally or otherwise any of the following provisions of the code of conduct:

1. A merchant banker in the conduct of his business shall observe **high standards of integrity and fairness** in all his dealings with his client and other merchant bankers.
2. A merchant banker shall render at all times **high standards of service, exercise due diligence,** ensure proper care and exercise independent professional judgements.
3. He shall wherever necessary, **disclose to the client possible source of conflict of duties and interests**, while providing unbiased services.
4. A merchant banker **shall not** make any statement or become privy to any act, **practise unfair competition**, which is likely to be harmful.
   - To the interests of other merchant bankers or
   - Is likely to place such other merchant bankers in a disadvantageous position in relation to the merchant banker, while competing for or executing any assignment.
5. A merchant banker **shall not make any exaggerated statement**, whether oral or written, to the client either about the qualification or the capability to render certain services or his achievement in regard to services rendered to other clients.
6. A merchant banker **shall always endeavour** to:

   (a) Render the **best possible advice** to the client having regard to the clients needs and the environment and his own professional skills; and

   (b) Ensure that all professional dealings are affected in a **prompt, efficient and cost-effective manner.**
7. A merchant banker **shall not**:

   (a) Divulge to other clients, press or any other party **any confidential information** about his client, which has come to his knowledge; and

   (b) **Deal in securities of any client company without making disclosure to the Board** as required under the regulations and also to the Board of Directors of the company.

8. A merchant banker **shall endeavour to ensure** that:
   (a) The investors are provided with **true and adequate information** without making any misguiding or exaggerated claims and are made aware of attendant risks before any investment decision is taken by them.
   (b) Complaints from investor are adequately dealt with.

News Article

SELL-OFF DEPT. WON'T LET BIG I-BANKS CORNER BIZ.	*Economic Times, 28 June, '10*

Appointment To Focus On Technical Bids, Not Fees.

Surabhi NEW DELHI

THE government plans to again tweak the norms for appointing merchant bankers to make managing public issues of state-owned companies more profitable and also create a level playing field.

Big merchant bankers quote abysmally low fees for managing issues to gain visibility, choosing even to bear charges like the cost of printing applications, filing fees to SEBI, and payments to NSE and BSE out of their own pockets. This discourages smaller ones from participation. Now, the disinvestment department plans to bear all these charges and rely largely on the technical bids for selecting merchant bankers to the issue.

Under the current norms, merchant bankers are expected to pay for activities like printing applications, filing fees to SEBI, and payments to NSE and BSE for use of software during book building, which can amount to about ` 15 crore to ` 20 crore per issue. But merchant bankers often quote appallingly low fees that do not include these costs. As a result, they pay these charges from their own pockets and incur severe losses while managing PSU issues. For instance, the six banks short-listed for managing the Coal India Ltd., Offer will collectively earn a mere ₹ 12,500.

SEBI TIGHTENS VIGIL ON ERRING I-BANKERS	*Economic Times, 28 June, '10*

NEW DELHI: Misdeeds in the past can make the future tough for i-bankers seeking to advise clients on public offers, as SEBI has upped the ante against those with a dark history. A SEBI scan will not only cover the i-banking entity concerned but also group entities, promoters, directors and key management persons.

❑❑❑

CHAPTER 14	PUBLIC ISSUE

14.1 PUBLIC ISSUE

Corporates may raise capital in the primary market by way of an initial public offer, rights issue or private placement. An Initial Public Offer (IPO) is the selling of securities to the public in the primary market. This Initial Public Offering can be made through the fixed price method, book building method or a combination of both.

Types of Public Issues

- IPO and FPO
- Fixed Price Issue and Book Building Issue

Issue type	Offer price	Demand	Reservations
Fixed Price Issue	Price at which the securities are offered and would be allotted is made known in advance to the investors.	Demand for the securities offered is known only after the closure of the issue.	50% of the shares offered are reserved for applications below ₹ 2 lakh and the balance for higher amount applications.
Book Building Issue	A 20% price band is offered by the issuer within which investors are allowed to bid and the final price is determined by the issuer only after closure of the bidding.	Demand for the securities offered, and at various prices, is available on a real time basis on the BSE/NSE website during the bidding period.	Generally, 50% of shares offered are reserved for QIBS, 35% for small investors and the balance 15% for HNI.

14.2 BOOK BUILDING

Book building is essentially a process used by companies raising capital through Public Offerings both Initial Public Offers (IPOs) or Follow-on Public Offers (FPOs) to aid price and demand discovery. It is a mechanism where, during the period for which the book for the offer is open, the bids are collected from investors at various prices, which are within the price band specified by the issuer. The process is directed towards both the institutional as well as the retail investors. The issue price is determined after the bid closure based on the demand generated in the process.

Book Building Process

- The Issuer who is planning an offer nominates lead merchant banker(s) as 'book runners'.
- The issuer specifies the number of securities to be issued and the price band for the bids.
- The issuer also appoints syndicate members with whom orders are to be placed by the investors.

- The syndicate members input the orders into an 'electronic book'. This process is called 'bidding' and is similar to open auction.
- The book normally remains open for a minimum period of 3 working days.
- Bids have to be entered within the specified price band.
- Bids can be revised by the bidders before the book closes.
- On the close of the book building period, the book runners evaluate the bids on the basis of the demand at various price levels.
- The book runners and the issuer decide the final price at which the securities shall be issued.
- Generally, the number of shares are fixed, the issue size gets frozen based on the final price per share.
- Allocation of securities is made to the successful bidders. The rest get refund orders.

BSE/NSE's Book Building System

- BSE/NSE offers a book building platform through the Book Building software that runs on the BSE/NSE Private network.
- This system is one of the largest electronic book building networks in the world, spanning over 350 Indian cities through over 7,000 Trader Work Stations via leased lines, VSATs and Campus LANS.
- The software is operated by book runners of the issue and by the syndicate members, for electronically placing the bids online real-time for the entire bidding period.
- In order to provide transparency, the system provides visual graphs displaying price vs. quantity on the BSE/NSE website as well as all BSE/NSE terminals.

14.3 BENEFITS OF LISTING

- Listing provides an opportunity to the corporates/entrepreneurs to raise capital to fund new projects/undertake expansions/diversifications and for acquisitions.
- Listing also provides an exit route to private equity investors as well as liquidity to the ESOP-holding employees.
- Listing also helps generate an independent valuation of the company by the market.
- Listing raises a company's public profile with customers, suppliers, investors, financial institutions and the media. A listed company is typically covered in analyst reports and may also be included in one or more of indices of the stock exchanges.
- An initial listing increases a company's ability to raise further capital through various routes like preferential issue, rights issue, Qualified Institutional Placements and ADRs/GDRs/FCCBs, and in the process attract a wide and varied body of institutional and professional investors.
- Listing leads to better and timely disclosures and thus also protects the interest of the investors.
- Listing on BSE/NSE provides a continuing liquidity to the shareholders of the listed entity. This in turn helps broaden the shareholder base.

Companies listed on BSE/NSE generally find that the market perception of their financial and business strength is enhanced.

14.4 PRINCIPAL STEPS IN AN IPO

The issue of securities to members of the public involves a fairly elaborate process, the principal steps of which are briefly described below:

- **Prospectus:** A draft prospectus is prepared giving out details of the company, promoter's background, management, terms of the issue, project details, modes of financing, past financial performance, projected profitability and others.
- **Approval of Board:** An approval of the board of directors of the company is required for raising capital from public.
- **Appointment of Lead Managers:** The lead manager is a merchant banker who orchestrates the issue in consultation with the company. The lead manager must be selected carefully.
- **Appointment of Other Intermediaries:** Several intermediaries like co-managers, underwriters, bankers, brokers and principal brokers and registrars, facilitate the public issue process. These may be selected on the basis of experience, expertise, credibility, and cost.
- **Filing of the Prospectus with SEBI:** The prospectus or the offer document communicates information about the company and the proposed security issue to the investing public. All companies seeking to make a public issue have to file their offer document with SEBI. The prospectus and application form (alongwith Articles and Memorandum of Association) must also be forwarded to the concerned stock exchange, where the issue is to be listed, for approval.
- **Filing of the Prospectus with the Registrar of Companies:** The prospectus is signed by the directors and then filed with the Registrar of Companies, where the issue is to be listed, for approval.
- **Printing and Despatch of Prospectus:** After the prospectus is filed with the Registrar of Companies, the company should print the prospectus (along with the application form).
- **Filing of Initial Listing Application:** Within 10 days of filing the prospectus, the initial listing application must be made to the concerned stock exchanges, along with the initial listing fees.
- **Promotion of the Issue:** To promote the issue the company holds conferences for brokers, press and investors. Advertisements are also released in newspapers and periodicals to generate interest among potential investors.
- **Statutory Announcement:** The statutory announcement of the issue must be made after seeking the approval of the lead stock exchange.
- **Collection and Processing of Applications:** After the close of the public issue, the application forms are scrutinized, tabulated and accordingly shares are allotted.
- **Establishing the Liability of Underwriters:** If the issue is undersubscribed, the liability of the underwriters has to be established.
- **Allotment of Shares:** According to SEBI guidelines, 50% of shares are reserved for QIB, 15% for HNI and 35% for Retail Individual Bidders. RIB is individual bidder who bids for less than ₹ 2,00,000.
- **Listing of the Issue:** The detailed listing application should be submitted to the concerned stock exchanges along with the listing agreement and the listing fee.

14.5 PRIVATE PLACEMENT

Raising of capital via private rather than public placement. The result is the sale of debt or equity securities to a single buyer/investor or to relatively few number of buyers/investors. Private placements do not have to be registered with organizations such as the SEBI because no public offering is involved. There is also no need for a formal prospectus or an underwriting agreement. A statement in lieu of prospectus is filed. The terms of the issue are negotiated between the company and the investors. The sale is generally conducted by a Merchant Bank who acts as an agent in bringing together the buyers and the sellers. The issuers are normally the listed public limited companies or closely held public or private limited companies which cannot or would not like to access the primary market. The securities are placed normally with the institutional investors, mutual funds, or other financial institutions.

Advantages of Private Placement:

The private placement market has grown phenomenally in recent years. This may be attributed to the following factors:

1. Accessibility 2. Flexibility 3. Speed 4. Lower issue cost.

14.6 BOUGHT OUT DEAL

Bought out Deal (BOD) is a process of investment by a sponsor or a syndicate of investors/ sponsors directly in a company. Such direct investment is being made with an understanding between the company and the sponsor to go for public offering in a mutually agreed time. Bought out deal, as the name suggests, is a type of wholesale sale of equities of a company. A company allots shares in full or in lots to sponsors at a price negotiated between the company and the sponsor(s). After a particular period agreed upon between the sponsor(s) and the company the shares are issued to the public by the sponsor(s) with a premium. After the public offering the shares are listed in one or more stock exchanges.

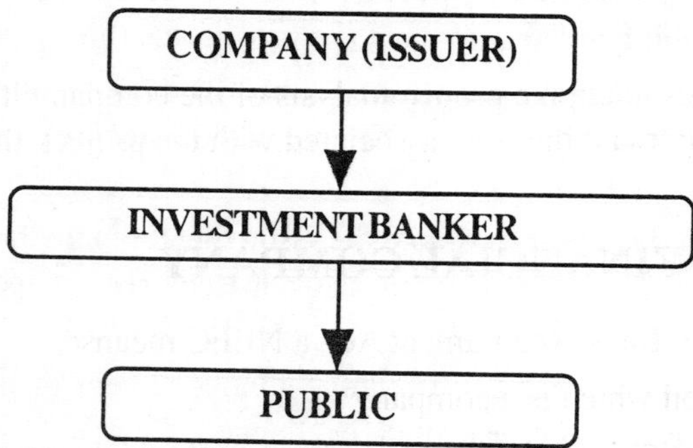

Advantages of BOD

(a) The company has the advantage of using the fund immediately without waiting as in case of direct public issue. In case of BOD the company gets funds instantly and is able to focus its attention on project implementation without worrying for source of investment. Bought out deals are ideally suited in circumstances when money needs to be arranged fast without which project may suffer. Lowering or eliminating issue cost is another advantage to the company.

(b) The time taken to raise money in the money in the capital market by a company takes as much as six months and this is very high for a company in the infancy stage.

(c) In case of a new and untried product it is easier to convince an investment banker for an investment in the company than the general public. Hence, BOD is an innovative method of financing for such companies.

(d) When the market sentiment is low and the secondary market is undergoing a bear phase, a company may not like to come to the market with a public issue. In such case BOD is a superior process to get fund for the company.

(e) The merchant bankers also gain from a BOD. The merchant banks expect a return of around 30% from a bought out deal, whereas private financing institutions expect a return of 40%-60% from a BOD. The gains can be tremendous provided the sponsors select proper issues and price it attractively to the investors.

(f) The investors also gain from the BOD in a way that they get good issues where some merchant bankers have already invested in it. The merchant bankers are professionals and can make proper appraisal of a company.

Drawbacks

(a) There is a fear of loss of management control because the sponsor is a holder of a large chunk of equities at one time. The sponsor may also influence the policy decision which may affect the functioning of the company.

(b) The investment banker who has to off-load the equities in the primary market at a later date is entitled to ask higher price for the risk taken by him. But this price may scare away the common investors, in case perceived excessive.

(c) If a company does not perform as per the expectations of sponsor or if the promoter does not cooperate with the sponsor later, the sponsor may have a tough time and may find its entire investment got eroded.

If a merchant banker does not make proper analysis of the company it may face a lot of problems with the BOD. Unless it evaluates all the risks associated with the project, there is every chance that the sponsor may burn his fingers.

14.7 NON-BANKING FINANCIAL COMPANY

According to the Reserve Bank Amendment Act, a NBFC means:

1. Financial institution which is a company
2. A non-banking institution which is a company and which has as its principal business the receiving of deposits under any scheme or arrangement or in any other manner or lending in any manner.
3. Such other non-banking institutions or class of such institutions with the previous approval of the Central Government.

Non-banking financial companies (NBFCs) are financial intermediaries engaged primarily in the business of accepting deposits and making loans and advances, investments, leasing, hire purchase, etc.

NBFC sector is characterized by a large number of privately owned, decentralized and relatively small-sized financial intermediaries. NBFCs are of various types, such as, loan companies (LCs), investment companies (ICs), hire purchase finance companies (HPFCs), equipment leasing companies (ELCs), mutual benefit financial companies (MNBCs) also known as Nidhis, banking companies (RNBSC). Loan companies, investment companies, hire purchase finance companies and equipment leasing companies are defined on the basis of the principal activity of their business. Customer orientation, concentration on the main financial centres and attractive rates of return offered by them are some of the reasons for their rapid growth. Primarily engaged in the area of retail banking, they face competition from banks and financial institutions. Depositors get higher returns in the form of interest but also face higher risk in certain cases in the form of nonpayment of dues.

Concept Testing

(a) *Greenshoe Option*

There is also a greenshoe option in case of an oversubscription of the issue. The greenshoe option, basically, gives the issuer company a right to allot an addition up to 15% of equity issue. This right can be exercised by the company in case of extra demand due to oversubscription of the issue and or extra funds required than earlier estimated to execute the project. The Company can exercise 'Greenshoe option' only if mentioned in offer document.

(b) *Reverse Book Building*

Securities and Exchange Board of India has issued the SEBI (Delisting of Securities) Guidelines 2003 for delisting of shares from stock exchanges which provide the overall framework for voluntary delisting by a promoter or acquirer through a process referred to as Reverse Book Building.

The promoter or acquirer shall appoint trading members for placing bids on the online electronic system. Investors may approach trading members for placing offers on the on-line electronic system. The shareholders desirous of availing the exit opportunity shall deposit the shares offered with the trading members prior to placement of orders. Alternately, they may mark a pledge for the same to the trading member.

The final offer price shall be determined as the price at which the maximum number of shares have been offered. The promoter/acquirer shall have the choice to accept the price. If the price is accepted, the acquirer shall be required to accept all offers up to and including the final price. If the quantity eligible for acquiring securities at the final price offered does not result in public shareholding falling below the required level of public holding for continuous listing, the company shall remain listed.

At the end of the book building period, the merchant banker to the book building exercise shall announce the final price and the acceptance (or not) of the price by the promoter/acquirer.

(c) *Corporate Governance*

Corporate governance refers to the distribution of rights and responsibilities among different participants in a corporate entity. Its core principles are fairness, transparency, accountability and responsibility. Corporate governance has emerged as an integral part of Corporate Financial Management practices in India. The SEBI has specified Corporate governance code and Corporate governance rating.

(d) *ASBA: Applications Supported by Blocked Amount in case of Application in Public Issue.*

(e) *SCODA: SEBI Committee on Disclosures and Accounting standards.*

(f) *SFIO: Serious fraud investigation office.*

News Article

PURE AUCTION METHOD MAY BE A GAME CHANGER FOR IPO'S

(Economic Times, Nov.,09)

Move will Allow Investors, Rather than Companies to Decide Pricing of Issues

ON MONDAY, the capital market regulator stepped in to change the way public share offerings happen. To begin with Securities and Exchange Board of India (SEBI) had announced a pure auction method of book building for follow-on public issues. Chances are this could be a precursor to a bigger change in the IPO market. A look at what it means:

What is the pure auction method of book building?

In this format, the company mentions a floor price. Investors are free to bid at any price above the floor price, and shares are allotted on a top-down basis, starting from the highest bidder.

How is it different from the existing form of book building?

In a typical book built issue, the merchant banker to the issue quotes the price band within which the investors have to bid. This band may not always represent the fair value. But investors wanting to participate in the issue have no choice but to bid within that band.

What are the benefits of the pure auction method?

It gives a more realistic picture of the demand for an issue. For instance, in a regular book-built issue, institutions have to factor an oversubscription while applying for the shares. If they intend to buy one lakh shares, they may had to bid for 10 or even 20 times that quantity, since the allotment is done on a pro rata basis. (If an issue is subscribed 20 times, then the investor will get only one share for every 20 shares he has bid). In a pure auction method, the institutions will bid only for the quantify they intend to buy, and quote a higher price, if need be, to ensure that they get the desired quantity. Retail investors will get the shares at a discount to what the institutional players have bid at, since SEBI has stipulated that retail be allotted shares at the floor price.

How is the pure auction format different from the Dutch auction format?

In a Dutch auction, potential investors enter bids for the number of shares they want to purchase at the price they are willing to pay. However, the price that each bidder pays is based on the lowest price of the successful bidders, or essentially the last successful bid. For instance, if the company has fixed the floor price at ₹ 50 per share, and the lowest bid is for ₹ 60, then the investors who have bid above ₹ 60 will also be allotted shares at ₹ 60 a piece. Google had raised $1.67 billion in 2004 through a Dutch auction.

What is SEBI's intention in introducing the pure auction method?

SEBI intends to improve the price discovery process by allowing investors, rather than companies, to decide on the pricing of the issue.

Is it mandatory for companies coming out with public issues to follow the pure auction format.

No, it is optional. Besides, SEBI will be experimenting this format with follow-on public offerings (FPOs), to begin with, and that too in only in the portion reserved for institutional investors.

What are the concerns of companies regarding the pure auction method?

Companies raising funds are particular about the profile of institutional investors participating in their public issues. In a pure auction method, short-term investors (like hedge funds, for instance) may bid aggressively, hoping to make a quick buck within a couple of days of listing. In the process, long-term investors who bid conservatively may lose out.

Dual Listing

What is dual listing?

Put simply, it's a process that allows a company to be listed on the stock exchanges of two different countries. The company's shares, which enjoy voting rights, can be traded on both the bourses.

When two companies in two countries enter into an equity alliance without an outright merger, dual listing means continued listing of the firms in both the countries. The key point to note here is that shareholders can buy and sell shares of both the companies on bourses in the two countries. In other words, if the Bharti MTN deal happens with a dual listing rider, a Bharti share can be sold on the Johannesburg Stock Exchange and vice versa.

How common is it?

Well, not exactly, mainly because of the complexities involved. However, there are enough examples to prove that it works: Royal Dutch Shell (UK/Netherlands), BHP Billiton (Australia/UK) Rio Tinto Group (Australia/UK), Unilever (UK/Netherlands)

Is it allowed in India?

No. Dual listing will need major amendments to key corporate laws of the country.

Like...

To begin with, the existing Companies Act and its proposed successor would both need to be amended.

In the case of a dual listed company, an investor can buy shares in one country and sell it in an overseas market. That would need the Indian rupee to be fully convertible, something that the central bank is yet to allow.

The Foreign Exchange Management Act (FEMA) too would need to be amended. Besides, domestic trading in shares denominated in foreign currency cannot happen without the permission of the Reserve Bank of India.

As it stands now, the proposed deal between Bharti and MTN does not require dual listing. However, if that happens, Bharti shares will have to be listed on the Johannesburg Stock Exchange, and MTN on NSE or BSE. In addition, the companies will need government permission to allow composition of a board identical to that of a foreign company.

How is it different from ADRs/GDRs?

In case of ADRs/GDRs, the companies deposit their equity shares with a custodian, say a bank, which in turn issues depository receipts to the investors. These receipts have all the rights, barring voting rights. Investors can convert ADRs/GDRs into underlying shares, which can be issued only within India and traded only on domestic bourses.

Other Updates

- An retail investor is one whose application amount is less than ₹ 2,00,000.
- The QIB portion, now closes a day before closing date. This RIB to gauge QIB response to the issue accordingly decide upon application.

❑❑❑

CHAPTER 15 PUBLIC SECTOR IN INDIA

15.1 EVOLUTION

Prior to Independence, there were few 'Public Sector' enterprises in the country. These included the Railways, the Posts and Telegraphs, the Port Trusts, the Ordinance Factories, All India Radio, few enterprises like the Government Salt Factories, Quinine Factories, etc., which were departmentally managed.

Independent India adopted planned economic development policies in a democratic, federal polity. The country was facing problems like inequalities in income and low levels of employment, regional imbalances in economic development and lack of trained manpower. India at that time was predominantly an agrarian economy with a weak industrial base, low level of savings, inadequate investments and infrastructure facilities. In view of this type of socio-economic set up, our visionary leaders drew up a roadmap for the development of Public Sector as an instrument for self-reliant economic growth. This guiding factor led to the passage of Industrial Policy Resolution of 1948 and followed by Industrial Policy Resolution of 1956. The 1948 Resolution envisaged development of core sectors through the public enterprises. Public sector would correct the regional imbalances and create employment. Industrial Policy Resolution of 1948 laid emphasis on the expansion of production, both agricultural and industrial; and in particular on the production of capital equipment and goods satisfying the basic needs of the people, and of commodities the export of which would increase earnings of foreign exchange.

In early years of independence, capital was scarce and the base of entrepreneurship was also not strong enough. Hence, the 1956 Industrial Policy Resolution gave primacy to the role of the State which was directly responsible for industrial development. Consequently the planning process (5-year Plans) was initiated taking into account the needs of the country. The new strategies for the public sector were later outlined in the policy statements in the years 1973, 1977, 1980 and 1991. The year 1991 can be termed as the watershed year, heralding liberalisation of the Indian economy.

The public sector provided the required thrust to the economy and developed and nurtured the human resources, the vital ingredient for success of any enterprise; public or private.

15.2 GLOBAL TREND

The public sector emerged as the driver of economic growth consequent to the industrial revolution in Europe. With the advent of globalization, the public sector faced new challenges in the developed economies. No longer the public sector had the privilege of operating in a sellers market and had to face competition both from domestic and international competitors. Further, in the second half of the 20th century in the developed economies, the political opinion started swinging towards the views that the intervention as well as investment by Government in commercial activities should be reduced to the extent possible.

Many eminent economists argued that Government must not venture into those areas, where the private sector could undertake job efficiently. Lot of emphasis was laid on market-driven economies, rather than State controlled and administered economies. The collapse of socialist economy of the Soviet block convinced the policy planners, around the world, that role of the State should be that of a facilitator and regulator rather than the producer and manager. It may be worth-mentioning that, in various countries, the turn towards liberalism including deregulation and decontrol also led to discontent amongst some sections of population as its benefits did not flow down to the weaker and disadvantaged sections of society.

Today, both public sector and private sector have become an integral part of the economy. There may not be much difference in working of these sectors in advanced countries, but in developing countries, the performance of public sector has considerable scope for improvement. It is also observed that pay packages are almost similar in both sectors in developed countries, but large differences exist in remuneration in the two sectors in developing countries, like ours.

The public sector provided the required thrust to the economy and developed and nurtured the human resources, the vital ingredient for success of any enterprise; public or private.

The main elements of the present Government policy towards public sector enterprises as contained in the National Common Minimum Programme (NCMP) are reproduced below:

(i) To devolve full managerial and commercial autonomy to successful, profit-making companies operating in a competitive environment

(ii) Generally, profit-making companies will not be privatized

(iii) Every effort will be made to modernize and restructure sick public sector companies and revive sick industry

(iv) Chronically loss making companies will either be sold-off, or closed, after all workers have got their legitimate dues and compensation

(v) Private industry will be inducted to turn-around companies that have the potential for revival

(vi) Privatization revenues will be used for designated social sector schemes

(vii) Public sector companies and nationalized banks will be encouraged to enter the capital market to raise resources and offer new investment avenues to retail investors.

The Government has made a clear commitment to empowering the CPSEs and their managements. It was recognised that public enterprises could not compete effectively with private entrepreneurs without freedom to function and operate commercially. Thus, the concept of Navratna and Mini-ratna was introduced with greater delegated authority, both financial and managerial. Government has realized that 'Navratnas', 'Mini-ratnas' and other CPSEs are required to grow and deliver on the promises they have made to their stakeholders. Other reforms have also been announced, such as professionalisation of the Boards of Directors of public sector enterprises and evaluation of performance of CPSEs through Memorandum of Understanding (MoU).

15.3 PERFORMANCE STATUS

Performance Status: Over the years, operations of CPSEs have extended to a wide range of activities in the manufacturing, engineering, steel, heavy machinery, machine tools, fertilisers, drugs, textiles, pharmaceuticals, petrochemicals, extraction and refining of crude oil and services such as telecommunication, trading, tourism, warehousing, etc., and a range of consultancy services. In 2006-07, there were 247 Central Public Sector Enterprises in India, as compared to 236 in 1997-98. The macro-view of overall performance of these numbers of CPSEs in the last 10 years is given in Table 1.The following observations are made regarding the performance of CPSEs during the last 10 years.

(a) The capital employed has increased from ₹ 2,49,855 crore in 1997-98 to ₹ 6,65,124 crore in 2006-07 recording a growth of 266%.

(b) Number of loss incurring CPSEs, it has come down from 100 in 1997-98 to 59 in 2006-07.

(c) Turnover increased to ₹ 9,64,410 crore in 2006-07, from ₹ 2,76,002 crore in 1997-98 recording a net worth growth of 349% increased from ₹ 1,34,443 crore to ₹ 4,52,995 crore in 2006-07 recording a growth of 337%.

(d) The turnover is equal to ₹ 9,64,410 crore in 2006-07, which is an increase of 349% in comparison to 1997-98 (₹ 2,76,002 crore). As regards Net worth, it has increased by 337% in 2006-07 in comparison to 1997-98 (₹ 1,34,443 crore), and is presently at ₹ 4,52,995 crore.

(e) Net profit has increased by 599% in 2006-07 in comparison to 1997-98 (₹ 13582 crore), and is currently to the tune of ₹ 81,550 crore. reported by companies under the cognate groups of Petroleum (₹ 33,442 crore), Telecommunications Services (₹ 14,126 crore), Power Generation (₹ 12,115 crore), Coal and Lignite (₹ 8,853 crore), Steel (₹ 7,612 crore), Minerals and Metals (₹ 5246 crore), Financial Services (₹ 2,828 crore), Transportation Services (₹ 2,210 crore) and Heavy Engineering (₹ 2,123 crore). Overall, the grand total of net profits of all the CPSEs put together was ₹ 81,549 crore during 2006-07, which indicates 17.28% growth over 2005-06.

Table 1. Growth of Investment in CPESs

Particulars	**Total Investment (₹ in crore)**	**Enterprises (Numbers)**
On the eve of the 1st Five Year Plan (1.4.1951)	29	5
On the eve of the 2nd Five Year Plan (1.4.1956)	81	21
On the eve of the 3rd Five Year Plan (1.4.1961)	948	47
At the end of the 3rd Five Year Plan (31.3.1966)	2410	73
On the eve of the 4th Five Year Plan (1.4.1969)	3897	84
On the eve of the 5th Five Year Plan (1.4.1974)	6237	122
At the end of the 5th Five Year Plan (31.3.1979)	15534	169
On the eve of the 6th Five Year Plan (1.4.1980)	18150	179
On the eve of the 7th Five Year Plan (1.4.1985)	42673	215
At the end of the 7th Five Year Plan (31.3.1990)	99329	244
On the eve of the 8th Five Year Plan (1.4.1992)	135445	246
On the eve of the 9th Five Year Plan (1.4.1997)	213610	242
At the end of the 9th Five Year Plan (31.3.2002)	324614	240
As on 31.3.2003	335647	240
As on 31.3.2004	349994	242
As on 31.3.2005	357939	237
As on 31.3.2006	403705	239
As on 31.3.2007	421089	247

Table 2

Sl. No.	Cognate Group	Turnover during (₹ Cr.)		% change over the previous year
		2006-2007	2005-06	
I.	**Mining**			
1.1	Coal & Lignite	34144	34607	-1.34
1.2	Minerals & Metals	14057	12384	13.51
1.3	Crude Oil	65165	54989	18.51
	Total (I)	**113365**	**101980**	**11.16**
II	**Manufacturing**			
2.1	Steel	49399	41742	18.34
2.2	Petroleum (Ref & Marketing)	515942	441744	16.80
2.3	Fertilizers	10452	9364	11.62
2.4	Chemicals & Pharmaceuticals	1180	975	21.02
2.5	Heavy Engineering	19454	15038	29.37
2.6	Medium & Light Engineering	10649	9560	11.39
2.7	Transportation Equipment	12535	9619	30.32
2.8	Consumer Goods	3133	1660	88.81
2.9	Agro-based Industries	245	173	42.04
2.10	Textiles	517	604	-14.37
	Total (II)	**623506**	**530478**	**16.03**
III.	**Electricity**			
3.1	Generation	41580	34633	20.06
3.2	Transmission	3608	3153	14.43
	Total (III)	**45188**	**37786**	**19.59**
IV	**Services**			
4.1	Trading and Marketing	94633	81212	16.53
4.2	Transport Services	2584[illegible]	25528	1.16
4.3	Contract & Construction services	[illegible]472	4453	22.90
4.4	Ind. Dev. & Tech. Consul. Services	3493	3246	7.61
4.5	Tourist Services	1037	671	54.38
4.6	Financial Service	12253	10185	20.30
4.7	Telecommunication Services	39638	41756	-5.07
4.8	Section 25 Companies			
	Total (IV)	**18235**	**167051**	**9.16**
	Grand Total (I + II + III + IV)	**964410**	**837295**	**15.18**

(*Source:* Public Enterprises-Annual survey of CPSES- 2006-07).

Table 3.

Sl. No	Cognate Group	2006-07 (₹ in crore)		2005-06 (₹ in crore)		% change
		Net profit/ Loss	No. of GPSEs	Net Profit/Loss	No. of GPSEs	Over the prev. years
I	**Mining**					
1.1	Coal & Lignite	8853.71	9	8215.72	9	7.77
1.2	Minerals & Metals	5246.05	10	4.39.23	10	29.88
1.3	Crude Oil	18335.46	3	16770.16	3	9.33
	Total (I)	**32435.22**	**22**	**29.25.11**	**22**	**11.75**
II	**Manufacturing**					
2.1	Steel	7612.7	6	5307.2	6	43.44
2.2	Petroleum (Ref & Marketing)	151.07.36	8	9411.17	8	60.53
2.3	Fertilizers	-2474.77	8	-1990.17	8	24.35
2.4	Chemicals & Pharmaceuticals	-123.45	14	-436.74	14	-71.73
2.5	Heavy Engineering	2123.34	10	976.54	10	117.43
2.6	Medium & Light Engineering	-29.3	24	-30.89	24	-5.15
2.7	Transportation Equipment	2209.06	10	1044.5	10	111.49
2.8	Consumer Goods	-212.92	12	143.15	12	-248.74
2.9	Agro Based Industries	-1.58	4	-21.31	4	-92.59
2.10	Textiles	-1338.62	5	792.6	14	-298.89
	Total (II)	**22871.82**	**101**	**15196.13**	**110**	**50.51**
III	**Electricity**					
3.1	Generation	10883.43	7	9078.79	7	19.88
3.2	Transmission	1232.73	2	1009.38	2	22.08
	Total (III)	**12115.73**	**9**	**10088.17**	**9**	**20.10**
IV	**Services**					
4.1	Trading and Marketing	432.49	18	357.81	18	20.87
4.2	Transport Services	1962.63	12	2527.8	12	-22.36
4.3	Contract & Construction services	-80.47	11	190.36	11	-57.73
4.4	Ind. Dev. & Tech. Consul. Services	373.44	15	355.65	15	5.00
4.5	Tourist Services	82.64	9	61.84	9	33.64
4.6	Financial Service	2827.62	16	2604.2	16	8.58
4.7	Telecommunication Services	14126.84	4	15226.71	4	-7.22
4.8	Section 25 Companies					
Total (IV)		**19725.19**	**85**	**20943.65**	**85**	**-19.22**
Grand Total (I + II + III + IV)		**81549.61**	**217**	**69536.12**	**226**	**17.28**

(*Source:* Public Enterprises-Annual survey of CPSES- 2006-07).

Note: In 2006-07, 9 operating units of National Textiles Corp. have stopped operations. Hence, total no. of Operational CPSEs has reduced to 217 from 226 in 2005-06.

Financial Ratios: The performance of CPSEs in terms of financial ratios in the last 10 financial years from 1997-98 to 2006-07 is shown in the Table 4:

C.E. Capital Employed **N.W.:** Net Worth

PBDITEP: Profit before Depreciation, Interest, Tax, Extraordinary item and Prior Period adjustment.

PBITEP: Profit before interest, Taxes, Extraordinary items and Prior Period Adjustment.

PBTEP: Profit before Taxes, Extraordinary items and Prior Period Adjustment.

4. Financial Ratios of CPSEs

(₹ in crore)

Particulars	1997-98	98-99	99-00	00-01	01-02	02-03	03-04	04-05	05-06	06-07
Sales to C.E.	110.47	117.01	128.47	138	122.77	137.32	139.43	147.56	143.24	145.0
PBDITEP to C.E.	21.24	21.31	20.54	20.91	22.97	24.38	28.15	28.26	24.42	26.77
PBTEP to NW	14.29	13.31	13.72	14.57	16.96	20.10	24.38	25.08	20.41	24.73
PBDITEP to T.O.	19.23	18.21	15.98	15.12	18.71	17.75	20.19	19.15	17.05	18.47
PBITEP to C.E.	14.89	14.99	13.95	14.72	16.21	17.39	21.01	21.50	18.33	20.91
PBITEP to T.O.	13.48	12.81	10.86	10.64	13.20	12.66	15.07	14.57	12.80	14.42
PBTEP to T.O.	6.96	6.35	5.66	5.45	7.99	8.49	11.28	11.51	10.12	11.62
Net Profit to T.O.	4.92	4.26	3.68	3.42	5.43	5.65	8.40	8.74	8.44	8.46
Net Profit to C.E.	5.44	4.98	4.73	4.72	6.66	7.75	11.71	12.90	12.09	12.26
Net Profit to N.W.	10.10	8.92	8.92	9.13	11.52	13.37	18.16	19.05	17.03	18.00
Divident Payout	26.57	37.35	38.07	52.77	31.06	42.57	28.85	31.84	32.56	32.87

(*Source:* Public Enterprises survey - 2006-07).

Contribution of CPSEs to the Economy and Central Exchequer: The share of output of CPSEs in GDP at market price stood at 8.23 per cent in 2006-07 and 8.21 per cent in 2005-06. The CPSEs made substantial contribution to the Central Exchequer through payment of dividends, interest on government loans and taxes and duties; the figures are shown in Table 5.

Table 5. Contribution of CPSEs to the economy

(₹ in crore)

Sl. No.	Particulars	2006-07	2005-06	2004-05	2003-04
I	**On Investment by CPSEs**				
1.	Dividend	18825.68	15200.85	15002.85	9596.45
2.	Interest	1975.08	138.22	731.67	794.32
	Total (I)	**20800.76**	**15339.07**	**15932.52**	**10390.77**
II	**Taxes and Duties**				
1	Excise Duty	64026.92	53278.48	44262.34	42963.75
2.	Customs Duty	11048.26	8601.18	10431.95	8408.67
3.	Corporate Tax	31997.93	26046.69	23613.61	17936.29
4.	Dividend Tax	383.12	3242.84	2742.48	1613.00
5.	Sales Tax	2817.25	5026.70	4487.80	3821.62
6.	Other Duties & Taxes	16654.04	13920.87	9132.97	3901.23
	Total (II)	**126927.54**	**110116.86**	**94671.15**	**78644.56**
	Grand Total (I + II)	**147728.30**	**125455.93**	**110603.67**	**89035.33**

The major share of contribution to Central Exchequer by the CPSEs was by way of payment of taxes and duties growth of 85.91% followed by dividend (11.74%) and interest (1.33%).

Revival of Sick CPSEs: The National Common Minimum Programme (NCMP) stipulates a strong and effective public sector, whose social objectives are met by its commercial functioning. Endeavour is to modernize and restructure sick CPSEs and revive sick industry. The chronically loss making CPSEs may be closed down or sold-off, after all the employees are paid their legitimate dues. The problem of sickness in CPSEs is addressed by the Administrative Ministries/Departments in the Government by evolving appropriate need based strategy concerning a particular CPSE. Some of the strategies for restructuring/revival of CPSEs including sick units on a long-term basis include:

- Revival through the process of BIFR;
- Financial restructuring;
- Formation of joint venture by induction of partners capable of providing technical, financial and marketing inputs; and
- Organizational restructuring and manpower rationalization through approved Voluntary Retirement Scheme (VRS).

In order to combat industrial sickness particularly with regard to the crucial sectors, where public money is locked up and for timely detection of sick and potentially sick industrial companies, Sick Industrial Companies Act (SICA) was extended to public enterprises in 1993; enabling sick public sector enterprises to be referred to a quasi-judicial body Board for Industrial and Financial Reconstruction (BIFR), to take appropriate measures for revival and rehabilitation of potentially sick industrial undertakings and for liquidation of non-viable companies.

Under the Sick Industrial Companies Act (SICA), 1985, a company is termed sick if at the end of any financial year, it has accumulated losses equal to or exceeding its entire net worth. Such industrial company is required to be referred to BIFR for formulation of rehabilitation/revival plan. Government set up a Board for Reconstruction of Public Sector Enterprises (BRPSE) in December 2004 to advise the Government inter alia on the measures to be taken to restructure/revive CPSEs.

The major share of contribution to Central Exchequer by the CPSEs was by way of payment of taxes and duties growth of 85.91% followed by dividend (11.74%) and interest (1.33%).

Revival of Sick CPSEs: The National Common Minimum Programme (NCMP) stipulates a strong and effective Public Sector, whose social objectives are met by its commercial functioning. Endeavour is to modernize and restructure sick CPSEs and revive sick industry. The chronically loss making CPSEs may be closed down or sold-off, after all the employees are paid their legitimate dues. The problem of sickness in CPSEs is addressed by the Administrative Ministries/Departments in the Government by evolving appropriate need based strategy concerning a particular CPSE. Some of the strategies for restructuring/revival of CPSEs including sick units on long-term basis include:

- Revival through the process of BIFR;
- Financial restructuring;
- Formation of joint venture by induction of partners capable of providing technical, financial and marketing inputs; and
- Organizational restructuring and manpower rationalization through approved Voluntary Retirement Scheme (VRS).

In order to combat industrial sickness particularly with regard to the crucial sectors, where public money is locked up and for timely detection of sick and potentially sick industrial companies, Sick Industrial Companies Act (SICA) was extended to public enterprises in 1993; enabling sick public sector enterprises to be referred to a quasi-judicial body – Board for Industrial and Financial Reconstruction (BIFR), to take appropriate measures for revival and rehabilitation of potentially sick industrial undertakings and for liquidation of non-viable companies.

Under the Sick Industrial Companies Act (SICA), 1985, a company is termed sick if at the end of any financial year, it has accumulated losses equal to or exceeding its entire net worth. Such industrial company is required to be referred to BIFR for formulation of rehabilitation/revival plan. Government set up a Board for Reconstruction of Public Sector Enterprises (BRPSE) in December 2004 to advise the Government inter alia on the measures to be taken to restructure/revive CPSEs, importance of the corporation. The pay scales of Chief Executives and full-time Functional Directors in CPSEs are determined as per the schedule of the concerned enterprise. As on 31.3.2007, there were 247 CPSEs. Out of 247 there are 54 Schedule 'A', 77 Schedule 'B', 48 Schedule 'C' and 06 are Schedule 'D' enterprises. The rest have not been categorized. The details of the Board level posts (whole-time) as in the year 2006-07 are given in Table 7.

Table 6. Number employees employed by the CPSEs

Year	Employ. (in lakhs) (excl. Casual & daily	Emoluments (₹in crore)	Emoluments (As % of Turnover) rated workers)	Per Capita Emoluments (₹)
1997-98	19.59	25385	9019	129582
1998-99	19.00	26254	8.46	138179
199-00	18.06	30402	7.81	168339
2000-01	17.40	38223	8.34	219672
2001-02	19.92*	38556	8.05	193554
2002-03	18.66	42169	7.36	225986
2003-04	17.62	43919	6.96	248481
2004-05	17.00	48629	6.53	286053
2005-06	16.49	46851	5.59	284123
2006-07	16.14	52574	5.45	325738

(2001*-02 the number of employees have increased due to corporations of DOT)

Table 7

Schedule	Chief Executives	Whole-time Directors*
Schedule A	54	201
Schedule B	77	181
Schedule C	48	67
Schedule D	06	-
Total	185	449

*(Directors draw salary one scale below the Schedule of the Company) CPSEs have been classified based upon the power vested in the Board of Directors of the company as Navratna, Mini-ratna (Category I and II) and others including profit making, loss making, etc. On 31.3.2007, number of CPSEs in this classification has been given in Table 9.

Table 9

Category	No. of CPSEs as on 30.5.2008
Navratna	16
Miniratna, Category I	41
Miniratna, Category II	13
Profit Making	156
Loss Making	59
Listed Companies	45
Non-listed Companies	202
Section 25 & Under Construction	32

Composition of the Board of Directors: The guidelines on professionalisation of Boards of Directors issued in 1992 provide that outside professionals should be inducted on the Boards of CPSEs in the form of part-time non-official Directors and that the number of such Directors should be at least one-third of the actual strength of the Board. In the case of listed CPSEs headed by Executive Chairman, the number of non-official Directors (independent Directors) should be at least half the strength of the Board. The guidelines also provide that the number of Government Directors on the Boards should not be more than one-sixth of the actual strength of the Board subject to a maximum of two. Apart from this, there should be some functional Directors on each Board, whose number should not exceed 50% of the actual strength. For 2006-07, the data for all CPSEs related to number of CMDs, Chairman, Directors (Functional and Independent) and Nominee Directors, etc., have been given in Table 8.

Table 8

Designation	No.
CMDs	122
Chair-Full Time	4
Chairman-Part Time	42
Managing Directors	33
Functional Directors	371
Independent Directors	306
Government Nominee Directors	474

15.4 DEVELOPMENTS IN RECENT YEARS – A CRITICAL OVERVIEW

Social & Economic Development: Independent India has exhibited more impressive price stability than most developing economies. The inflation rate was, on an average, in the single digit for almost all the years since independence. On the growth rate, the annual GDP growth in the decade of 1950s was 3.6 per cent, in the 1960s it was 4.0 per cent, in 1980s it was 5.6 pe rcent and in the 1990's (excluding the Gulf war crisis year 1991-92) it was 6.3 per cent. In the new millennium, the growth rate accelerated to 6.9 per cent; and during the period from 2003-04 to 2006-07 it has averaged 8.6 per cent. The changes in the social and economic developments that have taken place in the country since India became independent are quite substantial. The total outlay of the first Five Year Plan (from 1951-56) was ₹ 2,069 crore, which has increased to ₹ 66,632 crore for the tenth Five Year Plan (2002-07). The population of India in the year 1951 was around ₹ 36 crore and has increased to ₹ 103 crore as per the

2001 Census. The head count ratio of persons below poverty line has declined from the level of 54.9% in the year 1973-74 to 36% in 1993-94 (the latest year for which the NSS data was available). The decline in the urban poverty level from 48% to 36% is significant as it coincides with the period of rapid urbanization.

During the period since 1997, successive governments have carried forward the country's economic reforms in industrial, trade and financial sectors. The approach of the Government has been to gradually move towards comprehensive restructuring of the economy to reap the benefits of the fast changing global business environment. Some of the major changes during the past decade from 1.1.97 to 31.12.06 that have significantly contributed to economic reform in the country are:

(a) The Foreign Exchange Management Act (FEMA), 1999 replaced the Foreign Exchange Regulations Act (FERA), 1973 with the objective of 'facilitating external trade and payments' and 'promoting the orderly development and maintenance of foreign exchange market in India' including introduction of convertibility of rupees on current account.

(b) Further, the enactment of Fiscal Responsibility and Budget Management (FRBM) Act in 2003 marked a significant reform initiative taken both by Central Government and some States in the context of fiscal responsibility.

(c) The Insurance Regulatory and Development Authority Act, 1999 is a major milestone in liberalisation as it opens the way to private entry into the insurance business, which has been a Government monopoly.

(d) New Telecom Policy was implemented in 1999 to facilitate India's vision of becoming an IT superpower and develop a world-class telecom infrastructure in the country.

(e) Replacement of MRTP Act, 1969 by Competition Act of 2002, in view of the policy shift from curbing monopolies to promoting competition. The Competition Act was enacted that marks a conscious departure from the previous Monopolies and Restrictive Trade Practices Act (MRTP). The Competition Law aims at doing away with the rigidly structured MRTP Act and is more flexible. Also, the regulatory authority under the Act i.e., 'Competition Commission of India' is being set-up with the aim of centralizing under one umbrella all controls to eliminate the negative aspects of competition.

(f) Electricity Act, 2003 was enacted to create competitive environment which will result in enhancing quality and reliability of service to consumers.

(g) The Foreign Trade Policy was notified for the year 2004-2009 incorporating the Export and Import Policy for the year 2002-2007; several other initiatives have been taken for Export Promotion.

(h) The Foreign Direct Investment policy has been reviewed and liberalised to promote FDI in various sectors.

(i) Tax reforms have taken place in a major way including rationalization of both direct and indirect tax laws. Customs tariffs have been lowered and service tax net is being widened. The input tax credit for both excise duty and service has been streamlined. One of the important tax reforms has been introduction of State-level Value Added Tax to replace the Sales Tax. Introduction of Goods and Services Tax regime to be effective from 01.04.2010 is underway.

(j) A number of Rules and Regulations have been issued by the Securities and Exchange Board of India (SEBI), to develop the capital market on healthy lines and protect the investors' interests in securities.

(k) Special Economic Zones (SEZs) are being set up to enable hassle-free manufacturing and trading for export and to free the industry from the plethora of rules and regulations governing imports and exports.

If one looks at the changes that have taken place in the country during post-liberalization period when the New Economic Policy (NEP) of 1991 was announced, and more particularly from 1997 onwards, it becomes clear that India has opted for an open economy with greater reliance upon market forces. In a nutshell, global competition has ended Indian industry's monopoly, in local market and broken the shackles of 'License Permit Raj'.

15.5 NEW OPPORTUNITIES

In the competitive industrial scenario, one of the key components to increase the bottom line in the globalized economy is to find out how an enterprise leverages capability at a global level for procurement, sourcing and delivering all its products and services across markets far more rapidly and takes advantage by cross leveraging between various markets. In this context, Mergers and Acquisitions (M&A) have gained importance during the past few years and a storm of mergers of huge values have been notched-up. In response to the growing business and to release productive energies and to promote creativity of Indian businesses, the regulators have also issued guidelines to facilitate smooth transactions as well as making business restructuring tax neutral. Business consolidation of market share, synergies of operations, reduction of time and money in entering the domestic and foreign market, reducing uncertainty of market share, to meet end-to-end solution needs, buying out competition, realization of stock market valuations, create value for shareholders, etc., are some of the reasons leading to spur in M&A activities within India as well as promote overseas acquisitions by Indian companies.

Integration of Indian economy with global markets has thrown up new opportunities and challenges. Some of the public sector enterprises with strategic vision are actively exploring new avenues and have increased their activities to go in for mergers, acquisitions, amalgamations, takeovers and for creating new joint ventures. The Navratna CPSEs, which enjoy greater autonomy to incur capital expenditure and enter into joint ventures in India and abroad should avail of these opportunities for rapid growth overseas. Acquisitions, JVs and green field projects in Petroleum Sector have already taken place and are under active consideration in power, coal and mining sectors.

Another important initiative towards restructuring of pubic sector enterprises is 'Disinvestment' in select CPSEs. The statement of Industrial Policy of 1991 stated that in the case of selected enterprises, part of Government holdings in the equity share capital of these enterprises will be disinvested in order to provide further market discipline to the performance of public enterprises.

Some CPSEs have been such as Videsh Sanchar Nigam Ltd., (VSNL), Indian Petrochemicals Corporation Ltd., (IPCL), Maruti Udyog Limited (MUL), CMC Ltd., etc., have been privatized. In addition, there are CPSEs which have been acquired by other CPSEs by way of disinvestment and open bidding such as acquisition of IBP by Indian Oil Corporation Limited. There are also instances of acquisition of private firms by CPSEs as in the case of MRPL, which was a joint sector company and became a CPSE subsequent to acquisition of its majority shares by ONGC. There are also cases of domestic offerings, GDR listing, offloading of some equity shares in the market or to another organization, and forming joint ventures, by CPSEs.

□□□

15.6 LABOUR REFORMS

The first National Labour Commission, which had submitted its report in 1969, had promised a lot in the direction of social security, social welfare, wages, social insurance, industrial relations, industrial adjudication, collective bargaining, etc. In sequel to the recommendations made in the report of the National Commission on Labour, a series of enactments were passed. After a gap of around 30 years, the Second National Labour Commission (NLC) was constituted to suggest rationalization of existing laws relating to labour in the organized sector, and to suggest an umbrella legislation for ensuring minimum level of protection to the workers in the unorganized sector. The report was submitted in the year 2002 to the Government. The need for setting up of Second NLC was felt due to vast changes occurring in the economy during the last three decades particularly in the post-liberalization period.

15.7 HR PERSPECTIVE

Human Resources (HR) is one of the most complex and challenging fields of management, as it deals with the people dimension in business management. The biggest challenge now being faced by CEOs is HR as it plays a strategic role in the growth of an organization and thereby maximizing returns on investment. The HR management's role is required to be perceived as business strategic partner in the organization and it has to identify its key role with clarity in the context of organizational working as well as contributor to organization's strategy. Strategic HR practices help the organization in achieving a long-term and short-term goals through optimum utilization of human resources. This involves the development of human resources objectives, which are in alignment with the enterprise objectives. Thus, there is a new agenda in the role of HR and it has to come out from its traditional role of managing HR alone.

The changes in industrial scenario have sent clear signals to the public sector to revisit their Human Resources (HR) Management practices and formulate HR strategies with focus on profitability on a long-term basis. To achieve this, the thrust has to be on competitive HR policies and practices. HRM should now focus to build enterprises that change, learn, move and act faster than those of its competitors; and it is time to build competitive and not merely comfortable public sector enterprises. HRM of public sector enterprises is also required to keep pace with the changing legal and governmental regulations.

Human resources play an important role in development of businesses and is the main differentiator of excelling companies from other companies. In view of the growth in business, expanding market, high demand by consumers and change in technology, the biggest challenge being faced during the last decade by companies has been the need to meet their requirement for talented people. The rush for hiring of people is being seen in all the sectors such as IT and IT-enabled services, infrastructure, engineering, banking, airline, hospitality, biotech, medical, retail, etc. The demand-supply equation for talented professionals is heavily skewed in favour of the former; and as a result both attraction and retention have emerged as major challenges for HR professionals. The problem is not only limited within the country but it has become a global phenomenon, and even the MNCs and global recruitment firms are hiring people from India to meet their demands. However, in recent times, one can also see that the trend is gradually reversing and now expatriates are being assigned to or hired for Indian operations, and even a lot of expatriate Indians working abroad are coming back because India has now a lot to offer. The future outlook confirms that global nomad employees, who move from country-to-country on varying assignments will become a common feature.

CHAPTER 16

FINANCIAL MANAGEMENT IN SICK UNITS

The incidence of sickness, quite understandably, has been a cause of considerable concern to the government, financial institutions, and banks. This has been stated several times in the 'Economic Survey' prepared annually by the government.

16.1 DEFINITION OF SICKNESS

There are two ways of looking at insolvency. The stock-based insolvency occurs when the firm has a negative net worth implying that its assets are less than its debt. The flow-based insolvency occurs when the operating cashflows of the firm are not enough to meet its obligations.

A business firm may be regarded as sick if: (i) it faces financial embarrassment (arising out of its inability to honour its obligations as and when they mature), and (ii) its viability is seriously threatened by adverse factors.

16.2 CAUSES OF SICKNESS

Hence sickness may be caused by:

- Unfavourable external environment
- Managerial deficiencies

Unfavourable External Environment: The firm may be affected by one or more of the following external factors over which it may hardly have any control.

- Shortage of key inputs like power and basic raw materials.
- Changes in governmental policies with respect to excise duties, customs duties, export duties, reservation, etc.
- Emergence of large capacity leading to intense competition. E.g., Telecom.
- Development of new technology.
- Sudden decline in orders from the government.
- Shifts in consumer preferences.
- Natural calamities.
- Adverse international developments.
- Reduced lending by financial institutions.

Managerial Deficiencies: Management can be deficient in many ways. An attempt has been made below to classify managerial deficiencies function-wise. These shortcomings, singly or in combination, can induce sickness.

Production	Marketing
* Improper location	* Inaccurate demand projection
* Wrong technology	* Improper product-nix
* Uneconomic plant size	* Wrong product positioning
* Unsuitable plant and machinery	* Irrational price structure
* Inadequate emphasis on R&D	* Inadequate sales promotion
* Poor quality control (e.g., HMT) * Poor maintenance	* High distribution costs * Poor customer service
Finance	**Human Resources**
* Wrong capital structure	* Ineffective leadership
* Bad investment decisions	* Inadequate human resources
* Weak management control	* Overstaffing
* Inadequate MIS	* Poor organisational design
* Poor working capital management	* Insufficient training
* Strained relations with investors	* Irrational compensation

16.3 SYMPTOMS OF SICKNESS

Sickness does not occur overnight, but develops gradually over time. A firm which is becoming sick shows symptoms which indicate that trouble lies ahead of it. Some of the common symptoms are:

- ➢ Delay or default in payment to suppliers
- ➢ Irregularity in the bank account
- ➢ Delay or default in payment to banks and financial institutions
- ➢ Non-submission of information to banks and financial institutions
- ➢ Frequent requests to banks and financial institutions for additional credit
- ➢ Decline in capacity utilisation
- ➢ Poor maintenance of plant and machinery
- ➢ Low turnover of assets
- ➢ Accumulation of inventories
- ➢ Inability to take trade discount
- ➢ Excessive turnover of personnel
- ➢ Extension of accounting period
- ➢ Resort to 'creative accounting' which seeks to present a better financial picture than what it really is (e.g., Satyam).
- ➢ Decline in the price of equity shares and debentures.

16.4 PREDICTION OF SICKNESS

While the above symptoms suggest that the unit is in difficulty and may become potentially sick, it is not easy to reach a definitive conclusion about impending sickness on the basis of these symptoms. Financial ratios can be used for predicting industrial sickness with greater reliability.

Univariate Analysis: In univariate analysis, an attempt is made to predict sickness on the basis of single financial ratios.

Suppose we have a mixed sample of four sick (S) and four non-sick (N) firms with their ROI (for a given year) arranged in an ascending order as follows:

-5	-2	3	4		6	8	10	12
S	S	(N)	S	↑	N	N	(S)	N

Inspecting the above configuration, we choose a cut-off point, where the arrow is shown, to separate the sick group from the non-sick group - to the left of the cut-off point lies the sick group, to the right of the cut-off point lies the non-sick group. The cut-off point is chosen in such a way that the number of misclassifications is minimised. It may be noted

- Debt Equity Ratio
- ROI Ratio
- EBDIT/Sales
- OCF/Sales

Multivariate Analysis: Univariate analysis examines financial ratios individually but does not assess the joint predictive power of various combinations of ratios. Multivariate analysis, on the other hand, seeks to predict industrial sickness using a methodology that considers the combined influence of several variables (financial ratios in our context).

Where Z is the discriminant index, Xis are independent variables, and ais are coefficients of independent variables.

The use of multiple discriminant analysis for predicting business failure may be illustrated by a classic study conducted by E.I. Altman3. He studied a sample of 33 bankrupt firms along with a paired sample of 33 non-bankrupt firms. He examined 22 financial ratios with a view to selecting the 5 which jointly possessed the maximal power to predict bankruptcy. The discriminant function which discriminated best between the bankrupt and non-bankrupt firms is:

$$Z = 3.3\frac{\text{EBIT}}{\text{Total assets}} + 1.2\frac{\text{Net working capital}}{\text{Total assets}} + 1.0\frac{\text{Sales}}{\text{Total assets}} + 0.6\frac{\text{Market value of equity}}{\text{Book value of equity}}$$

$$+1.4\frac{\text{Accumulate dretained earnings}}{\text{Total assets}}$$

where Z is an index of bankruptcy.

A Z score less than 2.675 implies that the firm has a 95 per cent chance of becoming bankrupt within one year. However, Altman's analysis shows that the area between 1.81 and 2.99 may be regarded as a gray area. Thus $Z \leq 1.81$ predicts bankruptcy and $Z \geq 2.99$ nonbankruptcy.

Altman's original Z score model was developed for listed firms and manufacturing firms. He revised his model for unlisted firms and non-manufacturing firms. The revised model is:

$$Z = 6.56\frac{\text{Net working capital}}{\text{Total assets}} + 3.25\frac{\text{Accumulated retained earnings}}{\text{Total assets}} + 1.05\frac{\text{EBIT}}{\text{Total assets}}$$
$$+ 6.72\frac{\text{Book value of equity}}{\text{Total liabilities}}$$

According to his analysis:

$Z < 1.23$ indicates a bankruptcy prediction

$1.23 < Z < 2.90$ indicates gray area

$Z > 2.90$ indicates no bankruptcy

A Critique of Bankruptcy Prediction Models: Though various bankruptcy prediction models appear to possess some predictive value, it is very difficult to generalise about corporate failure for the following reasons:

1. We do not have a well-defined theory of corporate failure to guide empirical work.
2. Empirical studies are statistically flawed because they are retrospective in nature. As Johnson argues: Altman demonstrated that failed and non-failed firms have dissimilar ratios, not that ratios have predictive power. But the crucial problem is to make an inference in the reverse direction, i.e., from ratios to failures.

16.5 REVIVAL OF A SICK UNIT

When an industrial unit is identified as sick, a viability study should be conducted to assess whether the unit can be revived/rehabilitated within a reasonable period. Viability study suggests that the unit can be rehabilitated, a suitable plan for rehabilitation must be formulated. If the viability study indicates that the unit is "better dead than alive", steps must be taken to liquidate it expeditiously.

Viability Study: A reasonably comprehensive assessment of the various aspects of the working of a unit, a viability study should cover the following:

- Market
- Operations
- Finance
- Human resources
- Environment

The viability study may suggest one of the following:

(a) The unit can be revived by adopting one or more of the following measures: debt restructuring, infusion of funds, correction of functional deficiencies, granting of special reliefs and concessions by the government, replacement of existing management because of its incompetence and/or dishonesty.

(b) The unit is not potentially viable – This essentially implies that the benefits expected from remedial measures are less than the cost of such remedial measures.

Revival Programme: The revival programme usually involves the following:

Settlement with Creditors: A sick unit is normally in straitened financial circumstances and is not able to honour its commitments to its creditors (financial institutions, debenture-holders, commercial banks, suppliers, and governmental authorities). To alleviate its financial distress, a settlement scheme has to be worked out which may involve one or more of the following: rescheduling of principal and interest payment; waiver of interest; conversion of debt into equity; payment of arrears in instalments.

Provision of Additional Capital: Typically, a revival programme entails provision of additional capital. This may be required for modernisation and repair of plant and machinery, for purchase of balancing equipment, for sustaining a new marketing drive, and for enhanced working capital needed to support a higher level of operations. The additional capital has to be provided on concessional terms, at least for the initial years, so that the financial burden on the unit is not high.

Divestment and Disposal: The revival programme may involve divestment of unprofitable plants and operations and disposal of slow moving and obsolete stocks. The thrust of these actions should be to strengthen the liquidity of the unit and facilitate reallocation of resources for enhancing the profitability of the unit.

Reformulation of Product-market Strategy: Many business failures can be traced to an ill-conceived product-market strategy. For reviving a sick unit, its product-market strategy may have to be significantly reformulated to improve the prospects of its profitable recovery. This, of course, calls for a great deal of imagination and penetrating analysis.

Modernisation of Plant and Machinery: In order to improve manufacturing efficiency, plant and machinery may have to be modernised, renovated, and repaired. This may be essential for attaining certain cost standards and quality norms for competing effectively in the market place.

Reduction in Manpower: Generally, sick firms tend to be overstaffed. The revival programme must seek to reduce superfluous manpower. Remember an old managerial law: "The leaner the organisation, the greater are its chances of survival". Often a 'golden handshake' involving paying a significant retrenchment compensation is a better proposition than carrying redundant manpower on the payroll of the unit. E.g., Bajaj

Strict Control Over Costs: A profitable organisation can afford wastefulness and laxity in its expenditures. A tottering firm, seeking to regain its health and vigour, has to exercise strict control over its costs, particularly over its discretionary expenses. A zero-base review of all the discretionary expenses may be undertaken to eliminate programmes and activities which are a drain on the finances of the firm. E.g., HUL.

Streamlining of Operations: Manufacturing, purchasing, and selling operations have to be meticulously examined so that they can be streamlined. Value engineering, standardisation, simplification, cost-benefit analysis, and other approaches should be exploited fully to improve the efficiency of the operations. E.g., HUL.

Improvement in Managerial Systems: The managerial systems in the unit must be strengthened. In this exercise, greater attention may have to be paid to the following:

- Environmental monitoring
- Organisational structure
- Responsibility accounting

- Management information system
- Budgetary control

Workers' Participation: In general, workers' participation in management enhances employee commitment, motivation, and morale. Further, the suggestions offered by the workers result an improvements that lead to higher manufacturing efficiency and productivity. A sick organisation, which is being revived, can perhaps benefit even more from workers' participation in management. During the revival phase, the dedication, commitment, and support of workers is indispensable and meaningful workers' participation and involvement goes a long way in ensuring this.

Change of Management: A change in management may be necessary where the present management is dishonest and/or incompetent. It has been observed that a new chief executive, who is competent, committed, and uprighteous, can often bring about dramatic results. The classic example of this phenomenon was the dramatic turnaround of Chrysler Corporation under the stewardship of Lee Iacocca.

Merger with a Healthy Company: If a sick firm cannot pull itself by its own bootstraps, the option of merger with a healthy firm must be seriously explored. The healthy firm can leverage its resources to revive the sick firm. BOP with HDFC, Satyam with Mahindra.

16.6 DEBT RESTRUCTURING

Mechanisms for Debt Restructuring: Financially distressed companies that have difficulty in servicing their debt resort to debt restructuring aimed primarily at reducing the burden of debt.

Common Elements: Excluding the cases of Negotiated Settlement (NS) or a One Time Settlement (OTS) the common elements of debt restructuring schemes are as follows:

Interest Rate Relief: The contracted interest rate may be reduced if the borrower is not in a position to achieve cash break even.

Deferment of Past Interest Dues: The areas of interest, up to the restructuring date, are deferred and a repayment schedule spread over a period of time worked out.

Waiver of Penalties: Penalties levied in the form of compound interest and liquidated damages for non-payment of dues on time are generally waived.

Reschedulement of Loan Repayment: The loan repayment schedule is reworked, after assessing the cash flow position.

Reduction in the Loan Amount: In a situation where the borrower cannot potentially service the loan, lenders may write-off a portion of the loan.

CHAPTER 17

RISK MANAGEMENT AND DERIVATIVES

17.1 RISK MANAGEMENT

A risk management system must allow the management to deliberately accept risk such that the risk-return profile is consistent with its overall objectives.

The peculiarities of foreign exchange markets which result in risk:

- It operates as an over-the-counter market which implies exposure to credit risk.
- It is the only market which operates 24 hours a day which means that every open position is exposed to periods when it cannot be controlled.
- It is a multi-location market with no entry/exit barriers, therefore, competition is a variable factor. This results in market risk.
- Exchange rate fluctuate almost continuously which is the basis of rate risk.

The two entities which face exchange rate and interest rate based risk are the end-users, i.e.,, exporters, importers, individuals, etc., and banks who quote confirmed rates to these entities.

17.2 RISK VERSUS EXPOSURE

No.	Risk	Exposure
1	Risk can be defined as the possibility of a financial loss due to future uncertainties	Exposure can be defined as the gross value of the transaction amount on which loss could be incurred.
2	It is normally calculated in terms of domestic currency	It is normally determined in terms of foreign currency.
3	It should and can be controlled or managed through hedging transactions	Limiting exposure may adversely impact the volume of business growth and is therefore not normally attempted
4	Risk may be positive or negative	Exposure is always positive

17.3 HEDGING PROCESS

Hedging can be defined as a process or mechanism of reducing, minimizing or eliminating risk from a given transaction. A foreign exchange exposure is hedged or covered when the company takes certain steps to insulate itself from the adverse effects of exchange rate movements. The basic objective in hedging is to create a position in the foreign currency in the direction opposite to the one that exists so that ultimately the balance or net effect becomes zero. Hedging may be achieved through internal or external mechanisms.

17.4 INTERNAL HEDGING METHOD

Exposure Netting: Companies having both receivables and payables in a foreign currency, need not hedge receivables and payables separately, but can do so for the net position.

Denomination in Local Currency: The exchange risk can be completely avoided if the transaction is denominated in local currency. In such a case the exchange risk will be borne by the opposite party to the transaction.

Foreign Currency Accounts: In India, as per the Exchange Earners Foreign Currency (EEFC) account scheme, persons receiving foreign currency are entitled to retain in foreign currency 50% of the remittance received. The balance in this account can be used by the accountholder for purposes permitted in the exchange control regulations, including payment for imports. Thus, exchange risk is eliminated and the currency conversion cost can be avoided.

Leads and Legs: The manipulation of the timing of receipts and payments of foreign currency depending upon the expectations of change in currency values is known as leads and legs.

17.5 EXTERNAL HEDGING METHODS

A derivative can be defined as "a transaction or a financial instrument which derives its value through some other asset or security". Foreign currency derivatives derive their values from the value of the underlying currency.

Derivatives can be used for,

(a) hedging exchange rate risk
(b) speculation
(c) maximization of profits
(d) adjusting liquidity and hedging mismatched maturity risk (interest rate risk)

The commonly used foreign currency derivatives are:

(i) Foreign currency forward contracts.
(ii) Foreign currency swaps.
(iii) Foreign currency Futures contracts.
(iv) Foreign currency Option contracts.

Distinction Between Foreign Currency Swaps and Forward Contracts

No.	Swaps contracts	Forward contracts
1	Swaps involve simultaneous purchase and sale of equal amount of base currency which means there is no open exposure to rate change.	In forward contracts there is an outright purchase or sale of specific amount of base currency
2	Swaps can be viewed as a combination of spot and forward transactions.	They represent forward transactions only.
3	Swaps are available for longer maturity transactions extending beyond one year.	Forward markets are normally available only for transactions having maturity period of less than one year.

4	The currency swap covers both principal and interest payment.	To cover principal and interest payment through forward exchange market, a series of forward contracts of differing maturities and non-standard amounts would be required to hedge each cashflow separately.
5	Currency swaps are used to hedge liquidity and interest rate risk.	Forward contracts are used to hedge exchange rate risk.

American Options

American options are options that can be exercised on any day up to the expiration date. Most exchange traded options are American style options.

European Options

European options are options that can be exercised only on expiration date. European options are easier to evaluate than American options.

17.6 LIMITATIONS OF DERIVATIVES

Limitations of Derivatives

1. **Leveraging Increases Risk:** One of the important characteristic features of derivatives is that they help in leveraging resources. Thus, they are 'high risk-high-reward products'. There is a conscious acceptance of either high return or huge loss in all derivative instruments.
2. **Need for Regulatory Supervision:** To achieve the desired results, derivatives require appropriate accounting systems, efficient internal control systems and strict supervision. Regulations to restrict the use of derivatives for speculations are necessary.
3. **Need for Institutional Infrastructure:** An important feature for using derivative instruments like options, futures, etc., is the existence of an adequate institutional infrastructure. There has to be an effective surveillance process, a transparent price discovery process and standardisation of contracts and procedures.

Distinguish Between Domestic Foreign Currency Forwards and NDFs

No.	Domestic Forwards	NDFs
1	Applicable in onshore markets	Applicable in offshore markets
2	Operate in regulated markets	Operate in unregulated markets
3	Generally used by domestic participants	Generally used by non-resident participants
4	May not conform to CIP condition due to domestic demand supply factors	May not conform to CIP condition due to expectations in rate movements
5	Delivery is mandatory	No delivery involved
6	Conformity with CIP condition will increase with increased implementation of Capital Account Convertibility	Will increase implementation of Capital Account Convertibility, the need for this market will reduce.
7	On maturity currencies are exchanged	On maturity, profit/loss is exchanged.

Distinguish Between NDF and Currency Futures Markets

No.	NDF Market	Futures Market
1	Involves OTC contracts for purchase/sale of of notional amount of currency in future with no intention of delivery.	Involves exchange traded contracts for purchase/sale of specified currency amount in future which involve an intention to deliver on maturity.
2	Contract size and expiry is customised.	Contract size and maturity is standardised
3	Unregulated market.	Regulated market.
4	High credit risk.	No credit risk.
5	Cancellation with the same counterparty.	Cancellation through opposite contract on the exchange.
6	No institutional involvement.	Institutional settlement guarantee.
7	Profit or loss is cash settled in foreign currency on maturity.	Profit or loss adjustment through mark to market on a daily basis domestic currency.

Distinguish Forward Currency Contract and Future Currency Contract

Forward Contracts vs. Futures Contracts

No.	Forward Contracts	Futures Contracts
1	A forward contract can be defined as a contract between a bank and its customer in which the bank agrees to buy/sell a specific amount of foreign currency on a fixed forward period, at a rate decided on the date of the contract.	A futures contract can be defined as a contract between an exchange and an operator in which the operator agrees to buy/sell standardized amount of foreign currency for delivery on a standard maturity date in the future, at a specified rate.
2	Forward contracts are customized in terms of amount and settlement date.	Futures contracts are standardized in terms of amount and settlement date.
3	Settlement date of a forward contract can be any forward date.	All futures contracts maturing in a particular calendar month are settled on the last working day of the month in India.
4	A forward contract can provide 100% hedge to the customer.	Futures contracts do not provide 100% hedge to the operator.
5	A forward contract is a rigid transaction whose terms cannot be changed except with the original counterparty.	A futures contract is a flexible instrument which can be cancelled through an opposite transaction with the exchange.
6	Both parties to a forward contract carry credit risk.	Futures contracts do not involve credit risks because for both buyers and sellers, the counterparty is the exchange which guarantees the transaction. This called the 'Principle of Novation'.

17.7 INTEREST RATE ARBITRAGE

The equilibrium condition in terms of the CIP theory is represented by the relation,

$$\frac{F-S}{S} = \frac{(Rv-Rb)}{100} \times \frac{n}{12}$$

When this equality is satisfied, the cost of borrowing in one currency is equal to the investment yield earn on the other currency. Therefore, no arbitrage opportunity would exist.

When this equality is violated, it provides opportunity to earn arbitrage profit by borrowing in one currency and investing in the other.

When $\frac{F-S}{S} > \frac{(Rv-Rb)}{100} \times \frac{n}{12}$ arbitrage profit is derived by borrowing in the variable currency and investing in base currency. Similarly,

When  arbitrage gain is derived by borrowing in base currency and investing in the variable currency.

Role of RBI (Reserve Bank of India) in Foreign Exchange Management

The role of RBI in the exchange market is as follows:

- Monitoring and management of exchange rates without a predetermined target rate or range with intermittent intervention as and when necessary has been the basis of the Managed Float system followed in India.
- A policy to build a higher level of foreign exchange reserves, which takes into account not only anticipated current account deficits but also liquidity requirements arising from unanticipated capital outflows.
- A judicious policy for management of capital account transactions, with progressive liberalisation of such transactions.
- Balancing the external economy represented by the exchange rate and the internal economy represented by interest rates, inflation, money supply, etc.

❑❑❑

CHAPTER 18 FINANCIAL PLANNING

18.1 INTRODUCTION

Liberalization and globalization policies initiated by the government have changed the dimension of business environment. It has changed the dimension of competition that a firm faces today. Therefore, for survival and growth a firm has to execute planned strategy systematically.

To execute any strategic plan, resources are required. Resources may be manpower, plant and machinery, building, technology or any intangible asset.

To acquire all these assets financial resources are essentially required. Therefore, finance manager of a company must have both long-range and short-range financial plans. Integration of both these plans is required for the effective utilization of all the resources of the firm.

The Long-range Plan must Consider: (1) Funds required to execute the planned course of action. (2) Funds available at the disposal of the company. (3) Determination of funds to be procured from outside sources.

Benefits that Accrue to Firm out of the Financial Planning

1. **Effective Utilization of Funds:** Shortage is managed by a plan that ensures flow of cash at the least cost. Surplus is deployed through well-planned treasury management. Ultimately, the productivity of assets is enhanced.
2. Flexibility in capital structure is given adequate consideration. Here, flexibility means the firms ability to change the composition of funds that constitute its capital structure in accordance with the changing conditions of capital market. Flexibility refers to the ability of a firm to obtain funds at the right time, in the right quantity and at the least cost as per requirements to finance emerging opportunities.
3. Formulation of policies and instituting procedures for elimination of all types of wastages in the process of execution of strategic plans.
4. Maintaining the operating capability of the firm through the evolution of scientific replacement schemes for plant and machinery and other fixed assets. This will help the firm in reducing its operating capital. Operating capital refers to the ratio of capital employed to sales generated. A perusal of annual reports of Dell computers will throw light on how Dell strategically minimized the operating capital required to support sales. Such companies are admired by investing community.
5. Integration of long-range with the shortage plans.

Guidelines for Financial Planning

1. Never ignore the cardinal principle that fixed asset requirements be met from the long-term sources.
2. Make maximum use of spontaneous source of finance to achieve the highest productivity of resources.
3. Maintain the operating capital intact by providing adequately out of the current periods earnings. Due attention to be given to physical capital maintenance or operating capability.
4. Never ignore the need for financial capital maintenance in units of constant purchasing power.
5. Employ current cost principle wherever required.
6. Give due weightage to cost and risk in using debt and equity.
7. Keeping the need for finance for expansion of business, formulate plough back policy of earnings.
8. Exercise thorough control over overheads.
9. Seasonal peak requirements to be met from short-term borrowings from banks.

Forecast of Income Statement and Balance Sheet

There are three methods of preparing income statement:

1. Per cent of sales method or constant ratio method
2. Expense method
3. Combination of both these two

1. Per cent of Sales Method: This approach is based on the assumption that each element of cost bears some constant relationship with the sales revenue.

For example, raw material cost is 40% of sales revenue of the year ended 30.03.2007. But this method assumes that the ratio of raw material cost to sales will continue to be the same in 2008 also. Such an assumption may not hold good in most of the situations. For example, raw material cost increases by 10% in 2008 but selling price of finished goods increases only by 5%. In this case raw material cost will be 44/105 of the sales revenue in 2008. This can be solved to some extent by taking average for same representative years. However, inflation, change in Govt. policies, wage agreements, technological innovation totally invalidate this approach on a long-run basis.

2. Budgeted Expense Method: Expenses for the planning period are budgeted on the basis of anticipated behaviour of various items of cost and revenue. This demands effective database for reasonable budgeting of expenses.

3. Combination of both these two methods: Is used because some expenses can be budgeted by the management taking into account the expected business environment and some other expenses could be based on their relationship with the sales revenue expected to be earned.

18.2 FORECAST OF BALANCE SHEET

1. Items of certain assets and liabilities which have a close relationship with the sales revenue could be computed based on the forecast of sales and the historical database of their relationship with the sales.

2. Determine the equity and debt mix on the basis of funds requirements and the company's policy on capital structure.

Example: The following details have been extracted from the books of C Ltd., Income Statement

(₹ in million)

	2009	2010
Sales less returns	1000	1300
Gross Profit	300	520
Selling Expenses	100	120
Administration	40	45
Depreciation	60	75
Operating Profit	100	280
Non-operating income	20	40
EBIT (Earnings before interest and Tax)	120	320
Interest	15	18
Profit before tax	105	302
Tax	30	100
Profit after tax	75	202
Dividend	38	100
Retained earnings	37	102

Balance Sheet for the year 2008 (Forecast)

(₹ in million)

Particulars	Basis	Working	Amount
Assets			
Fixed Assets	Given		510
Add: Addition			100
			610
Depreciation		120 + 123	243
1. Net fixed assets			367
2. Investments			150
3. Current Assets and Loans and advances			
Cash at bank	$\frac{12}{1300}$	$\frac{12 \times 1690}{1300}$	16 (Rounded off)
Receivables	$\frac{128}{1300}$	$\frac{128 \times 1690}{1300}$	166

Inventories		$\frac{300}{1300}$	$\frac{300 \times 1690}{1300}$	390
Loans and Advances		$\frac{80}{1300}$	$\frac{80 \times 1690}{1300}$	104
4. Miscellaneous Expenditures		Given	24 + 19	43
Total				**1236**
Liabilities				
1. Share Capital				
Equity				120
Preference				50
2. Reserves and Surplus	Increase by current year's retained earnings			355
3. Secured Loan		$\frac{60}{1300}$	$\frac{60 \times 1690}{1300}$	78
Bank borrowings				40 (Difference - Balancing figure)
4. Unsecured Loan		60	60	
5. Current Liabilities and Provision				
Trade creditors		$\frac{250}{1300}$	$\frac{250 \times 1690}{1300}$	325
Provision for tax		$\frac{60}{1300}$	$\frac{60 \times 1690}{1300}$	75
Proposed Dividend	Current year given			130
Total Liabilities				**1236**

Extra Practise Problems

1. The Balance Sheet for the current year of a company is given below:

(All the figures are in ₹ lakh)

Liabilities	**₹**	**Assets**	**₹**
Equity Capital	100	Land and Building	200
Retained Earnings	120	Machinery	30
Term Loan	160	Furniture	30
Short-term Borrowings	120	Bills Receivables	100
Creditors	100	Debtors	60
Provisions	40	Stock	180
		Bank	40
Total	**640**		**640**

□□□

Other Information: Sales ₹ 800

V. Expenses ₹ 560

F. Expenses ₹ 160

The following are the projections for the next year :

1. The sales are expected to be ₹ 1,000.
2. F. expenses will increase by 25%.
3. No change in the ratio of variable expenses to sales.
4. Interest expenses will be ₹ 20.
5. No change in fixed assets. Ignore depreciation.
6. Bank balance and other current assets will increase in proportion to sales.
7. Tax to be provided at 35%. This will be the only provision next year.
8. Creditors will increase in proportion to sales.

You are required to prepare the projected income statement and balance sheet of the company for the next year.

If the company is required to raise funds (i.e., if liability side is less), they will be raised in the order of short-term borrowings, term loan and if required, equity capital. It is a policy of the company to maintain current ratio of minimum 1.25:1 and ensure that the long-term loans do not exceed 40% of total long-term funds.

If the asset side is less then the difference will be considered as cash balance available.

2. The balance sheet of Deepak Ltd., on December 31, 2009 is shown below:

Particulars	₹	Particulars	₹
Share Capital	150	Fixed Assets	400
Retained Earnings	180	Inventories	200
Term Loans	80	Receivables	150
Short-term Bank Borrowings	200	Cash	50
Accounts Payable	140		
Provision	50		
Total	**800**		**800**

The sales of the firm for the year ending on December 31, 2009 were 1,000. Its profit margin on sales was 6% and its dividend payout ratio was 50%. The tax rate was 60%. Deepak Ltd., expects its sales to increase by 30% in the year 2010. The ratio of assets to sales and spontaneous current liabilities to sales would remain unchanged. Likewise, the payout would remain unchanged.

Required

(a) Estimate the external funds requirement for the year 2010.

(b) Prepare "projected balance sheet" and "projected profit and loss account", assuming that the external funds requirement would be raised equally from term loans and short-term bank borrowings.

Recommended Book

"Complicated Financial Words Made Simple" by Pawan Jhabak, Himalaya Publication House, 2012.

❑❑❑

UNIVERSITY PAPER (NOV. – DEC. 2009)

(3 Hours) **[Total Marks 100]**

N.B: (1) The question paper has two sections: A and B Students must attempt questions from only one of these two sections.

(2) Total five questions are to be attempted. All five questions must be either from Section A or from Section B.

(3) On the top of the answer sheet the students must mention which Section they have chosen.

(4) Correct and to-the-point answers to theoretical questions will be assessed like practical problems. Thus, students attempting more theoretical questions will not be at a disadvantage.

(5) If students attempt more than five questions, only first five will be considered.

(6) All questions carry equal marks.

Section A

1. Elite India Ltd., a four-year young company, is growing rapidly. Presently it has 80,000 equity shares of ₹ 50 each and 10% debentures of ₹ 20,00,000.

The summary of income statement for last year is given below:

Sales		50,00,000
Less: V. Expenses	25,00,000	
F. Expenses	9,00,000	34,00,000
EBIT		16,00,000
Interest		2,00,000
EBT		14,00,000
Tax (35%)		4,90,000
PAT		9,10,000
EPS		11.38

The company further wants to expand its activities for which it is planning to make an additional investment of ₹ 20,00,000.

There are two financing options: either 40,000 equity shares of ₹ 50 each, or debt funds of ₹ 20,00,000 at 12% interest.

The company wants to assess its position for two levels of sales projections for next year, *viz.* ₹70,00,000 and ₹1,20,00,000.

The ratio of variable expenses to sales will remain the same next year and fixed expenses will be ₹ 13,00,000 at ₹ 70,00,000 sales and ₹ 26,00,000 at ₹ 1,20,00,000 sales.

For both the levels of sales projections the P/E ratio is expected to be 2.5 in case of debt option and 3 in case of equity option.

If the objective of the company is to maximize the market price of its shares then which financing option should it go for if the sales are ₹ 70,00,000 and if the sales are ₹ 1,20,00,000?

2. A company wants to assess the feasibility of a new project. It is not able to estimate the sales revenue and expenses and is not clear about sensitivity analysis. Using hypothetical figures explain to the company how it can do feasibility analysis of the project for three different levels *viz.*: pessimistic, expected and optimistic.
3. Explain with examples any two methods of corporate valuation which can be used to calculate the value of a company.
4. Explain the various financing options in respect of infrastructure projects.
5. What are the benefits to investors because of the existence of financial intermediaries?
6. Which are the important financial intermediaries in the Indian financial system? Explain.
7. (a) Explain the important functions of an investment banker and his role in primary Issue management.

   (b) Explain, in brief, the process and methodology followed by a rating agency to rate a financial instrument.
8. What are the possible causes of an industrial unit becoming a sick unit? What, according to you, can be a typical revival programme to revive a sick unit?
9. Answer any two of the following:
   (a) Explain the role of SEBI, in brief as the regulator of financial markets.
   (b) Explain in simple words 'Financial Interest Rate Swaps'.
   (c) Explain offshore/onshore instruments and multiple option bonds.
10. Explain in brief, any three, of the following:-
    (a) Due diligence
    (b) FIPB and joint venture formulation
    (c) Loan syndication
    (d) Process of bond valuation
    (e) Procedure of IPO
    (f) Any five factors which determine the capital structure of a company.

Section B

1. The balance sheet of International Trade Ltd., as on 31st March, 2008 is as under:

(All figures are in ₹ lakh)

Liabilities	**₹**	**Assets**	**₹**
Equity Capital (₹10 per share)	90	Building	150
10% Long-term debt	120	Machinery	75
Retained Earnings	30	Stock	50
Current Liabilities	60	Debtors	20
		Cash	5
Total	**300**	**Total**	**300**

The total assets turnover ratio of the company is 3, its fixed operating cost is 1/6 of sales and variable operating cost is 50% of sales. The corporate tax rate is 35%.

You are required to:

(i) Calculate the operating, financial and combined leverage

(ii) Calculate the market price of the share if the P/E multiple is 2.5

(iii) Calculate the level of EBIT if the EPS is (a) ₹ 15 (b) ₹ 25

2. The existing capital structure of Textile India Ltd., is as under:

Particulars	₹
Equity shares of ₹100 each	40,00,000
Retained Earnings	0,00,000
9 Preference shares	125,00,000
7% Debentures	25,00,000

The company wants to raise ₹ 25,00,000 for its expansion project for which it is considering the following options:

(a) Issue of 20,000 equity shares at a premium of ₹ 25 per share

or

(b) Issue of 10% preference shares

or

(c) Issue of 9% debentures

Company's return on capital employed is 12% (on existing as well as new funds) and corporate tax rate is 35%.

It is expected that the P/E multiples in case of the above three options would be 16, 13 and 12, respectively. Suggest the company, which alternative it should select and why?

3. (a) ABC Co. Ltd., has present value of net assets ₹ 100 lakh which includes cash balance of ₹ 10 lakh. It has 1,00,000 equity shares and no preference capital or debt funds. The company has to make the decision about declaring dividend. At the same time it is also exploring the possibility of investing in a new project. The company has three options:

(i) Do not declare any dividend and invest the available cash of ₹ 10 lakh in the new project. The present value of the future cashflows generated by this project is ₹ 20 lakh.

or

(ii) Pay ₹ 10 per share as dividend. This will take away the entire cash balance of ₹ 10 lakh

or

(iii) Pay dividend as suggested in the second option and also invest in a new project through a fresh equity issue of one lakh shares of ₹ 10 each. This investment will have the same effect on the company as in the first option, i.e., ₹ 20 lakh NPV from the project.

Give your recommendation to the company as to which is the best option if the company wants to maximize the shareholder value.

(b) The following information is available in respect of a company:

Capitalisation rate (Ke) = 0.12

EPS = ₹ 15

Rate of return on investment (r): (i) 0.15 (ii) 0.10

The company wants to know the effect on the market price of its shares under the two possibilities of r (i.e., 0.15 and 0.10) under the two options: (i) if it does not declare any dividend, and (ii) if it declares ₹ 15 as dividend.

Using Walter's model explain the results obtained by you.

4. The income statement and balance sheet of Five Star Ltd., is given below:

Income Statement

	₹ (in lakh)	
Sales	500	
Interest on Investments	10	
Profit on sale of old assets	5	
Total Income		515
Less: Manufacturing cost	180	
Admn. Cost	60	
Selling and distribution cost	50	
Depreciation	30	
Loss on sale of old	5	
Machine		325
EBIT		190
Less: Interest		20
EBT		170
Less: Tax (30%)		51
PATEPS 119 lakh/5 lakh		119
P/E ratio		₹23.82

Balance Sheet

Liabilities	₹	Assets	₹
Equity Capital (₹10 share)	50	Building	80
Retained Earnings	40	Machinery	70
Term Loan	60	Stock	10
Creditors	15	Debtors	12
Provisions	13	Bank	6
Total	**178**		**178**

The cost of equity and cost of debt is 10% and 12%, respectively. The company pays 30% corporate tax.

From the information given you are required to calculate the EVA. Also, calculate MVA on the basis of Market Value of equity capital.

5. Describe the important sources of financing long-term projects which can be used by the Indian companies. If they approach the financial institutions for long-term finances, what important norms and policies financial institutions would apply to provide such finances?

6. The Balance Sheet for the current year of a company is given below:

(All the figures are in ₹ lakh)

Liabilities	₹	Assets	₹
Equity Capital	100	Land and Building	200
Retained Earnings	120	Machinery	30
Term Loan	160	Furniture	30
Short-term Borrowings	120	Bills Receivables	100
Creditors	100	Debtors	60
Provisions	40	Stock	180
		Bank	40
Total	**640**	**Total**	**640**

Other Information: Sales ₹ 800

V. Expenses ₹ 560

F. Expenses ₹ 160

The following are the projections for the next year:

1. The sales are expected to be ₹ 1,000.
2. F. expenses will increase by 25%.
3. No change in the ratio of variable expenses to sales.
4. Interest expenses will be ₹ 20.
5. No change in fixed assets. Ignore depreciation.
6. Bank balance and other current assets will increase in proportion to sales.
7. Tax to be provided at 35%. This will be the only provision next year.
8. Creditors will increase in proportion to sales.

You are required to prepare the projected income statement and balance sheet of the company for the next year.

If the company is required to raise funds (i.e., if liability side is less), they will be raised in the order of short-term borrowings, term loan and if required, equity capital. It is a policy of the company to maintain current ratio of minimum 1.25:1 and ensure that the long-term loans do not exceed 40% of total long-term funds.

If the asset side is less then the difference will be considered as cash balance available.

7. Expain the important functions of either Credit Rating Information Services of India Ltd., (CRISIL) or Information and Credit Rating Services Ltd., (ICRA).
8. Which are the important financial intermediaries in the Indian financial system? How are they beneficial to the investors ? Explain.
9. Explain in brief, any three, of the following:
   (a) Important financial derivatives
   (b) MoU between government and a PSU
   (c) Venture capital funding in India
   (d) Revival of a sick unit and viability study
   (e) Regulation of financial markets in India
   (f) Procedure pertaining to IPOs.

(UNIVERSITY PAPER NOV. – DEC. 2010)

(3 Hours) [Total Marks : 100]

Instruction to Students

(1) Answer any **FIVE** questions. All questions carry equal marks.

(2) **Presentation** should be **neat** and **clean.** Marks will be deducted for **poor presentation.**

(3) All the **subquestions** of the main question should be attempted **together.**

(4) If students attempt more than **five** questions, only first **five** will be **considered.**

(5) Every **new question** should start on a new page.

1. Explain the important functions of either Credit Rating Information Services of India Ltd., (CRISIL) or Information and Credit Rating Services Ltd., (ICRA).

2. (a) Operating Leverage. Discuss the P/E ratio approach to stock valuation.
   (b) Describe evaluating the adjusted book value approach to corporate valuation.

3. A firm has total sales ₹ 9,00,000. It also has debt of ₹ 8,00,000 at 10% rate of interest. If the tax rate is 45%, calculate:
   (a) Operating Leverage
   (b) Financial Leverage
   (c) Combined Leverage

4. A Ltd., paid a dividend of ₹ 5 per share for 2009-10. The company follows a fixed dividend payout ratio of 30% and earns a return of 18% on its investments. Cost of capital is 12%. What is the price of the shares of A Ltd., as per Walter's model?

5. Explain in brief any three of the following:
   (a) Revival programme for a sick industrial unit
   (b) Procedure of pertaining to IPOs.
   (c) Regulation of Financial Markets in India.
   (d) Rationale of disinvestment in Public Sector Enterprise
   (e) Important sources of financing long-term projects in India
   (f) Financial Interest Rate Swaps

6. The following is the data regarding two Companies 'X' and 'Y' belonging to the same equivalent risk class:

	Company X	Company Y
Number of ordinary shares	90,000	1,50,000
Market price per share	₹ 1.20	₹ 1.00
6% Debentures	60,000	-
Profit before interest	₹ 18,000	₹ 18,000

All profit after debentures interest are distributed as dividends.

Explain how under Modigiani and Miller approach, an investor holding 10% of shares in Company 'X' will be better-off in switching his holding to Company 'Y'

7. The balance sheet of Deepak Ltd., on December 31, 2009 is shown below:

Particulars	₹	Particulars	₹
Share Capital	150	Fixed Assets	400
Retained Earnings	180	Inventories	200
Term Loans	80	Receivables	150
Short-erm Bank Borrowings	200	Cash	50
Accounts Payable	140		
Provision	50		
Total	**800**		**800**

The sales of the firm for the year ending on December 31, 2009 were 1,000. It profit margin on sales was 6% and its dividend payout ratio was 50%. The tax rate was 60%. Deepak Ltd., expects its sales to increase by 30% in the year 2010. The ratio of assets to sales and spontaneous current liabilities to sales would remain unchanged. Likewise the payout would remain unchanged.

Required:

(a) Estimate the external funds requirement for the year 2010.

(b) Prepare "projected balance sheet" and "projected profit and loss account", assuming that the external funds requirement would be raised equally from term loans and short-term bank borrowings.

8. Acme Ltd., is considering a capital project for which the following information is available:

Investment Outlay	1,000	Debt equity ratio	1 : 1
Project Life	10 Years	Depreciation (for tax purpose)	SLM
Salvage value	0	Tax rate	40%
Annual Revenues	2,000	Annual cost	1,400
Cost of equity	18%	(excluding depreciation -	
Cost of debt (post-tax)	10%	interest and taxes)	-

(a) Calculate the EVA of the project over its life.

(b) Compute the NPV of the project

(UNIVERSITY PAPER NOV. – DEC. 2011)

(3 Hours) **[Total Marks : 60]**

Instruction to Students

(1) Answer any **FIVE** questions. All questions carry equal marks.

(2) **All** questions carry **equal** marks.

(3) Answer **each** new question on a **fresh** page.

(4) Write all **sub questions** of a main question **together**.

(5) Don't write **extra** answers. Only first five will be **assessed**.

(6) Presentation should be **neat** and **clean.** Marks will be deducted for poor presentation.

1. The companies ACC Cements and Dalmia Cements belong to same risk class and are identical in every fashion except ACC Cements uses debt while Dalmia Cements does not. The leveraged company has ₹ 9,00,000 debentures carrying 10% rate of interest. Both firms earn 20% before interest and taxes on their total assets of ₹30 lakhs. Assume perfect capital markets, rational investors and so on; Both companies pay tax at 40% and capitalization rate for an all equity company is 15%.

   You are required to:

   (a) Compute the value of the two firms using the Net Income and Modigliani-Miller approach.

   (b) Using the M.M. approach, compute the overall Capitalization rate for both the companies.

2. (a) The following data is available for Modi Company Ltd.

Earnings per share	₹ 2
Internal rate of return	18%
Cost of Capital	16%

   If Walters Valuation formula holds, what will be the Price per share when the dividend payout ratio is 50%, 80% and 100%?

   (b) Lever Ltd belongs to a risk class for which the approximate capitalization rate is 12.5%. It currently has 1,00,000 shares selling at ₹ 80 each. The firm is contemplating the declaration of ₹ 6/- per share divided at the end of the current fiscal year which has just begun.

   Based on Modigliani and Miller model and assumption of no taxes, you are required to-

   (i) Calculate the share price at the end of the year, if dividend is not declared and dividend is declared.

   (ii) Assuming that the firm pays dividends, has net income of ₹ 25,00,000 and makes a new investment of ₹ 42,00,000 during the period, how many new shares must be issued?

3. The Balance Sheet of Ponds India Ltd as on March 31, current year is as follows:

Liabilities	Amount ₹ lakhs	Assets	Amount ₹ lakhs
Share Capital	300	Fixed Assets	750
Reserves & Surplus	210	Inventories	450
Long Term Loans	540	Receivables	360
Short Term Loans	300	Cash & Bank	90
Payables	180		
Provisions	120		
	1650		**1650**

Sales for the Current Year were ₹ 900 lakhs. For the next year ending on March 31, they are expected to increase by 20%. The net profit margin after taxes and dividend payout are expected to be 40% and 50% respectively. You are required to:

(a) Quantify the amount of external funds required.

(b) Determine the mode of raising the funds given the following parameters:

(i) Current ramtio should be 1.33

(ii) Ratio of fixed assets to long term loan should be 1.5

(iii) Long term debt to equity ratio should not exceed 1.06

(iv) The funds are to be raised in the order of –

– Short term bank barrowings

– Long term loans

– Equities

4. The following figures are available for ABC Ltd:

Net Sales	₹ 2,000 (lakhs)
EBIT as % of Net sales	12%
Capital employed	(a) Equity ₹ 600 lakhs
	(b) Preference shares ₹ 150 lakhs bearing 14% rate of dividend
	(c) Debt @ 16% - ₹ 400 lakhs.

You are required to calculate

(1) Return on the Equity of the Company.

(2) Operating leverage of the company given that its combined leverage is 3.

5. (a) The following information is available of Tata Steel Co Ltd., Calculate EVA:

14% Debt Capital	3000 (₹ lakhs)
Equity Capital	800 (₹ lakhs)
Reserve & Surplus	6200 (₹ lakhs)
Risk Free Rate	9%
Beta Factor	1.05
Market Rate of Return	19%
Equity (market) Risk Premium	10%
Operating Profit After Tax	2400 (₹ lakhs)
Tax Rate	35%

(b) Yes Ltd is considering financial Options. The key information is as follows:

(i) Total Capital of the three plans to be raised ₹ 20 lakhs

(ii) Plans of financing.

Plan	Equity	Debt	Preference Share	Total (₹ lakhs)
X	100%	—	—	20
Y	50%	50%	—	20
Z	50%	—	50%	20

(iii) Cost of Debenture is 8% and cost of preference share is 10%.

(iv) Tax rate is 30%

(v) Equity shares of face value of ₹ 10 will be issued at a premium of ₹ 10 per share.

(vi) Expected EBIT will be ₹ 8,00,000.

You are required to determine for each plan-

(1) Earning per share

(2) Financing Break Even Point.

(3) EBIT ranges among the plans of indifference.

6. Explain in brief any **Three** of the following:

(a) Symptoms of Sickness

(b) Private Placement

(c) Key Financial Intermediaries

(d) Important Sources of Financing Long-term Projects in India

(e) Due Diligence

(f) Procedure of IPO

7. (a) What are the major problems associated with disinvestment of PSUs in India?

(b) Describe and evaluate the adjusted book value approach to corporate valuation.

8. (a) What do you understand by financial derivatives? Explain in detail.

(b) Explain the important functions of Credit Rating Information Services of India Ltd. (CRISIL).